Unmanning Modernism

∼ Unmanning Modernism

Gendered Re-Readings

Edited by
Elizabeth Jane Harrison
and Shirley Peterson

The University of Tennessee Press • Knoxville

Permission to use material from the letters of Lytton Strachey granted by The Society of Authors as agents of
The Strachey Trust.

A Nightingale in Bloomsbury Square by Maureen Duffy © 1974 Maureen Duffy. Reproduced by kind permission of
Jonathan Clowes Ltd., London, on behalf of Maureen Duffy.

Quotations from *Alice Meynell: Prose and Poetry,* ed. Frederick Page, Viola Meynell, Olivia Sowerby, and Francis
Meynell (London: Jonathan Cape, 1947), used by permission of the Alice Meynell family.

The Well of Loneliness by Radclyffe Hall (New York: Anchor Books, 1990), © 1928 by Radclyffe Hall. Copyright
renewed 1956 by Una Lady Troubridge, executrix of the author.

An earlier version of Elizabeth Jane Harrison's "Zora Neale Hurston and Mary Hunter Austin's Ethnographic
Fiction" appeared in *MELUS* 21, no. 2 (Summer 1996). © 1997 MELUS, The Society for the Study of the Multi-
Ethnic Literature of the United States.

∞ The paper in this book meets the minimum requirements of the American National Standard for
Permanence of Paper for Printed Library Materials. The binding materials have been chosen for strength
and durability.
✿ Printed on recycled paper.

Library of Congress Cataloging in Publication Data

Unmanning modernism : gendered re-readings / edited by
Elizabeth Jane Harrison and Shirley Peterson. — 1st ed.
  p. cm.
Includes bibliographical references and index.
ISBN 0-87049-985-8 (cloth: alk. paper)
1. English literature—20th century—History and criticism—Theory, etc.
2. Modernism (Literature).
3. English literature—Women authors—History and criticism—Theory, etc.
4. American literature—20th century—History and criticism—Theory, etc.
5. American literature—Women authors—History and criticism—Theory, etc.
6. Feminism and literature.
7. Sex role in literature.
8. Women and literature.
9. Canon (Literature).
I. Harrison, Elizabeth Jane, 1960– . II. Peterson, Shirley, 1950– .
PR478.M6U53 1997
820.9'112—dc21   97-4761
                                                  CIP

∼ Contents

～ Introduction

> It is probable, however, that both in life and in art the values of a woman are not the values of a man. Thus, when a woman comes to write . . . she will find that she is perpetually wishing to alter the established values—to make serious what appears insignificant to a man, and trivial what is to him important. And for that, of course, she will be criticized; for the critic . . . will be genuinely puzzled and surprised by an attempt to alter the current scale of values.—VIRGINIA WOOLF, 1919

This collection of critical essays joins a growing chorus emerging since the 1970s that invites readers to reevaluate the gender politics informing literary modernism. In *The Gender of Modernism* (1990), Bonnie Kime Scott explains her enterprise as part of the discourse which arose from an evolving gender consciousness:

> Modernism as we were taught it at midcentury was perhaps halfway to truth. It was unconsciously gendered masculine. The inscriptions of mothers and women, and more broadly of sexuality and gender, were not adequately decoded, if detected at all. Though some of the aesthetic and political pronouncements of women writers had been offered in public, they had not circulated widely and were rarely collected for academic recirculation. Deliberate or not, this is an example of the politics of gender. (2)

Scott joins a host of critics, including Shari Benstock, Susan Gubar, Sandra Gilbert, Marianne DeKoven, Elaine Showalter, Jane Marcus, Rachel Blau DuPlessis, Susan Stanford Friedman, Mary Lynn Broe, Angela Ingram, Suzanne Clark, Marjorie Perloff, and Rita Felski, in sharpening, through the lens of gender, the modernist literary landscape.[1] These critics have raised provocative responses to such voices as Hugh Kenner's, who helped consecrate this period as "the Pound era," celebrating not only Pound's injunction to "make it new" but also cooperating in the enterprise to make it male.[2]

Even Scott acknowledges Pound's overwhelming presence in her "tangled mesh of modernists."[3] His influence and interaction with other writers is undeniable; yet the reemergence of Virginia Woolf, Gertrude Stein, and H.D. in the past twenty years as modernist figures[4] is of as much importance to the reconfiguration of modernism as Pound was to its earlier perception. The renewed interest of postmodern feminist readers and critics of Virginia Woolf brought into question her secondary status in the modernist canon as well as the basis for such hierarchical evaluations.[5] The flood of Woolf criticism and the concomitant proliferation of feminist literary studies in the past twenty-five years testify to the explosive force of what Marianne DeKoven termed in 1989 "the delineation of the (anti-) tradition of female Modernism" (191).

Woolf perhaps provides an apt response to the "im-Poundment" of modernism in her now canonical 1924 essay "Mr. Bennett and Mrs. Brown." Her comments, aimed at the Edwardian literary giants H. G. Wells, Arnold Bennett, and John Galsworthy, might well apply to her fellow modernists and their critical champions. She complains that the Edwardians "have made tools and established conventions which do their business. But those tools are not our tools, and that business is not our business. For us those conventions are ruin, those tools are death" (*Collected Essays* 1:330). Through this metaphor of literary construction, Woolf raises questions about narrative style, perspective, and subject matter that now seem germane to modernist studies, in particular those such as Scott's that theorize modernism from the perspective of gender identity. Woolf's categorical rejection of Edwardian "materialist" narratives doubtless propels her own narrative innovations, which earned her perhaps the sole female slot on the high modernist roster, although not without qualifications and caveats.[6] But the subsequent secondary status of Woolf through the 1960s indicates how the celebrated modernist "tools" have been efficiently used to erect a fortress as formidable as that of the Edwardians and as forbidding to women writers of the modernist era.

Since the 1970s feminist critics have interrogated the modernist tradition in an effort to recover a parallel female tradition;[7] two decades later, however, "female modernism" remains an amorphous term inciting even more questions. For instance, have texts by female modernists merely been excluded from the mainstream canon in a gesture of male prerogative, or is there an essential and valid aesthetic difference underlying the exclusion? Is it a mistake, as Benstock argues, "to assume that gender distinctions produce writing by women that differs from that of men in predictable or homogeneous ways" (31)? Has female modernism been too often defined *against* masculinist forms rather than interacting with them?[8] Should critics and readers attempt to define an alternate canon when the whole concept of canonization is problematic?

These are the questions that initiated this project. In 1991 we attended a National Endowment for the Humanities Summer Seminar on "The Female Literary Imagination in the First Half of the Twentieth Century," led by Susan Gubar. The issues we discussed that summer continued to intrigue several of us who had participated. Subsequently, we invited responses to the question of female modernism from a wider range of scholars. We deliberately chose not to impose any criteria or agenda on our contributors regarding the question of modernism, female or otherwise. As a result, our collection is multivocal and does not conform to either standard or revisionist paradigms of modernism as a period, a set of definitions, or a literary aesthetic. This collection is not intended to be representative of any particular writers or genres. With one exception (Maureen Duffy, a postmodernist influenced by Woolf), it fits the conventional time boundaries of Western modernism, roughly from 1910 to 1940, and all authors included in discussions are British or American. However, this is not by design nor meant to reinforce such limitations. Many of the essays challenge the concept of a modernist canon, whether mainstream or alternative. Others consider new techniques in fiction and compare or contrast them to accepted modernist aesthetics such as fragmentation and montage. Taken together, these essays add to the evolving concept of a gender-conscious modernism, practiced mostly by women writers who, like Woolf, employ new "tools" to "alter the established values."

As editors, we chose to work inductively rather than deductively, looking for common concerns among the essays rather than prescriptive definitions of female modernism. While we organize the essays alphabetically rather than thematically, what emerges reflects converging interests in essays engaged in the ongoing process we call "unmanning Modernism,"[9] a project designed to reopen the modernist debate to include modernism's (m)other tongue.

High Art versus Low Art

Increasingly, mainstream modernism is characterized as an elitist movement involving a closed circle of male writers who valorized high art as a defense against the rise of a feminized mass culture. In *After the Great Divide,* Andreas Huyssen discusses how "the modernism/mass culture dichotomy has been genderized as masculine/feminine" (x). He sees the exclusion of women and women writers from high culture as a corollary to the feminization, and consequent devaluation, of mass culture. Julie Taddeo's portrait of Lytton Strachey in "A Modernist Romance?: Lytton Strachey and the Women of Bloomsbury" reinforces this notion. While championing libertarian sexuality, Strachey and his male companions of Bloomsbury perpetuated Victorian ideas about women as the intellectual and emotional inferiors of men. At Cambridge, the secret society known as the "Apostles" extolled a "Greek way of life," that is, high culture, art, and homoeroticism, over debased contact with women, who were viewed as accessories or comforts to men. Strachey's long relationship with the artist Dora Carrington, his self-acknowledged "penwiper," is a case in point. This misogyny took shape as a consequence of the high/low art dichotomy reified by modernism.

Several essays in this volume argue that women writers of the period actually created high art, although they were not recognized for doing so. In "Gendering Modernism: H.D., Imagism, and Masculinist Aesthetics," Michael Kaufmann discusses H.D.'s development of imagism in a reevaluation of lyric form to high art.

He defines modernism as a "masculinist aesthetic" circumscribed by male writers' obsession with impersonality and objectivity. Joe Aimone's essay, "Millay's Big Book, or the Female Formalist as Modern," challenges assumptions about Edna St. Vincent Millay as a lesser artist by demonstrating the ironic personae, complex imagery, and innovative rhythms of her poetry. Similarly, in "Zora Neale Hurston and Mary Hunter Austin's Ethnographic Fiction: New Modernist Narratives," Elizabeth Harrison reconsiders the contributions of Hurston and Austin to illustrate their innovative experimentation with narrative, again collapsing the conventional boundaries between high and low art.

Other essays question whether the avant-garde belongs in the masculine domain of high art. Kornelia Tancheva's discussion of the Provincetown Players in "'I Do Not Participate in Liberations': Female Dramatic and Theatrical Modernism in the 1910s and 1920s" reveals how women modernist playwrights, particularly Neith Boyce, Louise Bryant, and Djuna Barnes, use subversive strategies in their drama to challenge male discourse as well as assumptions about high modernism's control by men. These playwrights' contributions to the avant-garde modernist theater contradict reputed masculinist aesthetics. Likewise, the British avant-garde lodged in Bloomsbury undergoes reexamination by Suzanne Young in "The Unnatural Object of Modernist Aesthetics: Artifice in Woolf's *Orlando*." Young illustrates how Woolf's focus on the "artificial" in *Orlando* resists the conventional tenets of high art. Through the use of masque and costume and the bisexual Orlando, the novel destabilizes notions of language, nature, and sexuality.

Sentimental Modernism

A correlative of the high/low art dichotomy is the debate over the sentimental and domestic subject matter that has also been designated female.[10] As Suzanne Clark maintains, "From the point of view of literary modernism, sentimentality was both a past to be outgrown and a present tendency to be despised" (2). The concurrent development of New Criticism helped discredit the sentimental as "obscene." Aimone and Tancheva each take up this question in connection with Millay and the Provincetown Players, respectively. Geneviève Morgan also argues that conventional readings of *Mrs. Dalloway* either overlook or simplify the children's story about Nurse Lugton's embroidery because of its domestic, thus sentimental (i.e., female), subject matter ("The Hostess and the Seamstress: Virginia Woolf's Creation of a Domestic Modernism"). Maria Frawley notes that the work of Alice Meynell lacked appeal in the modernist critical environment because of her maternal/sentimental concerns ("Modernism and Maternity: Alice Meynell and the Politics of Motherhood"). While Frawley argues the modernist dimensions of Meynell's maternal/sentimental poetry, Shirley Peterson explores the dark underside of the maternal in "Modernism, Single Motherhood, and the Discourse of Women's Liberation in Rebecca West's *The Judge*." These essays link the false equation of the maternal and sentimental to the devaluation of literary mothers in the modernist period.

New "Tools" of Language and Form

Many of the writers discussed in this collection, both like and unlike their male contemporaries, experimented with language and form to create what Shari Benstock terms "genderized writing" or "writing that situates itself creatively, politically, and psychologically within a certain space and time . . . [which] both mimed and undermined Modernist principles" (29). Benstock denies that this language is *écriture féminine,* although some contributors to this collection, notably Dagny Boebel, might disagree. In "The Sun Born in a Woman: H.D.'s Transformation of a Masculinist Icon in 'The Dancer,'" Boebel designates H.D.'s technique in her poem "The Dancer" as "Sapphic modernism," that is, an experimentation with form and syntax that creates space for female meanings. As such, it arrives at what Hélène Cixous calls "*jouissance.*" Aimone and Young also delineate a kind of female form in their essays on Millay and Woolf. These contributors indicate that the "genderized writing" they examine helps construct an alternative aesthetic to mainstream modernist methods of innovation. Aimone's exploration of Millay's ironic stance in her love ballads, for instance, demonstrates what Benstock calls "miming," or writing through traditional forms in order to expose disjuncture. Young points out that Woolf's self-conscious and "unnatural" style in *Orlando* not only questions conventional categories of sex and gender but also reveals anxieties about the "foundations of language and its relationship to the world" in the modern period. If, as Suzanne Clark explains, male modernists "practiced a politics of style, but . . . denied that style had a politics" (5), female modernists employed style as politics, not to deny or obscure it, but to emphasize their own displacement from public authority as well as to demonstrate the destabilization of language itself.

Point of View, Voice, Subjectivity

Another dimension of these essays concerns a radical reconsideration of point of view, voice, and subjectivity. Carolyn Heilbrun, Rachel Blau Du Plessis, and others have shown how the dominant male view imposed on women characters robs them of voice and agency.[11] With the advent of modernism, according to Clark, came "an écriture féminine which would rupture male conventions. But it did not make possible the appearance of a feminine subject in language" (7–8). The women writers discussed in this collection reconfigure poetic form to expose this limitation. For instance, Aimone and Boebel show how Millay and H.D. create male personas to underscore the irony of the objectifying male view. Likewise, Morgan illustrates Woolf's call for female subjectivity through validating her characters' domestic production.

The problem of female subjectivity is a byproduct of a heterosexual and patriarchal economy that fosters categorization and conformity at the cost of individuality and identity. As Loralee MacPike argues ("Is Mary Llewellyn an Invert? The Modernist Supertext of *The Well of Loneliness*"), Mary Llewellyn in *The Well of Loneliness* is not a textbook "invert"; consequently, she threatens the paradigm of the mannish lesbianism so neatly labeled by sexologists. Likewise, Peterson's essay shows how the unwed mother disrupts conventional, as well as feminist, definitions of sexual liberation. Both works indicate that, even at the margins of patriarchal culture, notions of female subjectivity and voice still reflect male authority. In other words, the internalization of male values retards the possibility of authentic voice for liminal characters.

The relevance of voice, however, is also expressed through silence. In her discussion of Djuna Barnes's play *To the Dogs,* Tancheva argues that the female protagonist asserts her presence through silence and gesture. At the beginning and end of the play she stands with her back to the audience "in a symbolic gesture of refusal to be known." Like Helen of Troy, she is voiceless, but in Barnes's creation, Helena is a subject, not object, who chooses her silence. In a related vein, Tancheva analyzes Boyce's *Enemies* and *Constancy* as ultrarealism, a theatrical technique that dissolves the boundaries between performers and audience. This approach challenges theater's conventional illusionism and initiates a new unity in stagecraft.

That women artists in particular transgress barriers between audience and actor, author and reader, is emphasized in Harrison's examination of Hurston's and Austin's ethnographic technique. Acting as participant-observers, these author/narrators establish an intimate relationship between tale teller and listener that bridges the gap between reader and narrative. Collapsing barriers between subject and object, art and audience, becomes a hallmark of these female modernist writers.

Plotting the Feminine

As Rachel Blau DuPlessis and Nancy Miller have argued, the question of plot marked a paradigm shift from nineteenth-century realism to early modernist texts.[12] Problems in the family romance plot emerge in Christine Sizemore's and Peterson's works on Woolf and West. In Sizemore's essay, "Virginia Woolf as Modernist Foremother in Maureen Duffy's Play *A Nightingale in Bloomsbury Square*," we see how the Oedipal plot, usually focused on desire for the father figure, here embodied as Freud, is replaced by the object of lesbian desire, Vita Sackville-West. Peterson's essay on *The Judge* notes the decentering of the heterosexual romance plot for the mother/daughter-in-law plot. Harrison's examination of Hurston's and Austin's "ethnographic fiction," which incorporates oral and literary techniques with social science strategies, undermines some of the structural underpinnings of conventional plot. Harrison foregrounds the ethnocentrism of dominant Anglo-European culture and its "plot" against those it oppresses. Tancheva's discussion of the experimental theatrical productions of the Provincetown Players demonstrates a range of departures from traditional theatrical practices. In particular, Barnes's rejection of action, plot, development, and conclusion arrests the audience's attention at a single moment that, Tancheva argues, marks the birth of the new modernist theater. Likewise, Morgan's reading of Woolf's sketch, *Nurse Lugton's Golden Thimble,* refuses the usual critical dismissal of this plotless children's tale, and finds its significance on a "structural, thematic, and semantic level" that privileges the moment over progression and development. Finally, and perhaps ironically, MacPike invites us to see through the traditional plot in *The Well of Loneliness* to disruptions in the text which recast the 1920s notion of sexual inversion. The realistic and teleological plot, she maintains, belies a more subversive text than what critics have generally seen.

Anxiety of Influence

Several essays qualify Harold Bloom's celebrated discourse on the anxiety of influence as a male phenomenon linked to the Oedipal struggle.[13] Sizemore's discourse on Duffy's struggle with Woolf spotlights the difference between *recovering* a female modernism and *recovering from* it. Unlike the "great tradition" of male authors against which subsequent male writers defined themselves, the foremothers of women's literature have not enjoyed a tenured place in the canon. Consequently, the matriarchs of the female tradition, as is allegorically illustrated in West's *The Judge,* for example, seem both benign and overpowering. Harrison's analysis of Hurston and Austin looks both backward and forward in terms of influence. The Boas school of anthropological study conditions and complicates the contributions of these writers while, at the same time, they become the foremothers to more contemporary African American and Native American female writers. In MacPike's essay on Radclyffe Hall, the influence of the sexologists is usefully problematized. While seeming to validate and make lesbian experience visible, their influence on writers such as Hall obscures other dimensions of lesbian identity.

The Canon?

We turn, finally, to the question of whether these women writers, or female modernists as we have called them, can be said to have established their own tradition or canon apart from or against mainstream modernism. Several problems emerge: Would not the process of establishing an antitradition be hierarchical itself? How does one determine which women writers fit the conventions of the alternate canon? Must the writers themselves be women or can men write female texts? What about the near absence of women of color among the writers discussed in this collection?

Eschewing a "representative" collection of women modernist writers, we have as editors, declined, perhaps by default, to decide who is "in" and who is "out" of such a canon. Some critics, like Benstock, have argued for a more inclusive, diverse modernist canon. Others, such as DeKoven and Gilbert and Gubar, subscribe to an alternative or parallel female tradition. In the introduction to *Tradition and the Talents of Women,* Florence Howe, while defending her own use of the singular form of the word *tradition,* warns against the dangers of creating new hierarchies through alternate canons: "to imagine a series of separate, 'monumental' traditions is only to establish (or to continue) a hierarchy among them, in which the traditional white male canon would survive dominant" (13). Janet Wolff describes another possibility: "The fact that women are absent from the modernist canon, therefore, is cause for critically examining the canon rather than for reluctantly accepting that modernism proved inaccessible to women" (61).

We believe that the authors of the essays included in this collection would, for the most part, agree with Wolff. Our modest goal is not so much to broaden the modernist tradition as to question its premises, to explore various responses by female literary artists to a unique cultural moment. We hope these essays will demonstrate, at the very least, that by focusing the lens of gender on modernism, our perspective will be radically and irrevocably changed.

Elizabeth Jane Harrison
Shirley Peterson

Notes

1. See Benstock, *Women of the Left Bank;* Sandra M. Gilbert and Susan Gubar, *No Man's Land: The Place of the Woman Writer in the Twentieth Century* (New Haven: Yale UP, 1988, 1989), vols. 1 and 2; Marianne DeKoven, *Rich and Strange* (Princeton: Princeton UP, 1991); Elaine Showalter, *A Literature of Their Own* (Princeton: Princeton UP, 1977); Jane Marcus, *Virginia Woolf and the Languages of Patriarchy* (Bloomington: Indiana UP, 1987); Rachel Blau DuPlessis, *Writing Beyond the Ending: Narrative Strategies of Twentieth-Century Women Writers* (Bloomington: Indiana UP, 1985); Susan Stanford Friedman, *Psyche Reborn: The Emergence of H.D.* (Bloomington: Indiana UP, 1981) and *Penelope's Web: Gender, Modernity, H.D.'s Fiction* (New York: Cambridge UP, 1990); Mary Lynn Broe and Angela Ingram, *Women's Writing in Exile* (Chapel Hill: U of North Carolina P, 1989); Marjorie Perloff, *Radical Artifice* (Chicago: U of Chicago P, 1991); Rita Felski, *The Gender of Modernity* (Cambridge: Harvard UP, 1995). See also Bonnie Kime Scott's *Refiguring Modernism,* vol. 1, *The Women of 1928* (Bloomington: Indiana UP, 1995).

2. See Hugh Kenner, Malcolm Bradbury, and James McFarlane, *Modernism 1890–1930* (New York: Penguin, 1976); Hugh Kenner, "The Making of the Modernist Canon," *Chicago Review* 34 (1984): 49–61; Hugh Kenner, *The Pound Era* (Berkeley: U of California P, 1971); Malcolm Cowley, *Exile's Return: A Literary Odyssey of the 1920's* (New York: Viking, 1951) and *A Second Flowering: Works and Days of the Lost Generation* (New York: Viking, 1973); Frederick Hoffman, *The Twenties: American Writing in the Postwar Decade* (New York: Collier, 1962).

3. See *The Gender of Modernism* 10, for Scott's "web" of modernist connections.

4. See Marcus, *Virginia Woolf*; DeKoven, *Rich and Strange,* on Stein; and Friedman, *Psyche Reborn,* on H.D.

5. In addition to Kenner, *The Gender of Modernism,* see also David Daiches, *The Novel and the Modern World* (Chicago: U of Chicago P, 1960) and *Virginia Woolf* (Norfolk, CT: New Directions, 1942).

6. See Jane Marcus, "Pathographies: The Virginia Woolf Soap Operas," *Signs* 17 (1992): 806–19.

7. In its most ubiquitous form, see Sandra M. Gilbert and Susan Gubar, *The Norton Anthology of Women's Literature,* now into a second edition.

8. See Michael Kaufmann's essay in this collection for an elaboration of this point.

9. We are indebted to our contributing writer Joe Aimone for the title of this collection.

10. See Ann Douglas, *The Feminization of American Culture* (New York: Doubleday, 1978).

11. See Rachel Blau DuPlessis, *Writing Beyond the Ending,* and Carolyn Heilbrun, *Reinventing Womanhood* (New York: Norton, 1979).

12. See Rachel Blau DuPlessis, *Writing Beyond the Ending,* and Nancy Miller, "Emphasis Added: Plots and Plausibilities," *The New Feminist Criticism: Essays on Women, Literature and Theory,* ed. Elaine Showalter (New York: Pantheon, 1985). 339–60.

13. See Harold Bloom, *The Anxiety of Influence: A Theory of Poetry* (New York: Oxford, 1973).

Works Cited

Benstock, Shari. *Women of the Left Bank: Paris, 1900–1940.* Austin: U of Texas P, 1986.

Clark, Suzanne. *Sentimental Modernism: Women Writers and the Revolution of the Word.* Bloomington: Indiana UP, 1991.

DeKoven, Marianne. "Gendered Doubleness and the 'Origins' of Modernist Form." *Tulsa Studies in Women's Literature* 8.1 (Spring 1989): 19–42.

Howe, Florence, ed. Introduction. *Traditions and the Talents of Women.* Urbana: U of Illinois P, 1991. 1–33.

Huyssen, Andreas. *After the Great Divide: Modernism, Mass Culture, Postmodernism.* Bloomington: Indiana UP, 1986.

Scott, Bonnie Kime. *The Gender of Modernism: A Critical Anthology.* Bloomington: Indiana UP, 1990.

Wolff, Janet. "Feminism and Modernism." *Feminine Sentences: Essays on Women and Culture.* Berkeley: U of California P, 1990. 51–66.

Woolf, Virginia. *Collected Essays.* 4 vols. New York: Harcourt Brace and World, 1966–67.

Millay's Big Book, or the Feminist Formalist as Modern

Joseph Aimone

> At best form gives concinnity, precision,
> paring of words and widening of vision,
> play for the mind, focus that is self-critical.
> Poets, and poems, are not apolitical.
> Women and other radicals who choose
> venerable vessels for subversive use
> affirm what Sophomore Survey often fails
> to note: God and Anonymous are not white males.
> "We always crafted language just as they did.
> We have the use, and we reclaim the credit"
> —MARILYN HACKER, *Taking Notice,* 1980

Few contemporary feminist poets (though perhaps a growing share) are as sanguine as Marilyn Hacker about the use of traditional forms. "Such forms remind us too much of Edna St. Vincent Millay," one can almost hear them say. Even feminist critics with their hearts set on some kind of recuperation of Millay concede first the hurdles her reputation puts between them and their goal, foremost often her formalism. Debra Fried, closest to my own views, introduces a scrupulous study of the complex insinuations of Millay's sonneteering by noting, "In a critical climate in which we are rediscovering the powerful experiments of American women poets in the modernist era, the tidy verses of Edna St. Vincent Millay have remained something of an embarrassment" (229). In *Masks Outrageous and Austere,* the second volume of her landmark historical study of American women poets, Cheryl Walker, equally embarrassed, identifies Millay as one of the last of the "nightingale" poets. Walker laments that "in truth, Millay was not really subversive" (164). In *Sentimental Modernism: Women Writers and the Revolution of the Word* Suzanne Clark situates her limited recuperation of Millay in a broader effort to recapture the sentimental, which Clark identifies as the repressed now returning to haunt the modernist and postmodernist text in the form of feminism (provided other feminists grasp her point and agree). But this recognition does not reelevate Millay to speaking with authority, especially regarding verse technique: "For her (passive?) repetition of conventional literary forms, the former gestures of power, is somehow feminine, slavish" (Clark 67). Even parenthetic doubts, while they hit on the crucial point of Millay's strategy of appropriation of male-dominated tradition, cannot undo Clark's clear vote of condemnation for Millay's "repetition."[1]

Such critics are not alone. In 1992 Amy Clampitt, a redoubtable contemporary poet, in a *New Republic* review of the recent Centenary Edition of Edna St. Vincent Millay's *Selected Poems,* sums up a common view of Millay: "Whatever else may be said of it, the poetry of Edna St. Vincent Millay is not modern" (44). I disagree with Clampitt, both about Millay and about the critical assumptions that underlie such a dismissive assessment. Millay was arguably an exemplary modern poet and an exemplary feminist poet.

Clampitt's reasons for her conclusion begin with oblique insinuation: She notes that Millay had harsh if casual words for the Armory show (which she attended) and for Duchamp (on a postcard). She faults Millay that she "failed to seek [Pound] out the year or two they were both in Paris" (44). Millay was by far the more widely published and often-read poet—but it seems she didn't know her proper place at the feet of the Master. Clampitt holds youthful fondness for poetry and Shakespeare in particular against Millay, explaining Millay's carefree use of archaic and literary locutions as a product of an overly bookish childhood, "[growing] up with book words and literaryisms" (Clampitt 45). Clampitt casually reproduces modernist prejudice against formal verse, claiming that "the effects produced by it are limited," and that "the bewilderments clutched at and grappled with by [William Carlos] Williams are beyond the ordering of anything so brittle" (Clampitt 45). This aesthetic of toughness, strength, and effectiveness sounds vaguely political or perhaps commercial, the preferred characteristics of a good district attorney in an era of rising crime or of a household cleaning utensil that gets the job done without breaking or requiring extra work. (One wonders if poetry really ought to be tough, strong, and effective, or at least whether that trio of utilitarian virtues are the most important values good poetry has.) But the killing blow is accusing Millay of a shallowness of intellect somehow directly a result of her formalism: "There is hardly any room for ambiguity of thought or feeling—for anything that critical analysis might take hold of or take apart" (Clampitt 45). Even Clampitt's praise of Millay (for she likes her as much as she can) suggests that what is right about Millay's best work is nothing Millay tried to achieve consciously: "a sensuous freshness that slips in and out of her work as regularly as the tide, inundating the formal music . . . with a vigor and a specificity from beyond itself" (Clampitt 45). In sum, Clampitt holds Millay too comfortable with conventionally elevated poetic diction, disrespectful of male modernists, too formal (and consequently limited, barred from serious thought), and at best the helpless vessel of an oceanic passion that only partly redeems her.

This attitude recapitulates in salient respects the dismissal John Crowe Ransom offered in "The Poet As Woman" in 1937. While Ransom would not so hastily equate form with incapacity for serious modern matter, his characterization of Millay as unintellectual and best when "sensuous freshness" is at hand anticipates Clampitt. It is only that Ransom's attitude toward women, his assumption that certain characteristics of her writing are essentially feminine, that might trouble a reader bred on contemporary poetry and ready to sympathize with Clampitt's jaundiced view of Millay. Conceding that Millay is an artist, he says, "She is also a woman. No poet ever registered herself more deliberately in that light. She therefore fascinates the male reviewer but at the same time horrifies him a little too. He will probably swing between attachment and antipathy, which may be the very attitudes provoked in him by generic woman in the flesh" (Ransom 76–77). The stereotype of feminine character that accompanies this gender anxiety translates into something very similar to Clampitt's assessment of Millay's writerly virtues and flaws. Here is Ransom's expatiation on the mental stance of women: "A woman lives for love, if we will but project that term to cover all her tender fixations upon natural objects of sense, some of them more innocent and far less reciprocal than men" (77). He concludes with backhanded praise: "man, at best is an intellectualized woman . . . [woman] is indifferent to intellectuality" (Ransom 77).

The resemblance between Ransom's patently masculinist attitude toward Millay and the conscientiously "contemporary poetic" ethos of Clampitt's review perhaps implies that sexism has gone underground and now appears as an ideology of modernism, at least in the criticism of poetry. Sandra Gilbert and Susan Gubar have suggested that male modernism in certain important respects is a reflection of male anxieties provoked by the emergence of women as potent political powers and literary progenitors, "words and works which continually sought to come to terms with, and find terms for, an ongoing battle of the sexes that was set in motion by the late nineteenth-century rise of feminism and the fall of Victorian concepts of 'femininity'" (Gilbert and Gubar, *No Man's Land* 1:xii). Denuded of explicitly antifemale ideas, the aesthetic of male modernism in its recent incarnations continues to propagate the taint of hostility that brought it into existence, ironically even in the mouths of women poets, for example, Clampitt. But if the objections raised against Millay were true, we have now entered a period of reconsideration of literary judgment that wants to rethink the modernist aesthetic (in whatever New Critical or more recent guise) as something other than a perfect culmination of or an obviously unquestionable improvement on all previous or possible future ways of thinking. We might find something has been missed in Millay's poetry that deserves attention and approbation.

Ironically, the objections brought under the aegis of the supposed modernist consensus against Millay are not even true. She is an intellectual writer, complex and ironic, a carefully modern stylist, with a clear sense of the contemporary and the cleanly elegant. And she is a postmodern eclectic user of verse forms archaic and recent, unbenighted by simpleminded wholesale rejections of traditional form.

Millay regarded herself as a modern poet, though she was a formalist. She collaborated with George Dillon on volume of translations from Charles Baudelaire's *Fleurs du Mal*. In the preface she authored for it she holds up Baudelaire as the inaugural modern poet. She diagnoses his appeal for modern readers as a matter of a certain "quality of mind" (Dillon xxx). She describes him in terms that make clear the value she places on intellectuality: "This was a poet of the intellect, a lover of order, of perfection in form, deploring superstition, sentimentality and romanticism" (Dillon xxxi). Her discussion of translation recognizes both the difficulties and the limited possibilities of success, with regard to sheer differences in vocabulary as much as differences in canons of versification between French and English. Amid this discussion she lays out her own attitude toward form: "To translate poetry into prose, no matter how faithfully and even subtly the words are reproduced, is to betray the poem. To translate formal stanzas into free verse, free verse into rhymed couplets, is to fail the foreign poet in a very important way" (Dillon vii). The grounds on which she accuses such betrayal is a concept of appropriate and necessary form:

> With most poets, the shape of the poem is not an extraneous attribute of it: the poem could not conceivably have been written in any other form. When the image of the poem first rises before the suddenly quieted and intensely agitated person who is to write it, its shadowy bulk is already dimly outlined; it is rhymed or unrhymed; it is trimeter, tetrameter, or pentameter; it is free verse, a sonnet, an epic, an ode, a five-act play. To many poets, the physical character of the poem, its rhythm, its rhyme, its music, the way it looks on the page, is quite as important as the thing they wish to say; to some it is vitally more important. To translate the poetry of E. E. Cummings into the rhymed alexandrines of Molière, would be to do Mr. Cummings no service. (Dillon vii)

Clearly Millay conceives of poetry as an intrinsically formal art. She accepts the possibility and even emphasizes the necessity of free verse. She is not a stylistic reactionary, but neither does she share the casual dismissal of traditional form as something "brittle," whose "effects . . . are limited." Free verse is for her one of a variety of technical choices rather than a kind of breakthrough into a bigger world. And given her insistence on the unity of intellectuality and formal perfectionism in the work of Baudelaire, it seems unlikely that she would accept an assumption (such as Clampitt's) that a traditional verse form, such as the sonnet, say, would have "hardly any room for ambiguity of thought or feeling—for anything that critical analysis might take hold of or take apart" (Clampitt 45). A cursory sample of her poetry will, in fact, show just the opposite.

It is customary to begin an examination of Millay's poetics with a look at "Renascence," since its tetrameter rhyming, its easy optimism, and its straining idealism exemplify the stereotyped thoroughly unmodern Millay. A better example of Millay's modernism is "Spring" from *Second April*:

To what purpose, April, do you return again?
Beauty is not enough.
You can no longer quiet me with the redness
Of little leaves opening stickily.
I know what I know.
The sun is hot on my neck as I observe
The spikes of the crocus.
The smell of the earth is good.
It is apparent that there is no death.
But what does that signify?
Not only under ground are the brains of men
Eaten by maggots.
Life in itself
Is nothing,
An empty cup, a flight of uncarpeted stairs.
It is not enough that yearly, down this hill,
April
Comes like an idiot, babbling and strewing flowers.

(Millay, Collected Poems 53)

This is free verse: freer than most free verse. The variations from regularity of line length are extreme. The line breaks emphasize or retard syntactic flow. The sentences are severely simple, for the most part. A grammatical break takes place in the first sentence, but the interrogatory appositive nomination of April forces emphasis on the preceding word, "purpose." The only inversion in the poem serves well the sarcastic irony it expresses, with "Not only under the ground are the brains of men / Eaten by maggots." The other images are also flatly unsentimental: the sun hot on the neck, the spikes of the crocus, the word "stickily" pulling the little red leaves out of their sentimental expectation, the mysteriously uncarpeted stairs, and finally, a babbling idiot tossing flowers. (One wonders if he drools!) And the poem is a kind of recognition of the irony of natural beauty for the disaffected subject and of the intellectually unsatisfying condition of human life. Yet this dark recognition is tempered by a hinted temptation simply to enjoy the sheer exuberance of April, a temptation that must be felt even if inevitably foregone by the uninnocent subject.

Even Millay's most simple verses, her most obviously traditional in form and diction, take on interesting resonance against the background of the wars of the sexes posited by Gilbert and Gubar. Consider "The Witch Wife":

She is neither pink nor pale
  And she never will be all mine;
She learned her hands in a fairy-tale,
  And her mouth on a valentine.

> She has more hair than she needs;
>   In the sun 'tis a woe to me!
> And her voice is a string of coloured beads,
>   Or steps leading into the sea.
>
> She loves me all that she can,
>   And her ways to my ways resign;
> But she was not made for any man,
>   And she never will be all mine.

The meter is a loose, folky, anapestic stanza, rhythmically identical to the limerick, but marked with different rhyming positions:

⏑ ⏑ — ⏑ — ⏑ —
She is neither pink nor pale,

⏑ ⏑ — — ⏑ ⏑ — ⏑ —
And she never will be all mine;

— ⏑ ⏑ — ⏑⏑ — ⏑ —
She learned her hands in a fairy tale,

⏑ ⏑ — ⏑⏑ — ⏑ —
And her mouth on a valentine.

The singsong rhythm creates a progressively more compelling cadence, as each stanza puts forth first a pair of lines between which we pause, then a pair without pause— the relentless beat slams on in the third line right into the fourth, skipping and galloping through iambs and anapests.

This chanting seems as unmodern as possible, with modernism's studied insistence on maturity. (Stephen Dedalus may remain stuck in a lifelong adolescent crisis, but he does not return to his nursery). And the archaisms, such as "'tis," belong in a nursery rhyme as easily as in the nineteenth century, not in a poem made after Pound's gospel. The odd formulations hardly reflect a modern purity of expression: How does one learn one's hands and mouth? How can a voice be a string of colored beads or steps to the sea? These seem more like infelicities than salubrious difficulties.

One might try to write off this poem as a bit of juvenile-oriented Gothicism. Only the word "resign" comes out of an unchildish lexicon. But all this "childishness" has a point: the speaker is male, and he is speaking of the intractability of woman. The nursery rhyme thinking is masculine thinking, bewailing the female's nonconformity to his desires, designs, and purposes. He objects that she is "neither pink nor pale," neither an unworldly and protected indoor thing nor weak or fearful. She has acquired power, "learned her hands," in the imagination, "a fairy-tale." And she has acquired both blatantly sexual beauty and the ability to speak, her mouth "on a valentine," which pattern of acquisition suggests the transformation of her objectification in the discourse of romantic love into a position of power to speak.

That she has "more hair than she needs" identifies her as excessive in the male economy—he thinks he knows what she needs, and he knows she has more than he thinks she ought to, the fact that it is only hair notwithstanding. Further, it troubles him that her sign of excess be seen "in the sun." The double significance of the female mouth, as beauty object and as threatening power, recurs in the third and fourth lines of the second stanza, as her voice becomes first "a string of coloured beads" and then the way to oblivion as "steps leading into the sea."

The speaker explains in the last stanza that she loves him "all that she can," a limited affection which he translates into her submission as "her ways to my ways resign." It is notable that he erases her agency, recording no resignation by her, only by her "ways." And he admits the incompatibility of his desire with her, but attributes the incompatibility to her nature rather than her choice, saying "she was not made for any man." He concludes with a frustration that reveals the full measure of domination his quasi-infantile masculine desire demands: "And she never will be all mine."

This ironic use of a childish formalism to make a feminist riposte to masculinist sexual politics does not exhaust Millay's modes of exploiting traditional forms. She is best known as a sonneteer. A glance at one of them will make obvious the degree to which her poetry's virtues are confined to what Clampitt calls "sensuous freshness that slips in and out of her work as regularly as the tide, inundating the formal music . . . with a vigor and a specificity from beyond itself" (45). Consider this untitled sonnet from *The Harp Weaver:*

> I, being born a woman and distressed
> By all the needs and notions of my kind,
> Am urged by your propinquity to find
> Your person fair, and feel a certain zest
> To bear your body's weight upon my breast:
> So subtly is the fume of life designed,
> To clarify the pulse and cloud the mind,
> And leave me once again undone, possessed.
> Think not for this, however, the poor treason
> Of my stout blood against my staggering brain,
> I shall remember you with love, or season
> My scorn with pity,—let me make it plain:
> I find this frenzy insufficient reason
> For conversation when we meet again.
>
> (Collected Poems 601)

The orientation is intellectual, detached if not passionless. And the graces of this poem are in its intellectuality and wit. Sexual attraction becomes, coolly, "a certain zest." The alliterative pairings of "needs and notions," "stout blood" and "staggering brain," "clarify" and "cloud" lay on a thickly ironic "literaryism." Millay's speaker sarcastically reduces sexual passion to "frenzy" and "frenzy" to "insufficient reason" in a blunt refusal to talk to a former lover. The reversal of the form's generic expectations is complete: A male voice, speaking to and of a female object with transcendent passion and lasting if unhappy devotion, has become a female voice, speaking to and of a male object with untranscendent passion and blithely temporary interest. Here is the patriarchal Petrarchan's nightmare come true, the unfaithful woman who casually uses and loses her lover like a toy, while maintaining an at once appealing and threatening self-possession, with as cerebral a rationale as any male modernist womanizer could boast of.

Now this biting "lightness" may tempt the male modernist (in flight already) to disparage Millay for lack of sobriety if not for lack of intellect. But the volume containing this sonnet also contains the narrative series "Sonnets from an Ungrafted Tree," which gives the story of a woman returning to manage the passing of her former lover. The nature of the original separation is unclear, but he is now unloved by her, and the tale holds a mood of Hardyian gloom and disillusion. In the final sonnet of the sequence, the female protagonist experiences her distance from her previous engagement with him:

> Gazing upon him now, severe and dead,
> It seemed a curious thing that she had lain
> Beside him many a night in that cold bed,
> And that had been which would not be again.
> From his desirous body the great heat
> Was gone at last, it seemed, and the taut nerves
> Loosened forever. Formally the sheet
> Set forth for her today those heavy curves
> And lengths familiar as the bedroom door.
> She was as one who enters, sly and proud,
> To where her husband speaks before a crowd,
> And sees a man she never saw before—
> The man who eats his victuals at her side,
> Small, and absurd, and hers: for once, not hers, unclassified.
>
> (622)

Note the Frostian simplicity of "that had been which would not be again." And the simile in the sestet, likening the woman's state at the funeral to that of a woman watching her husband speak publicly and recognizing her alienation from him, subtly inflects the separation imposed by his death with relief. Metrical devices aid this effect, as the accent of the foot hammers on "once" in "for once, not hers" and the delayed completion of the rhyme (the line is seven iambs long) with "unclassified" produces a sense of long-awaited resolution, loading the dry, Latinate word with excruciating emotion.

Millay uses free verse, nursery rhyme, and the sonnet with equal freedom and with a subtle intelligence in working out the gendered politics of the modern.

Millay's dramatic writing also argues for her seriousness as a modern writer, beginning with *Aria da Capo,* her first mature dramatic text.

Aria da Capo was written for and performed by the Provincetown Players and became an immediate success, with many other productions elsewhere soon after, as Millay explains in the author's note in the original Harper edition. It is a blank-verse masque, an expressionist tragic farce, replete with intellectual resonance, even anticipating in its black humor, logical impasses, and plot recursions perhaps Beckett's tramps or Stoppard's (or Pirandello's) caricatures. Two plots interweave in a complex metatheatrical interchange, both deceptively simple: Pierrot and Columbine banter blithely together, love-teasing and social commentary. Pierrot sets himself up first as a lover, then as a student who will "search into all things," then as a modern artist:

> PIERROT: . . . I am become
> A painter, suddenly,—and you impress me—
> Ah, yes!—six orange bull's eyes, four green pinwheels,
> And one magenta jelly-roll, m— the title
> As follows: Woman Taking in Cheese from Fire-Escape.
>
> (Millay, *Aria da Capo* 3)

Subsequently he takes up music "On a new scale. . . . Without tonality." He becomes a socialist: "I love / Humanity; but I hate people" (4). Columbine offers him a persimmon, which he refuses:

> I am become a critic; there is nothing
> I can enjoy. . . . However, set it aside;
> I'll eat it between meals.
>
> (7)

The happy repartee is interrupted by Cothurnus, called Masque of Tragedy in the dramatis personae, who runs Pierrot and Columbine off stage. When Pierrot, judging from appearances, says that Cothurnus is sleepwalking, Cothurnus replies with black irony, "I never sleep" (8). Cothurnus coaches two new characters, Thrysis and Corydon, through a rehearsal that slips in and out of its dramatic illusion, periodically prompted by Cothurnus from the playbook he holds, and occasionally interrupted by ejaculations from Pierrot and Columbine offstage. Thyrsis and Corydon initially resist Cothurnus's direction, complaining (as had Pierrot and Columbine) that this scene should come later in the play. They raise other objections, saying that they cannot build the wall their scene requires with only the tissue paper available on stage (though that is exactly what they will do). Thyrsis sums up unwittingly the project of the play as a whole when he says, "We cannot act / A tragedy with comic properties!" (10)

Thereafter unfolds a tragedy with comic properties, both in the sense that this tragedy has comic properties in general and in the specific sense of comic stage-properties: the aforementioned tissue, a bowl of confetti, and so on. In this tragedy, Thyrsis and Corydon are two shepherds meditatively tending their common flock. In proper bucolic fashion Corydon suggests they compose a song together. The subject of the song he proposes is "a lamb that thought himself a shepherd" (12). The hubris of the lamb will turn out to be the hubris of Thyrsis and Corydon. Thyrsis forgets his line and Cothurnus prompts him with "I know a game worth two of that" (12). Thyrsis picks up the thread of the script and suggests they build a wall instead of composing a song. They build a wall of tissue, separating the sheep of one from the sheep of the other. Each grows jealous of his own "property" as defined by the wall and envious of the other's. They mistrust each other, prompted by Cothurnus, who supplies at several junctures the forgotten line, "How do I know it isn't a trick?" (14) Thyrsis will not allow Corydon's sheep to drink the water which is only on Thyrsis's side of the wall. They both want to stop mistrusting each other but cannot. Corydon discovers jewels on his side of the wall, and Thyrsis offers to trade water for the sheep for jewels, but Corydon refuses. He claims to have given up his life as shepherd in favor of that of a merchant. And he becomes ambitious: "And if I set my mind to it / I dare say I could be an emperor" (21). Corydon contemplates the luxuries and fame that his great wealth can bring him, ignoring Thyrsis's warning that his sheep will die. Now, Thyrsis discovers a poisonous-rooted plant on his side of the wall, and when Corydon finally becomes thirsty, Thyrsis agrees to trade water for a necklace of Corydon's jewels. Thyrsis poisons Corydon with a bowl of offered water; Corydon in turn strangles Thyrsis to death as he dies himself of the poisoned water.

Cothurnus hides the bodies under the table at which Pierrot and Columbine had sat and calls them back on stage to do their scene again. Pierrot protests that the audience will not stand for the bodies to be left on stage while the farce is played. Cothurnus assures him that the audience will forget, though the bodies remain in plain sight. Pierrot and Columbine take up their exchange exactly where they had begun it, wondering what day it is, as if nothing had happened—or as if this state was implicit in the empty stage at the beginning of the play. The various postures of artist, socialist, critic, and so on, adopted by Pierrot as he verbally abuses Columbine, seem now to have been predicated on the tragedy of Thyrsis and Corydon having always already) happened. Their gendered byplay cohabits with the primal violence of equals entangled in deadly hostilities the origin of which they cannot remember, but which evolve out of a substitution of "a game worth two of that" for the collaborative production of a song. The song, were it possible to produce it, would be an admonitory one about a lamb that thinks it is a shepherd. Such a lamb among lambs is an equal with a delusion of superiority; and this same delusion is doubly present in the fatal competition of Thyrsis and Corydon.

It is hard to misread the intellectual complexity of this little play in light of later absurdist, existential, and minimalist drama in this century. The rest of Millay's dramatic writing may deserve a fuller examination on its own merits. But Millay also exploits the possibilities of dramatic polyvocality in works not intended for the stage. In 1937, the year John Crowe Ransom was damning her with faint praise for the feminine unintellectuality of her poetry, she published *Conversation at Midnight.* It is a closet drama of drawing-room conversation, the conversants exclusively male and educated but otherwise diverse enough: a stock-broker, a painter, a writer of short stories, a communist poet, a Catholic priest, a wealthy and liberal Euro-American aristocrat, an ad man, and a butler and chauffeur. The play explores the sometimes intractable differences of opinion between atheist and believer, communist and conservative, communist and liberal, and so on, spiced with discussions of "masculine" pursuits like hunting quail or women. The irony is thick.

The exclusion of women from the dramatis personae, plausible though it may be for the play's pretext, demands some explanation as the work of Millay, otherwise so committed to including a woman's view. I believe that one of Millay's untitled sonnets sums up nicely her sense of the literary politics of gender in a way that can shed some light on this exclusion:

> Oh, oh, you will be sorry for that word!
> Give back my book and take my kiss instead.
> Was it my enemy or my friend I heard,
> "What a big book for such a little head!"
> Come, I will show you now my newest hat,
> And you may watch me purse my mouth and prink!
> Oh, I shall love you still, and all of that.
> I never again shall tell you what I think.
> I shall be sweet and crafty, soft and sly;
> You will not catch me reading any more;
> I shall be called a wife to pattern by;
> And some day when you knock and push the door,
> Some sane day, not too bright and not too stormy,
> I shall be gone, and you may whistle for me.
>
> (*Collected Poems* 591)

The simple plot allegorizes the relationship of the woman writer to a male-dominated literary tradition as a marriage of woman and man. Her voice threatens revenge. She demands the return of her book, for which we may read something like control of the poetic imaginary. She offers him her kiss in exchange, knowing his presuppositions about her function as object of his desire. She questions, half-seriously it seems, whether he is her enemy or her friend, allowing that his answer may not be the same as hers. She reveals the events leading up to his theft of the book: he insulted her intelligence, presuming that her "little head" (read "small intelligence") and the "big book" (read, perhaps, "writing-in-general," the category of the literary itself) ill-matched. She offers to pose for him and show off what he might consider a more appropriate concern for her "little head," her latest item of millinery. She reassures him of her love casually, as if the assurance were unimportant as well as almost unneeded, "and all of that." Having lulled him, she becomes sarcastic, though we expect he may not catch her tone as she announces a campaign of deception, in which she will be "sweet and crafty" in concealing her interest in the "big book" from him. Finally, perhaps once she has that book in her possession, she will disappear from his domain, presumably into her own.

Reading this poem as a microcosm of Millay's attitudes about the situation of woman with respect to man and to the literary, this poem explains how she could want to write a serious bit of social commentary in verse and voice it entirely in male characters. In conforming to controlling expectations of the male-dominated literary tradition—that only men take up subjects like communism and liberalism, let alone quail hunting—Millay inscribes the female presence in its very absence: she doesn't let him see her reading.

Millay's campaign of deception may explain her broadly eclectic formalism also. *Conversation,* like Millay's work as a whole, makes evenhanded use of both traditional (even archaic) versification and free verse. Since both the tradition and the modernist "revolution" in verse technique are (or at least were for her) patently male-dominated affairs, her willingness to write in either formal or free-verse mode, her refusal to take sides, may betray a covert motive to get control of the "big book" rather than be read to by a self-important male who decides what she can understand with her "little head."

"Oh, oh, you will be sorry for that word" also allegorizes the relationship between Millay and her recent critical readers, theorists and poet alike. One way or another they treat her as somehow defective, citing as flaws her very strategies of deceptively occupying the expected positions in masculine poetics. They think she is out of her league up against contemporary feminists and canonical poets. They patronize her and take her book away. She offers, and they don't understand why, her flamboyantly feminized kiss and her thoughtful silence. Once we recognize her as a resourcefully ingenious and independent-minded poet, she has possession of the "big book," and they can go whistle.

Note

1. Jane Stanbrough, in perhaps the earliest of the feminist critical "recuperations" of Millay, characterizes Millay's entire poetics as inhabited by a congenital stance of tragic female vulnerability. In fact, I would not want to disagree with Stanbrough that Millay's "profound insight into her self's inevitable capitulation . . . makes Millay ultimately so vulnerable and her poetry so meaningful" (199), though I can imagine how this view might be seen as ultimately itself a capitulation to John Crowe Ransom's ill-taken dismissal of Millay as "the poet as Woman." As capitulation and recapitulation may be rusing signs of defeat, I can't help finding a bit more to Millay's acquisition of the dominant masculine poetics. (Even vulnerability, if it were all she were about, and it isn't, can be a weapon.) The most recent reassessment, in the third volume of Gilbert and

Gubar's *No Man's Land, Letters from the Front,* traces the historic rewriting of Millay by a masculinist critical tradition with much more sense of Millay's power.

Works Cited

Clampitt, Amy. "Two Cheers for Prettiness: Edna St. Vincent Millay, *Selected Poems: The Centenary Edition,* Edited and with an Introduction by Colin Falck." *New Republic* 6 Jan., 13 Jan. 1992.

Clark, Suzanne. *Sentimental Modernism: Women Writers and the Revolution of the Word.* Bloomington: Indiana UP, 1991.

Dillon, George, and Edna St. Vincent Millay, trans. *Flowers of Evil: From the French of Charles Baudelaire with the Original Texts and a Preface by Miss Millay.* New York: Harper & Brothers, 1936.

Fried, Debra. "Andromeda Unbound: Gender and Genre in Millay's Sonnets." *Critical Essays on Edna St. Vincent Millay.* Ed. William B. Thesing. New York: G. K. Hall, 1993.

Gilbert, Sandra M., and Susan Gubar. *No Man's Land: The Place of the Woman Writer in the Twentieth Century.* Vol. 1, *The War of the Words.* New Haven: Yale UP, 1988.

————. *No Man's Land: The Place of the Woman Writer in the Twentieth Century.* Vol. 3, *Letters from the Front.* New Haven: Yale UP, 1994.

————. *Shakespeare's Sisters: Feminist Essays on Women Poets.* Bloomington: Indiana UP, 1979.

Hacker, Marilyn. *Collected Poems.* New York: Harper & Row, 1956.

————. *Taking Notice.* New York: Knopf, 1980.

Millay, Edna St. Vincent. *Aria da Capo: A Play in One Act.* New York: Harper, 1920.

————. *Collected Poems.* Evanston, IL: Harper & Row, 1956.

————. *Conversation at Midnight.* New York: Harper & Row, 1937.

Ransom, John Crowe. *The World's Body.* New York: Scribner's, 1938.

Stanbrough, Jane. "Edna St. Vincent Millay and the Language of Vulnerability." In Gilbert and Gubar, *Shakespeare's Sisters.* 183–99.

Walker, Cheryl. *Masks Outrageous and Austere: Culture, Psyche, and Persona in Modern Women Poets.* Bloomington: Indiana UP, 1991.

The Sun Born in a Woman: H.D.'s Transformation of a Masculinist Icon in "The Dancer"

Dagny Boebel

Among H.D.'s so-called lost works of the 1930s (Owens 49) was her long poem "The Dancer," both a "tribute to the achievement and perfection of the female artist" (Martz xxvii) and a protest against the ideological appropriation of the image of the female dancer by masculinist modernists, who tended to share the following notions.

First, the modern era is threatened with intellectual and social chaos. Susan Gubar and Sandra Gilbert suggest that a significant portion of the alarm expressed by intellectuals and artists in the early years of the twentieth century at cultural decline and advancing disorder was concern, in fact, over the advance of women into positions of influence and power in the arts, in politics, and in the professions. Among these upholders of the phallic order was Ezra Pound, who conceptualized originality as "the phallus or spermatozoid charging, head-on, the female chaos" (qtd. in *Sexchanges* xi).

Second, the artist's best ally in this crusade against chaos is the mostly masculine Tradition. In "Tradition and the Individual Talent," T. S. Eliot uses a metaphor that suggests that the modern artist must approach this Tradition like a mature and discriminating lover. To this Tradition—and to the task of artistic creation—he must surrender himself: "What happens is a continual surrender of himself as he is at the moment to something which is more valuable. The progress of an artist is a continual self-sacrifice, a continual extinction of personality" (589–90). It might be said that Eliot represents the relation of the male artist to the male Tradition, as well as to the act of artistic generation, in masculine, orgasmic (and homoerotic) terms: to achieve success is to die.

Finally, the literary work that results from this surrender or "death" of the individual artist will be pure form, free of any intruding personal or political statement. Through this "process of depersonalization," Eliot notes, "art may be said to approach the condition of science" (590). By valorizing science, and art that is scientific, Eliot extends into literature the longstanding "exclusion of women" from science (Schiebinger 3). In imitation of the hard (culturally masculine) facts that comprise scientific "truth," T. E. Hulme prescribes a "hard" and "dry" poetry. Hulme believes the aim of the poet should be similar to the aim of the scientist: "accurate, precise, and definite description" (12). Poetry, in short, must abandon all that has traditionally been associated with the feminine (romantic) side of the cultural binary: mystery, feeling, wetness (12).

H.D. seems to have studied closely the prescriptions of Eliot and Hulme, for in "The Dancer" she gives Apollo the voice of a masculinist modernist. Insisting that the female dancer dance *his* message *his* way, Apollo dictates to her balletic movements designed to deform her body into a phallic stylus. Not unlike this demanding Apollo, poets like Yeats and Mallarmé and critics like Heppanstall often interpreted and evaluated the art of modern female dancers, of Loie Fuller and Isadora Duncan, for example, according to the demands of masculinist modernist ideology. H.D.'s images in "The Dancer" suggest that she has created a dancer who performs both Loie Fuller's illusionary transformations and Isadora Duncan's leaps. By uniting in one dancer the characteristic dance movements of Fuller and Duncan, H.D. reappropriates the work of both of these important modern dancers for feminist, or Sapphic, modernism,[1] which, in contrast to masculinist modernism, exhibits the following qualities.

First, like masculinist modernists, feminist, or Sapphic, modernists studied the Tradition, but they did this to find traces of and to give voice to their lost, silenced, and suppressed mothers. Sapphic modernist art was generated by an expressivity based in a life-giving and life-enhancing "maternal and sororal" (Gregory 132) connection. Sapphic modernists did not perceive artistic creation as the surrender of or as the death of the artist.

Second, feminist, or Sapphic, modernist artists, like H.D., Djuna Barnes, Radclyffe Hall, and Virginia Woolf, saw through the masculinist insistence that art be without personal and political message; such insistence on purity was belied by formalistic prescriptions that privileged masculinity. Sapphic modernists abandoned the formalistic strictures of their male colleagues, daring to give expression to the suppressed and denigrated soft, moist female body. In *Notes on Thought and Vision* (1919), for example, H.D.'s metaphor for origination is the soft, moist jellyfish "placed like a foetus in the body" (19). The work of feminist modernists became increasingly personal, increasingly visionary, increasingly political, but they maintained the modernist critical, intellectual, and ironic edge.

Finally, like masculinist modernists, feminist, or Sapphic, modernists experimented with form, but not to become "hard." Through their experiments with form and syntax, they created space for female meanings.

Space for female meanings is created in the "The Dancer" when both the poet and the dancer liberate themselves from masculinist dogma and unite in an ecstatic expression of feminine *jouissance*. The poem begins, however, in a phallic aesthetic mode. A poet "from the west," who has adopted a masculinist ideology, identifies the dancer "from the east" as Other, as "witch" and as "nature." The poet maintains an analytical detachment, threatening in its insistence on control, until the third section. There the poet clearly recognizes the dancer as deity and as life-source. In the next two sections the poet follows the dancer through a series of transformations, rich in their associations with female divinity and creativity. In the sixth section, the poet recognizes Apollo as a tyrant, who has claimed the dancer as "my mistress . . . my stylus" (VI.30–31). In the next two sections, the poet sings to the dancer and claims her as "my sister"; however, Apollo is still recognized as "our Master." In the final sections of the poem, the poet, now clearly identified as female, names the dancer Rhodocleia, a figure H.D. identifies in her poem "The Master" as "heart of the sun" (XII.20) and as "that Lord become woman" (XII.25). She is also "laurel-tree" ("The Dancer" X.26), or Daphne, who stole from Apollo the powers of generativity and of rational speech. The bond between the dancer and the poet is expressed through images of Sapphic erotic ecstasy. Sappho expressed such a bond in her poems, H.D. believed.

The dance images in "The Dancer" suggest a blending together of the artistry of Loie Fuller and Isadora Duncan, two American modern dance innovators who had died only a few years before the poem was written. Female erotic bonding was sometimes noted, both in the art and lives of Fuller and Duncan. Like Loie Fuller, who was being posthumously honored at a French exhibition in the early 1930s (Kermode 151), H.D.'s dancer is a mistress of illusionary metamorphoses. Fuller had stunned her audiences by transforming herself into butterflies, flowers, and flames through elaborate costuming and lighting effects. But H.D.'s dancer is also capable of performing the leaps which marked the dances of Isadora Duncan, who shocked Fuller by dancing "nude, or nearly so" (Fuller 227). Duncan claimed, in *The Art of the Dance,* that she followed the advice of ancient Greek philosophers who wrote, "O Woman . . . come in simple tunics, letting us see the line and harmony of the body beneath" (Duncan 73). H.D. represents these Fuller-like transformations and Duncanesque leaps through linguistic image, through rhythm, and even concretely through the arrangement of the lines on the page. H.D.'s dancer, like Fuller and Duncan, liberates herself from the rules of ballet, which are to dance what syntax is to language.

Although Fuller was taken aback by the younger dancer's "nude" performances, she introduced Isadora Duncan to European audiences, and for a short time, despite their different styles of performing, Duncan danced with Fuller's company. But Fuller was not the only one who was shocked. Although Duncan's own company was later to bring forth, to some observers, images of Sappho on Lesbos (Heppanstall 271), a very young Duncan was amazed by the open expressions of Sapphic eroticism she found on her first introduction to Fuller's company: "in a magnificent apartment, I found Loie Fuller surrounded by her entourage. A dozen or so beautiful girls were grouped about her, alternately stroking her hands and kissing her. . . . I was completely taken back by coming upon this extreme attitude of expressed affection, which was quite new to me. . . . In the midst of these nereid, nymphs, iridescent apparitions, there was a strange figure in a black tailor-made. . . . I was at once attracted by this personality but felt that her enthusiasm for Loie Fuller possessed her entire emotional force" (*My Life* 94–96).

It is not surprising that, only a short time after they joined forces, Fuller and Duncan broke with each other in Budapest (Blair 54). However, although their styles were different, both dancers were social and artistic revolutionaries. Duncan, a Marxist who was accused of being a feminist, appreciated Fuller as "an extraordinary genius. . . . Unbelievable. Not to be repeated or described" (*My Life* 95). And that Loie Fuller thought of herself as a feminist is clear, for she reprints in her autobiography the following review of her performances: "'The other evening I had, as it were, a vision of a theatre of the future, something of the nature of a feministic theatre. Women are more and more taking men's places. They are steadily supplanting the so-called stronger sex. The court-house swarms with women lawyers. The literature of imagination and observation will soon belong to women of letters. . . . Just watch and you will see women growing in influence and power; and if, as in Gladstone's phrase, the nineteenth century was the working-man's century, the twentieth will be the women's century'" (282). To this male journalist, the female modern dancer delineated the rising importance of women in culture. Other male viewers, however, found a feminist meaning for female modern dance too threatening. They suppressed such an interpretation, in favor of the notion that the female dancer was dancing *their* meaning.

A similar, but much earlier, fear of the meaning of female dancing has been noted by historian David Underdown. The association of the image of the dancing woman with liberation and power disturbed Puritans in seventeenth-century England. At that time, Puritans attacked revels, which had come to be identified with the image of the dancing woman, that is with "an unacceptable degree of [female] sexual freedom" (48). This dancing woman is viewed by cultural historian Enid Welsford as a rebel who in her dance took on the identity of the *mommo,* a suppressed underworld goddess. The dancer/*mommo* rocked the ground and threatened the patriarchal edifice. Welsford notes the linguistic link between the words *revel* and *rebel* and between the reveler's dramatic dancing, called the *momerie* or *mumming,* and the *mommo* (359).

The fear of subversion through female silent expressive art continued into the twentieth century. This image still connoted to some males a threat to civilized order. In "Ballets," for example, Mallarmé suggests that the dancer embodies many of the qualities Welsford found in the image of the *mommo.* He viewed her as embodying "some elemental aspect of earthy form" (112). He omits, however, Welsford's association of this "elemental aspect" with feminine rebellion. He inscribes her body with *his* meaning: "the illiterate ballerina . . . that sorceress . . . through her always ultimate veil, she will give you back *your* concepts in all their nakedness, and silently inscribe *your* vision as would a Symbol—which she is" (115; emphases added).

Mallarmé doubtless thought he was flattering Fuller when he called this highly conscious artist who "sometimes kept her electricians at work all through the night to achieve her effect" (Fuller 258) an "enchantress . . . working . . . by instinct" (qtd. in Kermode 154). Female modern dancers, however, tended to view themselves as artistic and, in some cases, even as social revolutionaries. Unfortunately, the views of these women tended to be discredited or ignored.

Only by silencing the dancer herself could she become, for masculinist modernists, *the* representative modern artist. To modernist male poets and critics, female dancers represented "in visible form the incomprehensible image of art in the modern world" (Kermode 154). Consequently, dance held a predominant position among the arts in the first third of the twentieth century (Sweeney 65). Both the high status of the art and the idealization of the female dancer are curious phenomena, given the fact that modern dance was distinctly a "mothered" art, an art based in female experience. Virtually all of its early theorists, performers, choreographers, teachers, and company managers were women.

Isadora Duncan, raised in a family of women, traced the origins of her art to the music and poetry she learned from her mother and grandmother. She also saw the crushing effect of marriage, which "annihilated" the "glorious voice" of her Aunt Augusta (*My Life* 19). Like ballet, marriage prescribed a discipline, or a "syntax," that silenced women. Duncan abandoned both traditional marriage and traditional dance—ballet. She viewed ballet as "a false and preposterous art . . . which deformed the female body" (Blair 29). In "The Dance of the Future" (1903), Duncan writes, "All the movements of our modern ballet school are sterile movements because they are unnatural . . . under the skirts, under the tricots are dancing deformed muscles. Look still farther—underneath the muscles are deformed bones. . . . The ballet condemns itself by enforcing the deformation of the beautiful woman's body!" (263). Such deformation and violation of the female reveals the misogynistic aims of the inventors of this art. Because ballet reflected the corrupt, hierarchical, aristocratic, and sexist court in which it originated, Duncan deemed it an inappropriate art form for American children, who were being raised to revere democratic principles:

> The real American type can never be a ballet dancer. The legs are too long, the body too supple and the spirit too free. . . . The Minuet is the expression of the unctuous servility of courtiers of the time of Louis XIV. . . . Why should our children bend the knee in that fastidious and servile dance. . . . Rather let them come forth with great strides, leaps and bounds, with lifted forehead and far-spread arms, dancing the language of our pioneers. . . . When the American children dance in this way, it will make of them Beautiful Beings worthy of the name of Democracy. (*The Art of the Dance* 49–50)

Duncan believed that her dances expressed the freedom and lack of hierarchy that characterize both female friendships and American democracy. However, Duncan was far from appreciated as an innovator, a liberator, and a theorist. Dance critic Rayner Heppanstall was especially savage in his critique of Duncan in "The Sexual Idiom" (1936). In that essay, Heppanstall blasts Duncan for being a feminist whose schools of dance elicited the image of "Sappho and the Isle of Lesbos" (271). He belittles Duncan as a theorist, mocking her interest in philosophers such as Nietzsche and Kant—"as though an Isadora might have something to do with Pure Reason" (269). He attacks Duncan's rejection of ballet in order to "dance the freedom of woman . . . [to] help womankind to a new knowledge of the possible strength and beauty of their bodies" (*The Art of the Dance* 63). Heppanstall strongly moves against this new subjective style. In his view, it is only ballet that can erase from the female dancer the "sin" of her femaleness: "a woman on her points, 'because of change in significant line and stress and action, ceases to be significantly a woman. She becomes an idealised and stylized creature of the Theatre.' And there is a kind of eternal virginity about her. She is inaccessible. She remains unravished" (274).

But, amidst all this pique, Heppanstall makes the intriguing suggestion that Duncan's rejection of ballet was the equivalent of a writer rejecting syntax: "Ballet . . . is very like what . . . pure syntactical and geometrical logic and form are in the making of Literature" (279). His construction of literature follows, not surprisingly, a masculine modernist definition. Duncan rejects ballet, the syntax that deforms (deforms) the Woman. Interestingly, Heppanstall, in what may be an inversion of the Medusa myth, seems to be saying that unless she is deformed by balletic syntax, a woman dancing is a monster too dangerous to look upon. Because he had avoided danger by never watching Duncan dance, Heppanstall believed himself to be her ideal critic: "I never saw Isadora Duncan dance. That, I believe, may well be my best qualification for writing about her. For it seems that nobody who did see her was able to tell about her sanely" (267).

The poet/critic in H.D.'s "The Dancer" also seems concerned about falling under the spell of an enchantress and losing detachment and objectivity. Like T. E. Hulme, and perhaps like the young H.D., this poet seems to believe that the aim of poetry is "accurate, precise, and definite description" (12). Near the beginning of the poem, the poet follows Hulme's advice to the letter:

> I watch intent
> as one outside with whom is the answer;
> intelligence alert,
> I am here to report,
>
> . . . .
> I am perfectly aware,
> perfectly cold. (II.7–10, 14–15)

It is almost impossible for the reader to think of this gazing poet as female, even though we know that a female poet can adopt a theory of the subject which structures perceptions in ways that are normatively male: a hierarchy is established that does violence to the subordinate term. The poet in H.D.'s poem, who might even be H.D. in her early imagist stage, claims a hierarchically higher position than that of the female dancer, who is treated as a mere object and threatened with further violence:

> nothing is hidden/from me . . .
> if you make one false move,
> I will slay you. (II.26–29)

The dancer responds to these threats by deconstructing through her dance the hierarchy the poet has asserted. H.D. represents the movements of the dance through concrete notation. The dancelike arrangement of the lines on the page creates a visual image of Isadora Duncan in the midst of a leap, arms outstretched, legs separated, toes of her bare feet pointed, outlining the way she is depicted in the drawings of Walkowitz. The section begins with the three one-word lines, each stating the word "fair." The repetition establishes the unity of the three voices in the poem, that of the poet, of the dancer, and of Apollo. At this "turning point," so to speak, the poem and the dance mirror each other. The speakers unite into a *we* in the subsequent line, raising a rhetorical question:

> Fair
> fair,
> fair,
> do we deserve beauty? (III.1–4)

The answer follows in three more single-word lines, in which the word *fire* marks a shift away from preceding conventional images in which the woman functions as a mere fantasy. As the constructed object of the masculine (Apollonian) gaze, she had mirrored back to men their own truth. In a Promethean act of re-creation, H.D.'s metaphors reconnect the feminine with fire, that is, with the female artist's own desire, with her own source of power:

> pure,
> pure
> fire. (III.5–7)

In the lines that follow, the syntax is broken, signaling that the separation of subject and object, structured into phallic syntax, is overcome. It is a separation which the formerly "perfectly cold," "classical" poet had validated. The oxymoronic joining of fire and ice signals the end of this separation; the feminine power—"fire," "redrose"—buried in the icy grave of the Tradition, that is, of the phallocentric myth, is exposed and released:

> loveliest
> O strong,
> ember

> burns in ice,
> snow folds over ember;
> fire flashes through clear ice
> pattern frozen is red-rose . . . (III.12–18)

In *The Wise Sappho,* H.D. writes that Sappho breaks the syntax in order to provide space where flowers, that is, female meanings, can grow: "[R]eading deeper we are inclined to visualize these broken sentences and unfinished rhythms as rocks—perfect rock shelves and layers of rock between which flowers by some chance may grow" (58). The metaphoric valorization of female existence out of a coincidental (or fatal) formation does not only reinsert a Promethean subjectivity but also demonstrates the natural and (almost) aesthetic power of a recreative sexual symbol.

Apollo imperiously and brutally stakes his claim on the dancer, commanding her,

> dance for you are my mistress,
> you are my stylus,
> you write in the air with this foot
> . . . .
> your taut frame is one arrow,
> my message . . . (VI.30–32, 37–38)

However, she escapes. Together, the poet and the dancer create an art of Sapphic love. The images are feminine—a circle, opening, closing and opening again; butterflies; the moon-flower; and water:

> O love in a circle
> of opening,
> of closing,
> of opening:
> you are every colour of butterfly,
> now in a frail robe, you are a white butterfly,
> burning with white fervour,
> you are moon-flower
> seen in water. (V.15–23)

These images are unlike the phallic images prescribed by Apollo; he insistently demands that the dancer dance *his* message:

> your flung hand
> is that pointed arrow,
> your taut frame
> is one arrow,
> my message . . . (V.35–39)

Both dancer and poet escape Apollo's possessive tyranny and express a specifically feminine divinity through the image of the laurel tree, whose "under-current of sap" is like the "slow / beat of our hearts" (IV.9–10). They reject Apollo's ballet and syntax and find freedom. In "The Laugh of the Medusa," Hélène Cixous counsels women to "write through their bodies." They can only do this by "sweeping away syntax": "We've been turned away from our bodies, shamefully taught to ignore them, to strike them with that stupid sexual modesty. . . . Women must write through their bodies, they must invent the impregnable language that will wreck partitions, classes, and rhetorics, regulations and codes. . . . Such is the strength of women . . . sweeping away syntax" (256). Isadora Duncan swept away syntax, and Heppanstall was afraid to look at the "impregnable" message. In fact, as a masculinist modernist, he condemns her for *carrying* a message: "She speaks always the 'message' of her Art. . . . She was, in fact, a bit of a feminist, a good deal of a suffragette. She wasted a lot of enthusiasm, for instance, on Emancipation" (275).

Abandoning ballet, Duncan believed, liberated the female body to "write" female meanings. The meaning could be enthusiastically received, as it was in the case of Loie Fuller's admirer, quoted above. Or it could be condemned. There is, however, a third possibility: misinterpretation.

And, indeed, comparing what female dancers said about their art with the interpretations of their masculine spectators reveals that the high status of dance was, perhaps, more a testimony to the power of the pen in male hands to rewrite the dancers' meanings than it was an understanding and acceptance of the dancers' messages. Under male scrutiny, the female dancer performed the function that women have always performed in patriarchal culture, a function Virginia Woolf succinctly described in *A Room of One's Own* as "looking-glasses possessing the magic and delicious power of reflecting the figure of man at twice its natural size" (35). And indeed, such fantasy representations are to be found in works such as Yeats's "Byzantium" and Valéry's "Philosophy of the Dance": onto the figure of the dancer we see projected their own visions, fantasies, and desires.

The phenomenon of projection dominates the early stanzas of "The Dancer." In these stanzas, both a poet and Apollo seek to control the female dancer through proprietary interpretation. The poem contains three distinct speakers. First, there is a poet "from the west." For awhile, that voice willingly subordinates itself to a second speaker, the tyrant Apollo, who is known simply as the "Sun/ . . . Lord." Finally, late in the poem, the dancer, too, who has up to that point expressed herself solely through bodily movement, is given voice.

Early in the poem, the poet assumes a Western/masculine stance from which the female dancer is viewed as "witch" and "nature," as Other and object:

> you are a witch
> you rise out of nowhere;
> the boards you tread on,
> are transferred
> to Asia Minor
>
> . . . .

> I worship nature
> you are nature. (I. 13–17, 29–30)

This poet, like other modernists, views dance as both the most elemental and the most modern of the arts: it is silent, pure form, free of personal or political message. James Johnson Sweeney writes that dance is the "gesture behind speech," the "rhythmic pattern beneath all" (66). However, the female modern dance is revolutionary and political. Its rejection of ballet is a rejection of a phallic "syntax," which, as both the poet and the dancer in H.D.'s poem come to understand, validates masculine power. Balletic syntax, as Heppanstall agrees, silences the feminine text. For this reason, he applauds it. The ballet is a modern form of the ritual sacrifice of the feminine, a sacrifice that Stravinsky's modern ballet, *Rite of Spring* (1911–13), reenacts.

Words, too, can be lethal, Luce Irigaray argues. She charges that the syntax of discourse is also political syntax and a means of masculine "self-representation" (*This Sex Which Is Not One* 132). Words, Irigaray points out, can make women "disappear" ("When Our Lips Speak Together" 69). When this happens, *nothing* is left. *Nothing* (no-thing) is one of the words for *woman* in Renaissance English. *Nothing* could also mean *chaos,* equated by Edmund in *King Lear* with the goddess Nature. H.D. may be playing with these meanings when she has her poet boast, "nothing is hidden / from me" (441). This *nothing* can be the *woman,* or the feminine *chaos,* to which Ezra Pound had referred, a *nothing* that is hidden indeed from this Apollo loyalist. The poet does not see a woman dancing, but an "abstract" (442), perfectly writing Apollo's—and the poet's—poem:

> You can not betray us
> not the Sun
> who is your Lord;
> for you are abstract,
> making no mistake,
> slurring no word
> in the rhythm you make,
> the poem,
> writ in the air. (III. 32–40)

Here, H.D.'s poet comes close to echoing Mallarmé, who had written, in "Ballets," that the female dancer is "*not* a girl, but rather a metaphor . . . with miraculous lunges and abbreviations, writing with her body. . . . Her poem is written without the writer's tools" (112; emphasis added).

Through the words of both Mallarmé and H.D.'s poet, the woman artist, like all good masculinist modernist artists, disappears. Yeats goes almost as far in "Among School Children," which ends with the dancer, who is likely a female, "disappeared" into her art:

> O body swayed to music, O brightening glance,
> How can we know the dancer from the dance? (ll. 63–64)

To each writer, it is the *female* artist, the dancer, who represents the extinction of the personal in art, even though, as I have noted above, when T. S. Eliot sets forth this notion in "Tradition and the Individual Talent," he seems to envision the "surrender," or "extinction," as happening to a male artist: "What happens is a continual surrender of himself as he is at the moment to something which is more valuable. The progress of an artist is . . . a continual extinction of personality" (590). The words *surrender* and *extinction* suggest a sexual metaphor. The something "more valuable" is the art, to which artist surrenders. It is, therefore, natural to find such "surrender" and "extinction" epitomized in a female artist, a dancer. And, in fact, when Mallarmé watched Loie Fuller perform a dance in which she created the illusion that she had been transformed into a flame, he saw her "made dead" (Kermode 155).

In "The Dancer," however, H.D.'s fire images revitalize; they do not kill. The "flame heat" of crimson rhododendrons "melts" the cold, detached, objective verse of the first two sections into an expression of loving unity between the female dancer and the poet. Finally, the dancer speaks; she addresses the poet as her "singing sister" (IX.23). The masculinist modernism articulated by writers such as T. S. Eliot and T. E. Hulme, and at first adopted by H.D.'s poet, has been replaced by a new kind of modernism, a Sapphic modernism, that H.D. extracts from her reading of the poetry of Sappho and articulates in her essay *The Wise Sappho*.

According to *The Wise Sappho,* the power of Sappho's poetry is that it is *not* objective, impersonal, or difficult, qualities valued by modernists like Hulme and Eliot. Nevertheless, Sappho's poetry was revered by these and other modernists, so much so that, according to Susan Stanford Friedman, they accepted and validated the few women poets they did "largely because of Sappho's influence" (*Psyche Reborn* 10). Imagist poet Richard Aldington, whom H.D. married in 1913, praised Sappho as "the most famous of all women" (Robinson 13), and Ezra Pound, for a time H.D.'s lover, included Sappho among the few authors who could teach new methods of "charging words," a suggestive image given his notion of originality as "*charging,* head-on, the female chaos" (28). Pound probably thought of the young Hilda Doolittle as a second Sappho when he named her "H.D., Imagiste" (Friedman, "H.D." 86). Like Sappho's, Doolittle's "hard, crisp lines without excess words or sentiment" (86) fulfilled masculinist modernist demands. However, Friedman notes, Pound's naming—and circumscription—was both premature and unfortunate:

> [T]he forces of history—particularly its cycles of cataclysmic violence—created in H.D. the need for her to develop a more explicitly gendered discourse. . . . H.D.'s later long sequence poems featured the poet as prophet wandering in the wilderness of the modern world . . . forg[ing] new myths that might give meaning to a world shattered by war, technology, and alienation. But unlike the epics of male modernists, H.D.'s poems center on the consciousness of the female poet who finds a potent force for healing in the presence of female divinity. ("H.D." 86)

The creative turning point for H.D. seems to have been the birth of her daughter Perdita in 1919 and the establishment of her relationship, shortly before that birth, with Bryher. Her new aesthetic was articulated in *Notes on Thought and Vision*, written in 1919 but unpublished until 1981. Friedman describes the work as "uterine moments of psychic suspension in a seeming sea enclosed in a globe" ("H.D." 88).

Like the masculinist modernists, H.D. turned to the tradition for confirmation of her aesthetic insights. Like them, she found this confirmation in Sappho. But unlike them, H.D. found validation in Sappho for the "maternal and sororal instinct" she recognized as the origin of her own poetic gift (Gregory 132). Sappho's poetry and the female dancer raised for H.D. what Jacqueline Rose has defined as "[t]he question of the woman's body as language (what, of that body, can achieve symbolisation). The objective is to retrieve the woman from the dominance of the phallic term and from language at one and the same time" (Rose 54).

H.D.'s *Wise Sappho* is an important modernist document, for in it, H.D. proclaims that Sappho's poetry is not impersonal. It is, rather, a woman's very personal expression of love for her female friends. She is expressing, not repressing, her personality and passionate feelings: "This woman whom love paralysed till she seemed to herself a dead body yet burnt, as the desert grass is burnt, white by the desert heat; she who trembled and was sick and sweated at the mere presence of another, a person, doubtless of charm, of grace, but of no extraordinary gifts perhaps of mind or feature—was she moderate, was she wise? Savonarola standing in the courtyard of the Medici (some two thousand years later) proclaimed her openly to the assembled youthful laity and priests of Florence—a devil" (64). This aristocratic "devil," a breaker of boundaries, was democratic enough to "construct from the simple gesture of a half-grown awkward girl, a being a companion, an equal . . . a sister, a muse" (65). Like H.D., she was both daughter and mother: "It is reported that the mother of Sappho was named Cleis. It is said that Sappho had a daughter whom she classed Cleis" (66). According to H.D., neither Sappho nor her poems are hard and dry. Sappho is "a pseudonym for poignant human feeling . . . she is the sea itself, breaking and tortured and torturing, but never broken" (67).

H.D. renders Sappho's artistic credo as follows: "'I sing not to please any god, goddess, creed or votary of religious rite—I sing not even in abstract contemplation, trance-like, remote from life, to please myself,' but says this most delightful and friendly woman, 'I sing and I sing beautifully in order to please my friends—my girl-friends'" (62).

Following Sappho, their cultural mother, H.D.'s poet and the dancer finally unite to create an Isle of Lesbos, their own "wild-wood":

> O wild wood,
> let no serpent
> with drawn hood
> enter,

> know the world we know; . . .
> let no mortal ever know
> mysteries
> within the fold
> of purple
> and of rose. . . . (XI.2–6, 9–13)

Know is, doubtless, used in the biblical sense; the "fold / of purple / and of rose" are female genital images.

When the rose merges with fire, patriarchal culture's masculine image of divine enlightenment—the sun—takes on a feminine identity. The fire (sun) is within, not outside: the "fire flashes through clear ice . . . and snow covers / the flame heat / of purple / of crimson" (III.17, 22–25). Apollo, the distant—and distancing—male sun, is replaced by the flaming purple or crimson flower: "the sun / born in a woman" (III.33–34).

Although Loie Fuller had been dead for several years when H.D. wrote "The Dancer," this birth image may be a reinterpretation of Fuller's *Danse de Feu,* or flame dance. Much earlier, in 1893, Mallarmé had concluded his ecstatic response to Fuller's *Danse de Feu* by noting that the dancer was "retracted into a silence . . . ecstatically stretched . . . *made dead*" (Kermode 155; emphasis added). What Fuller had hoped her viewer would see, however, was closer to H.D.'s image. For Fuller had written in her *Autobiography* that she had lit a red lantern from below the stage to achieve the effect of a dancer becoming "herself a flame" (264). Fuller also contradicts the interpretation of Gustave Fréville, cited by Kermode, that the flame is destructive and, most likely, masculine: The flame "caresses her dress, seizes her entirely, and, inexorable lover, is sated by nothing short of nothingness" (152).

Kermode writes, "Years later Yeats was pretty certainly remembering this dance . . . in his 'Byzantium'":

> Dying into a dance
> An agony of trance,
> An agony of flame that cannot singe a sleeve. (qtd. in Kermode
> 152, ll. 30–32)

The "death" of the artist that Mallarmé, Fréville, and Yeats perceived in Fuller's dance follows masculinist modernist dogma: the female dancer surrenders herself to and is consumed by her art, metaphorically the masculine flame/lover. Such envisioning has a phallic base. By contrast, artistic fulfillment can be envisioned in gynocentric terms, as giving birth. H.D.'s image is suggestive of Fuller's attempt to represent through her dance female creative energy and power—herself *as* "flame"—not what her male viewers saw, a woman being consumed by masculine power.

In "The Dancer," two female artists, a poet and a dancer, escape phallic violence through sisterhood. They exchange words with each other. Rhodocleia, formerly the *wife* of the sun and now a sun herself, invites the poet, her "sing-ing sister," to

> stare with me
> into the face of Death,
> and say
> Love is stronger. (IX. 3 5–3 8)

When her sister-poet responds, she describes dance movements antithetical to those she and Apollo had tried to force on the dancer earlier in the poem:

> Rhodocleia,
> rhododendron,
> sway, pause, turn again:
> rhododendron,
> O wide rose,
> open, quiver, pause
> and close. (X. 1–7)

The opening, quivering, pausing, and closing of the "wide rose" expands the earlier gynocentric image of "love in a circle." The poet writes an *écriture féminine* that origi-nates in the rose, opening, quivering, pausing, and closing, not in the "taut" phal-lus. In *The Wise Sappho* roses appear frequently: "[R]oses . . . the stains are deep on the red and scarlet cushions, on the flowering cloak of love" (57). The rose has al-ways been the flower of the goddess. It was also a female genital image in Arab and French troubadour poetry, and still is, Barbara Walker notes "a common French metaphor for 'maidenhead'" (434). Rose (*rhodo*) images occur repeatedly in "The Dancer": wide rose, Rhodocleia, rhododendron—also oleander, or rosy branch, as well as rhododaphne, from Daphne, the laurel goddess (Walker 449). Cleia in Rhodocleia may also be a reference to Cleia, or Cleis, the name both of the mother and the daughter of Sappho (Owens 5 1).

H.D. consulted the Tradition and found the feminine myth—"the flame heat / of purple" (III. 2 3–24)—burning beneath the "snow" of the patriarchal version of the story of Daphne and Apollo. In "The Dancer" she re-presents this myth. The dancer is Rhododendron, Rhodocleia, rose tree, laurel tree, into which, according to the myth, the fleeing Daphne was metamorphosed. Walker writes that rhododendron was the Greek name for the oleander hedge and that "Pythian priestesses [brought] on their oracular frenzies" by chewing its leaf (449). Owens notes that "the rhodo-dendron . . . is often considered to be a symbol of creativity in Celtic heraldic tra-ditions" (5 1). Long before the patriarchal myth made the laurel into an image of female disempowerment, it was, as rhododaphne, a site of female divinity and power. H.D. retrieves rhododaphne's ancient power, for the flowering tree is nei-ther still nor silent; it dances and speaks prophecies. Nor is it cold: its roses are flames. As H.D. had praised Sappho's liberation of language from the constrictions of syntax, so does she, in "The Dancer," enable a woman's liberation from Apollonian choreography. According to Joyce Owens, H.D.'s "dancer . . . recover[s] . . . language and the authority to name" (49).

The final dance in the poem is very different from the syntactical "ballet" prescribed by Apollo. The dancer creatrix leaps out of and dives under the sea, traditionally an image of female generativity:

> Leap as sea-fish
> from the water,
> toss your arms as fins
> dive under. (XIII. 1–4)

Such dancing is what both Martha Graham and Isadora Duncan called Dionysian dancing. It was popular in ancient Greece among women and other dominated people, but feared and despised by elite males. Through such dancing, the body revealed itself, Graham writes, as "free . . . victorious" (qtd. in Hanna 134).

It was the freedom Isadora Duncan admired in the dances of her own pupils in 1914: "I sat in a loge watching my pupils dance. At certain parts of the programme the audience rose and shouted with enthusiasm and joy. . . . These were indeed the gestures of the Vision of Nietzsche: "Zarathustra the dancer, Zarathustra the light one, who beckoneth with his pinions, one ready for flight, beckoning unto all birds, ready and prepared, a blissfully light-spirited one" (*My Life* 301).

Isadora Duncan rejected the "syntactic" rules of dance. Loie Fuller preached freedom from the "educational processes in so far as dancing is concerned" (68). H.D.'s dancer liberated herself from the "rules" of Apollo and became the "sun / born in a woman." The female dancer liberated herself from being a victimized icon. She is no "stylized creature," as Heppanstall would have her be. She is woman; she generates her own light and heat. Speaking her own language, she personifies, as Owens asserts, "feminine creative and spiritual strength" (50). She is the "sun / born in a woman."

Note

1. In "Expatriate Sapphic Modernism: Entering Literary History," Shari Benstock uses the term *Sapphic Modernism* to "redefine modernism in ways to acknowledge its Sapphic elements." Benstock's failure to cite H.D.'s "The Dancer" and *The Wise Sappho* is a surprising oversight.

Works Cited

Blair, Fredrika. *Isadora.* New York: William Morrow, 1986.

Cixous, Hélène. "The Laugh of the Medusa." Trans. Keith Cohen and Paula Cohen. *New French Feminisms.* Ed. Elaine Marks and Isabelle de Coutivron. New York: Schoken Books, 1981. 245–64.

Duncan, Isadora. *The Art of the Dance.* 1928. New York: Theatre Arts, 1969.

———. "The Dance of the Future." *What Is Dance?* Ed. Roger Copeland and Marshall Cohen. Oxford: Oxford UP, 1983. 262-64.

————. *My Life.* 1927. New York: Liveright, 1955.

Eliot, T. S. "Tradition and the Individual Talent." *Literary Criticism and Theory.* Ed. Robert Con Davis and Laurie Finke. New York: Longman, 1989. 587–93.

Friedman, Susan Stanford. "H.D." *The Gender of Modernism.* Ed. Bonnie Kime Scott. Bloomington: Indiana UP, 1990. 85–92.

————. *Psyche Reborn: The Emergence of H.D.* Bloomington: Indiana UP, 1981.

Fuller, Loie. *Fifteen Years of a Dancer's Life.* Boston: Small, Maynard, 1913.

Gilbert, Sandra M., and Susan Gubar. *No Man's Land: The Place of the Woman Writer in the Twentieth Century.* Vol. 2, *Sexchanges.* New Haven: Yale UP, 1989.

Gregory, Eileen. "Rose Cut in Rock." *Signets.* Ed. Susan Stanford and Rachel Blau Duplessis. Madison: U of Wisconsin P, 1990. 129–54.

Hanna, Judith Lynne. *Dance, Sex, and Gender.* Chicago: U of Chicago P, 1988.

H.D. "The Dancer." *H.D.: The Collected Poems, 1912–44.* Ed. Louis L. Martz. New York: New Directions, 1983. 440–50.

————. "The Master." *H.D.: The Collected Poems, 1912–44.* Ed. Louis L. Martz. New York: New Directions, 1983. 451–61.

————. *Notes on Thought and Vision and The Wise Sappho.* San Francisco: City Lights Books, 1982.

Heppanstall, Rayner. "The Sexual Idiom." *What Is Dance?* Ed. Roger Copeland and Marshall Cohen. New York: Oxford UP, 1983. 267–88.

Hulme, T. E. "Romanticism and Classicism." *Critiques and Essays in Criticism.* Ed. Robert W. Stallman. New York: Ronald P, 1949. 3–16.

Irigaray, Luce. *This Sex Which Is Not One.* Trans. Catherine Porter with Carolyn Burke. Ithaca: Cornell UP, 1985.

————. "When Our Lips Speak Together." *Signs* 6.11 (1980): 69–70.

Kermode, Frank. "Poet and Dancer Before Diaghilev." *What Is Dance?* Ed. Robert Copeland and Marshall Cohen. New York: Oxford UP, 1983. 145–60.

Mallarmé, Stéphane. "Ballets." *What Is Dance?* Ed. Roger Copeland and Marshall Cohen. New York: Oxford UP, 1983. 111–15.

Martz, Louis L. Introduction. *H.D.: The Collected Poems, 1912 -44.* By H.D. New York: New Directions, 1983. xi–xxxvi.

Owens, Joyce. "The Muse's Dance: H.D.'s 'The Dancer' as Spiritual Metaphor." *Women and Language* 16.1 (1993): 49–52.

Pound, Ezra. "How to Read." *The Literary Essays of Ezra Pound.* Ed. T. S. Eliot. Norfolk, CT: New Directions, n.d. 15–40.

Robinson, David M. *Sappho and Her Influence.* Boston: Marshall Jones, 1924.

Rose, Jacqueline. "Introduction—I." *Feminine Sexuality.* By Jacques Lacan. Ed. Juliet Mitchell and Jacqueline Rose. New York: Norton, 1982. 27–57.

Schiebinger, Londa. *The Mind Has No Sex?* Cambridge: Harvard UP, 1989.

Sweeney, James Johnson. "Sweeney, 1937." *Martha Graham.* Ed. Merle Armitage. Brooklyn, NY: Dance Horizons, 1966. 63–70.

Underdown, David. *Revel, Riot and Rebellion.* New York: Oxford UP, 1985.

Walker, Barbara G. *The Woman's Dictionary of Symbols and Sacred Objects.* San Francisco: Harper & Row, 1988.

Welsford, Enid. *The Court Masque*. Cambridge: Cambridge UP, 1927.

Woolf, Virginia. *A Room of One's Own*. 1929. New York: Harcourt Brace Jovanovich, 1957.

Yeats, William Butler. "Among School Children." *The Poems*. Ed. Richard J. Finneran. 14 vols. Vol. 1 of *The Collected Works of W. B. Yeats*. New York: Macmillan, 1989. 215–17.

Works Consulted

Valéry, Paul. "Dance and the Soul." *Selected Writings of Paul Valéry*. New York: New Directions, 1950. 184–98.

———. "Philosophy of the Dance." *What Is Dance?* Ed. Robert Copeland and Marshall Cohen. New York: Oxford UP, 1983. 55–65.

Walkowitz, Abraham. *Isadora Duncan in Her Dances*. Girard, Kans.: Haldeman-Julius, 1945.

∽ Modernism and Maternity: Alice Meynell and the Politics of Motherhood

Maria Frawley

The relationship of motherhood to feminism has been—and continues to be—fraught with a range of individual, social, and cultural anxieties. Witness one version of the debate in the pages of *The New York Times Magazine*, which testifies to the powerful hold that the two concepts—equally resistant to definition—have on the public imagination. In an essay titled "Sperm in a Jar," Anne Taylor Fleming chronicled the emotional upheavals of her unsuccessful bid to become pregnant at the age of thirty-eight, arguing that the cultural training she received in 1960s America little prepared her to recognize the values of childbearing. "Not only am I infertile," Fleming wrote, "but, worse, a cliché, a humbled renegade haunting the national imagination, held up as some sort of dupe of feminism, rather a double dupe of the sexual revolution and the women's revolution" (55). Fleming's essay elicited widespread reaction, and the *Times* reprinted three letters in a subsequent issue, all in some way critical of Fleming's message. One respondent wrote: "It is hard for me to believe that I am the only woman in the world who, long ago, walked happily away from the drudgery of child care." Another woman wrote: "I might disagree with her characterization of Virginia Woolf and Simone de Beauvoir as 'barren.'" Still another wrote: "Fleming stops just short of blaming her infertility on her feminist past. Infertility is neither the wages nor the fruits of feminism."[1]

The issues raised in this discussion echo those analyzed by Susan Faludi in *Backlash: The Undeclared War Against Women,* her 1991 study of cultural myths about and assaults on feminism waged throughout the 1980s.[2] Yet—as the references to Woolf and de Beauvoir imply—we cannot attribute the contradictory anxieties generated by the uneasy alliance between motherhood and feminism solely to our own historical moment, shaped as it is by technological innovations that redirect our understanding of reproductive control. As Faludi pointed out, the history of women's rights is characterized not by steady progress but by peaks and valleys, and the rhetoric associated with the debate today hearkens back to recent and more distant pasts.[3] Indeed, one can locate proto-versions in periods of history that predate what has come to be associated with the feminist movement.

In this essay I want to explore how a preoccupation with motherhood helps to elucidate the feminism surfacing in the work of Alice Meynell, a British essayist and poet who lived from 1847 until 1922. Writing on a wide range of subjects, only some of which were identifiably feminist, Meynell helped to establish what might be thought of as the discourse of modern maternity, one characterized by a refusal of the sentimental and a corollary attention to the anxieties of motherhood. Rather than endorse—and consequently stabilize—a maternal ideal championed by Victorian domestic ideology, Meynell's work celebrates what she calls in a poem titled "A Letter from a Girl to Her Own Old Age" the "shifting phases" of womanhood, a phrase chosen to capture the social and psychological ambivalence that Meynell associated with women.[4] Resisting the lure of a consistent representational focus, Meynell deliberately approached the subject(s) of motherhood indirectly, a technique that helped her to challenge essentialistic assumptions about maternity. Through a notoriously spare and sometimes riddle-like style of writing, Meynell stylistically reinforced her themes of anxiety and ambivalence, thus helping to demarcate a place for women's writing within modernism.

Literary historians have for years considered Meynell a paradigmatic figure of the fin de siècle in Britain—a poet, essayist, and editor both Victorian and not-Victorian; modernist and yet not-modernist. While she published her first collection of poems, *Preludes,* in 1875, the bulk of her work was published in the 1890s and onward, beginning with the collections *Poems* and *The Rhythm of Life* in 1893 and continuing to *Last Poems,* published in 1923, and *Essays of Today and Yesterday,* published in 1926. Thus, her published writing hovers between the literary periods associated with pre- and postsuffrage feminism, reflecting and helping to construct the gender politics and anxieties of female liberation that critics like Shirley Peterson associate with the emergence of modernism.

Seemingly traditional in her choice of subject matter, Meynell's austere lyrical style of poetry marked her as strikingly innovative in her understanding of and approach to language. Yet, as Valerie Sedelak has written, "[m]ost people have never heard of Alice Meynell" (33). Kathy Alexis Psomiades attributes the "loss" of Meynell from the annals of British literary history to a more widespread lack of understanding of literary production in Britain at the turn of the century and to a disregard for the ways that Meynell coded feminist messages into her often oblique poetry (197).

Although largely forgotten now except by scholars of women's writing, her poetry was widely acclaimed in her day, with Dante Gabriel Rossetti praising her poem "Renouncement" as "one of the three finest sonnets ever written by women" and John Ruskin calling several of her poems "the finest things I have yet seen or felt in modern verse."[5] Like many of the male poets more traditionally associated with modernism, Meynell's work was clearly thought of as "high art," a status confirmed by the fact that she was suggested as a possible successor to "Tennyson as England's Laureate" (Schlack 111). In another recent study of Meynell, Kathy Psomiades stresses "her considerable reputation . . . with both middle and high-brow audiences, to the extent that male poets and essayists such as Max Beerbohm saw her as a competitor" (197). Meynell was at least as well known for her essays as for her poetry, and she wrote a weekly column for women in the *Pall Mall Gazette* during the 1890s. Although raising seven children during these same years, her journalistic career enabled her to proclaim support for women's rights and, in addition to writing in favor of suffrage, she served as president and vice-president of suffrage societies (Schlack 111).

Meynell's public recognition and literary stature were not unconnected to her "private" role as a mother. Like Elizabeth Gaskell before her, Meynell's public image became one in which her status as a mother was inextricably, and seemingly naturally, linked to her professional work. In fact, motherhood seems to have legitimized Meynell's ambition, in essence making some of her activities more palatable to a public still largely governed by the domestic ideology of the "separate spheres" that literary historians have come to associate with middle-class Victorian culture.

Although not published until 1947, Vita Sackville-West's biographical introduction to the centenary volume *Alice Meynell: Prose and Poetry* exemplifies much about the relationship between motherhood and profession that undergirded Meynell's public identity. Sackville-West admits to never having met Meynell, describing her as "a legend" who "retains the quality of a legend still" (8). In her tribute, she establishes Meynell's genealogy within a particular class and emphasizes the domesticating forces of her upbringing. Describing the decision of Meynell's parents to return from travels abroad to permanently reside in England during their children's adolescence, Sackville-West writes: "The ruinous palaces and disorderly billiard-rooms were replaced by a solid house in the Isle of Wight, where the Babes, the sweet Babes, the Angels of their mother's diary learnt to discard their Genoese dialect and to converse in the approved Victorian manner with the young men they met at croquet parties, concerts, and dances" (12). Sackville-West encourages her readers to view Meynell's mother as the ideal embodiment of Victorian motherhood—sacrificing a penchant for the exotic to a class- and gender-specific version of the domestic, which in this passage is symbolized by the "solid" house, the "approved" language, and, perhaps most significantly, the evolution of Meynell and her sister from "sweet Babes" and "Angels" into sexual women available for the marriage market.

The transition of Meynell from this period to that of her married life is glossed over, and the portrait of the domesticated Meynell that follows foregrounds the pleasures of her private life while suggesting the ways in which it accommodated her professional aspirations. Of her subsequent life as the wife of journalist Wilfrid Meynell and mother of seven children, Sackville-West writes: "She was happy in her personal life; she loved the man she had married; she loved the seven editors with their small heads clustered underneath her busy table" (16). While evidently most eager to portray her domesticity, she also alludes to the cracks in the picture. "Mrs. Meynell was no needlewoman," she writes simply, and then goes on to report that Meynell's daughter "relates that [her parents] were commonly so absorbed that the children temporarily lost their names and were all indiscriminately called 'Child'" (14). Although she presents Meynell's flaws as a mother (and she presents no others), she also uses her status as Mother to shield her from criticism. Sackville-West encourages readers of the centenary volume to accept Meynell's feminism by representing her first and foremost as a mother, as the syntactical arrangement of the following representative statement suggests: "This mother, this journalist, this hostess, this poet, held strong views about the position of women in a world controlled by men" (21).

Meynell's public identity maintained a tenuous balance between domestic and professional duties, and the ideological uneasiness is equally apparent in a eulogistic section titled "Prefatory Poems" that follows in *Alice Meynell: Prose and Poetry,* which echoes the adulatory tone of Sackville-West's introduction. In this section Meynell is represented as an enchanting embodiment of "passionless passion, wild tranquillities" in a poem titled "Her Portrait" by Francis Thompson (l. 268). She is seen as having a body like "sharp honey assuaged with milk" in "Alicia" by the doting family friend Coventry Patmore (l. 6). In "To A.M." by George Meredith she is "virginally majestic" (l. 8). And in G. Rostrevor Hamilton's "The Library, Greatham (A Memory of Alice Meynell)" she "trace[s] to far horizons the unrest / Of young desire on Earth's maternal breast" (ll. 11–12). Anxieties about Meynell's sexuality clearly entered into each of these tributes and frame the essays and poems that follow in the volume. Moreover, the anxieties generate—if in some cases implicitly—from her status as a mother. In their combination of opposites (the passion with the passionless; the wild with the tranquil; the exciting with the nurturing; the innocent with the majestic; and the restless with the comforting) Meynell is represented as what the Victorians conceived as either dangerous or impossible: the sexualized mother, the desiring and desirable woman with the "maternal breast."

The ideological contradictions evident in the introductory material from *Alice Meynell: Prose and Poetry* owe something to Meynell, who encouraged these "impossible representations" through her own literary treatment of motherhood. As Beverly Schlack has written, "Meynell was fascinated by the relationship of gender to creativity. In the regenerative world of physical nature, in the creative world of art, in her biological role as mother, *woman* is the creative principle in Meynell's metaphysics, and she explored tirelessly the intricate interrelationships existing among woman as nature, nature as woman-mother, and woman poet linked to nature" (115). Angela Leighton credits Meynell with writing the "first, serious, adult poems, by any poet, about biological motherhood," a subject about which she felt "considerable emotional ambivalence" (257).[6] Leighton places Meynell within a study of Victorian women writers, but her symbolic status as the sexualized mother-writer suggests her anachronistic status in that collection. Meynell's attitude toward and treatment of maternity, emphasizing as it does ambivalence, helps concurrently to suggest something of the uncertain place of women's writing within emerging modernist literature.[7]

To appreciate the range of ways that Meynell explored motherhood in her writing entails navigating between her poetry and her prose, for both evidence an ongoing and interconnected interest in representing and analyzing the psychological and social experiences of motherhood. Meynell seems to have found both forms—poetry and prose—individually inadequate to the task and thus necessary to one another. Of particular interest are five of her twelve books of essays: *The Children* (1897), *Ceres' Runaway* (1909), *Mary, The Mother of Jesus* (1912), *Childhood* (1913), and *Wayfaring* (1928), each of which contains essays that deal indirectly with mothering, often, for example, by delving into child psychology and development and implying that such a perspective can only be understood by a mother.

I want to read several short essays collected in a volume titled *Essays* under the heading "The Darling Young" in relation to several of Meynell's poems, most particularly "Cradle Song at Twilight."[8] Meynell credited the phrase "The Darling Young" to Francis Thompson, a family friend and, like Coventry Patmore, a devout worshipper. The phrase encourages her readers to believe that the essays that follow (i.e., "Fellow Travellers with a Bird," "The Child of Tumult," "The Child of Subsiding Tumult," "The Unready," "That Pretty Person," "Under the Early Stars," and "The Illusion of Historic Time") will treat their subject sentimentally, but in each case Meynell subverts the sentimental in a range of ways.[9] Each essay represents motherhood indirectly by focusing instead on the experience of the child from an adult and presumably female perspective. Moreover, each elucidates Meynell's understanding of the contradictions underwriting cultural notions of maternity.

On their surface, these essays are primarily concerned with child development and invoke a rhetoric of behavioral understanding familiar to fans of T. Berry Brazleton or Penelope Leach. Often Meynell directs her essays to the frustrated parent in need of advice: "But even the naughty child is an individual, and must not be treated in the mass," she writes in "The Child of Tumult" (*Essays* 235). Her credentials are not those of the medical establishment, of course; and rather than establishing her authority by announcing something akin to "I know, because I am a mother," she simply assumes the stance. Although she relays anecdotal accounts of raising children, she never directly refers to her own experience. The strategy reflects her understanding that her readership is well aware of her status as mother-author. Yet by distancing herself from the purely personal, she also suggests a desire to legitimize her observations as objective.

Meynell's deliberately unsentimental picture of childhood coexists with a Romantic vision of the child. In "The Child of Tumult," for instance, she writes: "With the other incidents of childish character, the crowd of impulses called 'naughtiness' is perfectly perceptible—it would seem heartless to say how soon" (235). Her in-tent is not to arm parent-readers with disciplinary advice but rather to encourage their patience and understanding: "The work is not easy, but a little thought should make it easy for the elders to avoid the provocation which they—who should ward off provocations—are apt to bring about by sheer carelessness" (241). Similarly in "The Unready" she writes: "It is rashly said that the senses of children are quick. They are, on the contrary, unwieldy in turning, unready in reporting, until advancing age teaches them agility. This is not lack of sensitiveness, but mere length of process" (247).

Although Meynell's wry tone is designed to appeal to parent-readers who have endured similar frustrations, her sympathy is clearly with the children of whom she writes. She represents children as embodying unpredictability, freedom, and adven-ture. In describing the child's gradual acquisition of language in an essay titled "Fel-low Travellers with a Bird," for instance, she writes: "There is something very cheer-ful and courageous in the setting-out of a child on a journey of speech with so small baggage and with so much confidence in the chances of the hedge. He goes free, a simple adventurer" (*Essays* 232). In "Under the Early Stars" she writes of summer-time dusk, when "children strike some blow for liberty," arguing that "when twi-light comes, there comes also the punctual wildness. The children will run and pursue, and laugh for the mere movement—it does so jolt their spirits" (259). What seems predictable here to the parents is the "wildness"—or unpredictability—that the playful child represents. Underwriting each of these depictions of childhood playfulness is the assumption that, through observation of the child at play, the par-ent may vicariously enjoy again something of uninhibited liberty.

Meynell frequently draws on Romantic rhetoric to voice a desire for the free-dom of the child. In "The Illusion of Historic Time" her statement that "[c]hildhood is itself Antiquity—to every man his only Antiquity" (*Essays* 264) cannot help but remind one of the more famous Wordsworthian pronouncement that the "child is father of the man." Wordsworthian notions of the child are evident as well in an essay titled "The Influential Child," which appears in the centenary volume, and which also associates children with the element of "wildness" that so appealed to Meynell: "It is their own landscape, their own hour, that moves children not to words but to emotions. Great views, I think, give them a more ordinary and grown-up pleasure; they do not love formal gardens, even Italian formal gardens; and on this point cer-tainly the child is not the father of the man. But hill-sides in wild flower, calm sum-mer seas, and those aspects and phases of landscape to which Tennyson gave his perfect word in return for a perfect emotion—these are wonderful to children" (*Prose and Poetry* 310).

Meynell's literary response to childhood helps ultimately to reveal the roots of her feminism and its relationship to modern motherhood. Consider, for example, a passage from "The Child of Tumult":

Only to a trivial eye is there nothing tragic in the sight of these great passions within the small frame, the small will, and, in a word, the small nature. When a large and sombre fate befalls a little nature, and the stage is too narrow for the action of a tragedy, the disproportion has sometimes made a mute and unexpressed history of actual life or sometimes a famous book; it is the manifest core of George Eliot's story of "Adam Bede," where the suffering of Hetty is, as it were, the eye of the storm. All is expressive around her, but she is hardly articulate, the book is full of words—preachings, speeches, daily talk, aphorisms, but a space of silence remains about her in the midst of the story. And the disproportion of passion—the inner disproportion—is at least as tragic as that disproportion of fate and action; it is less intelligible, and leads into the intricacies of nature which are more difficult than the turn of events.

It seems, then, that this passionate play is acted within the narrow limits of a child's nature far oftener than in a nature adult and finally formed. (*Prose and Poetry* 295–96)

The voice that opens this homiletic passage is that of sympathetic mother who feels compassion for the frustrations experienced by the young child. Meynell moves rhetorically, though, from childhood experience to tragedy and from everyday life to the novel. Although she likens Hetty Sorrel to the young child with the "small nature," readers of George Eliot's *Adam Bede* (and thus, most of Meynell's readers) are far more likely to associate Hetty with her sexuality, the "sin" of unwed motherhood, and infanticide. Implicitly, Meynell asks her readers to sympathize with Hetty, to recall the freedom that she represents in the beginning of the narrative when acting only on desire, and to see her at the narrative's end as a victim of a linguistic deprivation that symbolizes the larger deprivation of a society unable to accept her sexuality. The voice of the literary critic becomes interwoven with that of the mother pleading for sympathetic understanding for her child. Although she returns at the end of the passage from the tragic fate of Hetty Sorrel to the "passionate play" of the child, her message resonates throughout the remainder of the essay. Meynell's essays thus can hardly be reduced to treatises on child development, as a concern with sexual politics surfaces in varying ways, complicates the subject matter, and creates a resistance to resolution.

Meynell's interest in the psychological and social positioning of the child underwrites much of her poetry as well, from the *Poems* of 1893 to the works collected in the 1901 volume *Later Poems,* and finally to poems in the collection *Last Poems,* issued in 1923. In "San Lorenzo's Mother," a poem from the early collection, for example, Meynell adopts the form of a dramatic monologue in order to capture the anguish of a mother separated from her child: "I had not seen my son's dear face / (He chose the cloister by God's grace) / Since it had come to full flower-time" (*Poems* ll. 1–3).[10] The personal predicament of the mother is by the poem's end transformed by her religious faith, one ironically established by its resistance to transformation: "I might mistake my dearest son / But never the Son who cannot change" (ll. 24–25). In another variation of the dramatic monologue, "A Letter from a Girl to Her Own Old Age" gives the figure of the mother greater psychological complexity by constructing the mother/daughter relationship within one "self," as it were.

The "girl" of the poem addresses her "old age" as a suffering mother; she is the "time-worn woman" (*Poems* l. 2) and "silent one" (l. 13) who reminds her daughter "Of the great hills that stormed the sky behind thee / of the wild winds of power that have resigned thee" (ll. 14–15). Collapsing traditional temporal distinctions between the past, present, and future in a maneuver typical of much of Meynell's poetry, as of modernist literature in general, her narrator suggests the impossibility of separating youth from old age, daughter from mother:

> And we, so altered in our shifting phases,
> Track one another 'mid the many mazes
> By the eternal child-breath of the daisies. (ll. 40–42)

As in "San Lorenzo's Mother," Meynell's speaker is plagued by her sense of change and yet comforted by what seems eternal. The daughter's voice then becomes the voice of the feminist unwilling to champion woman's silence as empowering because she recognizes the debilitating consequences of her ambivalent condition:

> I have not writ this letter of divining
> To make a glory of thy silent pining,
> A triumph of thy mute and strange declining. (ll. 43–45)

The poem ends with an oblique statement by the daughter of her psychological predicament. She describes herself as

> The one who now thy faded features guesses,
> With filial fingers thy grey hair caresses,
> With morning tears thy mournful twilight blesses. (ll. 55–57)

"A Letter from a Girl to Her Own Old Age" represents the mother as silent, but she nonetheless "speaks" powerfully and almost continually to her daughter. This seemingly contradictory thematic is reinforced stylistically as Meynell combines the daughter's "morning" tears with the "twilight" state of old age, a twilight at once "mournful" and "bless[ed]."

Perhaps the poem most central to understanding Meynell's perspective on motherhood is "Cradle-Song at Twilight," a work Angela Leighton has aptly described as an "odd, deceptively simple little poem" with multiple points of reference (259), and that Beverly Schlack describes as "a disconcerting song of wished-for flight" (118). In its entirety, the poem reads:

> The child not yet is lulled to rest.
>   Too young a nurse, the slender Night
> So laxly holds him to her breast
>   That throbs with flight.
>
> He plays with her, and will not sleep.
>   For other playfellows she sighs;

An unmaternal fondness keep
Her alien eyes. (*Poems* ll. 1–8)

The restlessness of the young child serves as Meynell's springboard not for a sooth-ing lullaby but rather for a study of subjectivity. Meynell goes on to depict the inte-riority of the nurse, or Night, who has taken over (or been given) the motherly duty of inducing sleep. With its ambiguous references to the "breast / That throbs with flight," the desire "for other playfellows," and the "unmaternal fondness" that char-acterizes her "alien eyes," the poem illustrates well the anxiety about the sexuality of the mother (in this case displaced onto the nurse and Night) that marked repre-sentations of Meynell herself.

"Cradle-Song at Twilight" utilizes language and recalls ideas that surfaced in Meynell's essays as well. In "That Pretty Person," published in *Essays,* she wrote that "as the primitive lullaby is nothing but a patient prophecy (the mother's), so was education, some two hundred years ago, nothing but an impatient prophecy (the father's) of the full stature of mind and body" (252). "Under the Early Stars," an-other Meynell essay, concludes with the intriguing message: "If English children are not rocked to many such aged lullabies, some of them are put to sleep to strange cradle-songs. The affectionate races that are brought into subjection sing the primi-tive lullaby to the white child. Asiatic voices and African persuade him to sleep in the tropical night. His closing eyes are filled with alien images" (261). With its jux-taposition of the English to the Asiatic and African and with its curious blending of social and political commentary, the passage evidences Meynell's interest in using motherhood to simultaneously suggest states of subjection and of subjectivity. The cradle song that would seem to announce an uncomplicated maternal love is made "strange" in several ways. On one level, it is distanced from its supposed source, sung not by the mother herself but by the servant she employs to mother her chil-dren. The "mother" of this cradle song is thus not the child's biological parent but a representative of what Meynell calls the "affectionate races," an African or Asian person who serves both the child she rocks and the white mother for whom she works. The child's night, traditionally the province of protective domesticity, is made tropical and exotic. The passage ends with the child falling off to sleep but taking with him "primitive" and "alien" images—images not unlike those that character-ized the Night/nurse in the poem "Cradle-Song at Twilight." Emphasizing the alien and exotic within the nursery and stressing the physical and psychological distance between mother and child, Meynell reconfigures the domestic within the more modernist thematic of exile.

Reading "Cradle-Song at Twilight" alongside "Under the Early Stars" helps to elucidate important complexities within Meynell's writing. Angela Leighton has recognized one level of sociopolitical commentary implicit in "Cradle-Song at Twi-light," writing that Meynell's "refusal to explain the identity of this child cradler" may imply that "she is a too young 'single mother' with an illegitimate child," or that "she represents that other, darker side of motherhood, whose real thoughts, contrary to all the conventions, are 'unmaternal' and 'alien'" (260). But "Under the Early Stars" suggests complexities of greater reach within the poem. With their similar attention to the "primitive" lullaby, the restlessness that characterizes both its singer and its recipient, and the subjection that marks the "mother" figure, be she biological or substitute, both "The Pretty Person" and "Under the Early Stars" are fundamentally ambivalent about the role of the mother, who has distanced herself from her child. The eroticism of the mother or mother-figure ultimately soothes the child to sleep, and the child takes these "alien images" with him as he slumbers. The poem in particular leans tonally toward the menacing, but Meynell nowhere suggests that the child is endangered by his symbolic immersion in "the tropical night." On the contrary, her association of childhood with freedom, adventure, and unpredictability everywhere implies an attraction to all that is considered exotic or "wild."

In her later poetry Meynell continued to explore the position of the mother and the meaning of motherhood from a range of psychological and social perspectives. In poems such as "Parentage," "The Modern Mother," and "Maternity" from *Later Poems* and "To the Mother of Christ the Son of Man" from *Last Poems* motherhood serves as either a source of destructive guilt or a monument of grief. "Parentage," for example, ends with the enigmatic sentence: "And she who slays is she who bears, who bears" (*Poems* l. 12). In "The Modern Mother," Meynell writes that

> This mother, giver of life, death, peace, distress,
> > Desired ah! not so much
> Thanks as forgiveness; and the passing touch
> Expected, and the slight, the brief caress. (*Poems* ll. 16–19)

In "Maternity" the center of interest is a woman whose child died, newly born, ten years before. A short poem like "Cradle-Song at Twilight," "Maternity" ends,

> Ten years ago was born in pain
> > A Child, not now forlorn.
> But oh, ten years ago, in vain,
> > A mother, a mother was born. (*Poems* ll. 5–8)

Concluding the poem this way, Meynell emphasizes not just the grief of the mother at losing her child, but more specifically the feeling of purposelessness that she associates with this maternal experience. In this way, her representation of maternity, emphasizing as it does here futility and loss, is reminiscent of modernist poems such as T. S. Eliot's *The Waste Land*, which underscored the barrenness of modern culture and its institutions. Like the essays, Meynell's poetry emphasizes through its representation of motherhood what Angela Leighton describes as "a troubling knowledge of separation and difference" (259). One could also argue that the phrase "separation and difference" describes more generally the place of Meynell's writing, as well as that of other women writers, in the history of female modernism.

In *Victorian Poetry: Poetry, Poetics, and Politics,* Isobel Armstrong writes that Meynell's poetry does not "possess the reach and ambition" of nineteenth-century women poets: "It is not simply their smallness of scale, or their thematics of love and religion . . . that persuades one of the more restricted world of these lyrics. It seems that the preoccupation with silence places the feminine in any empty space, that which is not there, making it seem without a context in which to exist. The disappearances and vanishing points explored in her work presage the eclipse of women's poetry in the twentieth-century—or, at least, the steady refusal of women's poetry by modernism" (482–83). It seems possible to agree with Armstrong's description but to draw very different conclusions regarding Meynell's significance. It is worth recalling that Meynell rarely wrote directly about motherhood but accessed it instead via representations of childhood that depend on her readers' empathy with—one might even say desire for—the liberties of a seemingly unrestricted world. The anxieties of liberation that more typically characterize female modernism are displaced in Meynell's writing through an examination of the mother/child relationship that foregrounds complexities of female subjectivity. It is also worth reminding ourselves of the wealth of interpretive possibility raised by poems such as "Cradle-Song at Twilight" in which Meynell resists the lure of the sentimental and subverts claims to the naturalness of the maternal.

While it is impossible to glean straightforward political commentary from Meynell's literary representations of motherhood and childhood, it is clear that such representations are as essential to understanding her feminism as are her more overtly feminist activities—her work in support of suffrage, for example. Read in conjunction, Meynell's poetry and prose addresses and, importantly, refuses to resolve the complexities of the mother/child bond or the difficult relationship between psychological and social dimensions of motherhood. As G. K. Chesterton wrote in 1923, Meynell "took so much thought for neglected truths, and especially neglected truths that told in favour of women" (10). The motherhood that Meynell represented is, like the motherhood we know today, fraught with a range of anxieties, but in her works these anxieties become the source of its interest, its energy, and its power, rather than the symptoms of its despair.

Notes

1. The letters are signed by L. A. Farrow, Roswitha T. Both, and Glenda E. Gilmore. All appear in the Letters section of The New York Times Magazine 10 July 1994: 8.

2. The implied debate about the relationship of motherhood to feminism is no less prominent a feature in intellectual circles: the challenge of articulating it moved into the elite upper echelons of literary theory in the 1980s—in the work, for example, of Hélène Cixous, Luce Irigaray, and Julia Kristeva—and continues to influence scholars in disciplines as diverse as sociology, philosophy, religion, history, and political science. For a good overview of the way that each of these theorists invoke and deploy the idea of maternity as it relates to feminism, see Domna Stanton.

3. A good example of its manifestation in the recent past would be when the publication in 1976 of Adrienne Rich's *Of Woman Born* incited widespread commentary. In 1977 Kathleen Barry wrote that "in *Of Woman Born,* Adrienne Rich returns motherhood to women. And she returns it with feminist vision" (302), an assertion that implies both that motherhood naturally belongs within feminism and that it had been taken from it. Yet she also acknowledges that Rich's book, despite its enormous influence, was widely condemned as "partisan writing," evidencing, among other things, the author's "rage against men" (302).

4. "A Letter from a Girl to Her Own Old Age" is reprinted in the Selected Poems section of the centenary volume, Alice Meynell: Prose and Poetry (London: Jonathan Cape, 1947) (l. 40). All references to works in this edition will hereafter be cited parenthetically in the text by page number, or, in the case of poetry, line numbers.

5. These two comments appear in advertisements for Meynell's *Poems* published by Burns Oates & Washbourne, Ltd. that appear in the unpaginated end pages of Meynell's *Essays.* The Rossetti comment is quoted by William Sharp in this advertisement.

6. To her credit, Leighton attends in her introduction to the difficulties of dating literary periods with any precision and acknowledges that many of her choices would either predate or succeed traditional datings of the Victorian period.

7. The status of motherhood within modernist literature is no less problematic than in Victorian literature. Despite its reputation as the great age of the domestic ideal, Victorian literature is noteworthy for the way it marginalizes the mother figure, often ironically making her powerful presence felt precisely by emphasizing her absence.

8. *Essays by Alice Meynell* (London: Burns Oates & Washbourne, 1930). The first edition of this volume was published in 1914. References to essays are to this edition.

9. In this sense, Meynell's works might be said to participate in what some literary historians have analyzed as emerging modernist efforts to discredit sentimental literature, thought to be the province of women writers. In an analysis of the relationship of sentimentalism to modernism, Suzanne Clark argues that restoring an understanding of the ways in which modernism does value the sentimental enables a better appreciation of modernism's contradictions as well as "the sense of great struggle over subjectivity that the resulting contradictions precipitated" (4).

10. The poetry from these volumes (as well as several others) are collected in *The Poems of Alice Meynell: Complete Edition* (New York: Charles Scribner's Sons, 1923). References to poems in this edition will be cited parenthetically in the text by page number and by line numbers.

Works Cited

Armstrong, Isobel. *Victorian Poetry: Poetry, Poetics, and Politics.* New York: Routledge, 1993.

Barry, Kathleen. "Reviewing Reviews: *Of Woman Born.*" *Chrysalis* 2 (1977). Rpt. in *Adrienne Rich: Reviews and Re-Visions, 1951–1981.* Ed. Jane Roberta Cooper. Ann Arbor: Michigan UP, 1984. 302.

Chesterton, G. K. "Alice Meynell." *Dublin Review* 172 (Jan. 1923): 1–12.

Clark, Suzanne. *Sentimental Modernism: Women Writers and the Revolution of the Word.* Bloomington: Indiana UP, 1991.

Faludi, Susan. *Backlash: The Undeclared War on American Women.* New York: Crown Publishers, 1991.

Fleming, Anne Taylor. "Sperm in a Jar." *New York Times Magazine* 12 June 1994. 52–55.

Hamilton, G. Rostrevor. "The Library, Greatham (A Memory of Alice Meynell)." *Alice Meynell: Prose and Poetry.* Ed. Frederick Page, Viola Meynell, Olivia Sowerby, and Francis Meynell. London: Jonathan Cape, 1947. 33–34.

Leighton, Angela. *Victorian Women Poets: Writing Against the Heart.* Charlottesville: UP of Virginia, 1992.

Letters. *The New York Times Magazine* 10 July 1994. 8.

Meredith, George. "To A. M." *Alice Meynell: Prose and Poetry.* Ed. Frederick Page, Viola Meynell, Olivia Sowerby, and Francis Meynell. London: Jonathan Cape, 1947. 32.

Meynell, Alice. *Alice Meynell: Prose and Poetry.* Ed. Frederick Page, Viola Meynell, Olivia Sowerby, and Francis Meynell. Introduction by Vita Sackville-West. London: Jonathan Cape, 1947.

———. *Essays.* London: Burns Oates & Waterbourne, 1930.

———. *The Poems of Alice Meynell.* New York: Charles Scribner's Sons, 1923.

Patmore, Coventry. "Alicia." *Alice Meynell: Prose and Poetry.* Ed. Frederick Page, Viola Meynell, Olivia Sowerby, and Francis Meynell. London: Jonathan Cape, 1947. 32.

Psomiades, Kathy Alexis. "Poetry by Women." *Nineteenth-Century Contexts* 16.2 (1992): 193–99.

Sackville-West, Vita. Introduction. *Alice Meynell: Prose and Poetry.* By Alice Meynell. Ed. Frederick Page, Viola Meynell, Olivia Sowerby, and Francis Meynell. London: Jonathan Cape, 1947. 7–26.

Schlack, Beverly Ann. "The 'Poetess of Poets': Alice Meynell Rediscovered." *Women's Studies* 7 (1980): 111–26.

Sedelak, Valerie F. "Alice Meynell's 'A Thrush Before Dawn': A Response to Sound." *MAWA Review* 2–3 (Summer/Fall 1986): 33–37.

Stanton, Domna C. "Difference on Trial: A Critique of the Maternal Metaphor in Cixous, Irigaray, and Kristeva." *The Poetics of Gender.* Ed. Nancy K. Miller. New York: Columbia UP, 1986. 157–82.

Thompson, Francis. "Her Portrait." *Alice Meynell: Prose and Poetry.* Ed. Frederick Page, Viola Meynell, Olivia Sowerby, and Francis Meynell. London: Jonathan Cape, 1947. 27–31.

Zora Neale Hurston and Mary Hunter Austin's Ethnographic Fiction: New Modernist Narratives

Elizabeth Jane Harrison

As twentieth-century "regional" or "ethnic" writers, Zora Neale Hurston and Mary Hunter Austin have suffered from a neglect of their literary strategies in favor of an analysis of the cultural context of their narratives. By focusing on the incorporation of this content, we might reconsider the place of each author in the modernist American canon. Far from simply recording or romanticizing "primitive" African and Native American cultures, these two authors critique the relationships among narrator, subject, and audience, and construct complex narrative structures which incorporate oral forms. Their narrative techniques, what I define as "ethnographic fiction," link them to so-called high modernists like James Joyce, Virginia Woolf, and William Faulkner, whose experiments with multiple points of view and oral narratives can no longer be considered unique.

Although modern psychology's influence on the development of stream-of-consciousness narrative is widely recognized, anthropology's effect on fiction writers of the modernist period is often overlooked.[1] Many people know that Zora Neale Hurston trained under anthropologist Franz Boas at Columbia University in the late 1920s, and some literary critics have studied Hurston's anthropological writings. But few have focused on how Hurston used her training in ethnography to develop new fictional forms. Likewise, critics analyze Mary Austin's stories about Native American cultures in the southwestern United States without considering seriously how her theories of what she termed "Amerindian" folklore may have affected her own literary methods. Unlike Hurston, Austin never studied anthropology in an institution; nevertheless, as I will demonstrate, the two authors were influenced both directly and indirectly by new anthropological concepts developed by Boas and his contemporaries.

During the early part of the twentieth century, a schism was occurring in anthropology between the evolutionists and the historians. Franz Boas and his school represented the latter approach, which stressed what today we call "cultural relativism," or the idea that no race or culture is inherently superior to another.[2] Boas's *The Mind of Primitive Man* (1913) was a remarkably influential book, which no doubt affected Hurston's ethnographic research, since she studied under him, and must have been familiar to Austin as she completed work on Native American literature and traditions for *The American Rhythm* (1930).[3] Both Hurston and Austin demonstrate and challenge the idea of Boas's cultural relativism in their narratives. Following the anthropologist's concepts, their writings valorize "primitive" cultures and question innate racial characteristics. But through their own research and reading in the field, the authors developed narrative strategies which also question ideas of "objective" knowledge and "accurate" reportage, ideas which, as a trained social scientist, Boas could ill afford to reject.[4]

As women, moreover, the two authors establish a different perspective than their male contemporaries who had previously dominated the social sciences. Occupying a unique stance as female researchers and literary artists, Hurston and Austin ultimately subvert Boas's method of participant-observer ethnography.[5] The following pages will discuss Hurston's *Mules and Men* and *Tell My Horse* and Austin's *Land of Little Rain, Lost Borders,* and *One Smoke Stories* to demonstrate how both authors create a new genre of "ethnographic fiction" from their knowledge and incorporation of anthropological methods. As committed cultural relativists, Hurston and Austin prepared literary audiences for an acceptance of new social science tenets and thus helped disseminate changing views of culture. In this way they function as precursors for contemporary, postmodern writers of ethnic fiction.

One of the major methods of modern anthropology popularized by Franz Boas was a more interactive model of collecting material called participant-observer ethnography. Instead of remaining an aloof, "objective" outsider, the collector might actually enter into the culture to take part in its rituals. Participant-observer ethnography posited a new relationship between narrator/observer and subject/material. In her first book of folklore, *Mules and Men* (1935), Hurston uses this strategy. The author began her project of collecting African American folklore in 1927 while she was Boas's student at Columbia. The narrator, Zora, who simultaneously does and does not represent Hurston herself, takes part in storytelling sessions on the porch of the local store, rather than passively describing only what she sees. At first this narrative technique appears as a simple framing device. The reader follows Zora on her folklore-collecting journey from Eatonville to Polk County, Florida, and finally on to New Orleans to observe hoodoo. But the relationship between the narrator and the tales she collects is complicated by the slippage that often occurs between the frame and the material. The narrator tells as well as reports jokes and folktales in the frame story; the act of observation is not separated from the reportage of data as in traditional ethnography.

Hurston represents herself in the text as both educated ethnographer and as one of the "folk" whom she travels to study. In the introduction she intimates that as a native of Eatonville she will be able to gather stories there "without hurt, harm or danger." But collecting from "the Negro," she tells us, is difficult "because he is particularly evasive" and "offers a feather-bed resistance" to outsiders. The point of view of the introduction then shifts to "we"—Hurston places herself as one of the observed: "we let the probe enter, but it never comes out" (2).[6] Constantly shifting perspectives throughout *Mules and Men,* the narrator Zora manipulates her audience and implicitly asks her readers to question the accuracy of the material she collects. Whose voice, after all, do we trust?

To become an "insider," Hurston the narrator hints, an observer must surrender "objectivity," revealing a problem with Boas's participant-observer method. However much her mentor stressed surrendering aloofness, he maintained traditional scientific attitudes toward "accurate" reportage. Hurston's shifting points of view challenge the efficacy of such a method. "Subjects" will only reveal when and what they want to, perhaps never to outsiders, no matter how much researchers try to enter into the culture they wish to study. The narrator's final tale, which closes the book, confirms Hurston's skepticism about objective reportage. The story of Sis Cat conflates narrator, author, and material into one. The tale teller who invents the "lie" and the author who records it are Sis Cat; and the Rat, who has been doubly duped by her "lies," represents Hurston's presumably white audience. The tale itself becomes both folklore material and a gloss of the text's ultimate purpose. The "manners" that Sis Cat learns to use after catching her Rat demonstrate the narrator's method of gathering and reporting data. As an anthropologist, it seems, Hurston has learned a new way of storytelling ("lying") rather than adopting Boas's "scientific" method.[7] However, the author can only reveal her strategy indirectly through analogy and symbol so as not to threaten the anthropological label of her study or risk rejection from her teacher and sponsor.[8]

In Hurston's second collection of folklore, *Tell My Horse* (1938), the author modifies her narrative strategy. Unlike *Mules and Men,* an academic investigation supported by Boas, the research for *Tell My Horse* was funded by two successive Guggenheim Fellowships and developed as a project expressly for Mrs. Osgood Mason, Hurston's wealthy white patron. Mason literally owned the material Hurston collected. Consequently, Hurston's purpose and audience shifted. She was not to appeal to a scholarly reader but to one who held more popular, or stereotypical, views of African American and Caribbean culture. Furthermore, Hurston was more of an outsider herself in Jamaica and Haiti than she had been on her native territory in the United States.

The author's relationship with her "subjects" is represented in the curry goat feed incident in chapter 2 of *Tell My Horse.* First, Hurston must assure her audience that although she is not Jamaican, she can still offer her reader "inside" information. She reports: "They did something for me there that has never been done for another woman. They gave me a curry goat feed. That is something utterly masculine in every detail. Even a man takes the part of a woman in the "shay shay" singing and dancing that goes on after the feed" (11).

Not only is she privileged to take part in an authentic cultural event despite her outsider status, but her gender is also overlooked. In fact, it is perhaps because of her academic status that she is able to overcome her gender. As Hurston soon reveals, Jamaican society is patriarchal and denies independent action for women. Ethnographer Zora must convince her audience that she has not been denied access to the culture she has come to study. Later in the chapter she makes another intimate appeal to her audience, inadvertently revealing her anxiety about the role she has assumed: "The band began playing outside there in the moonlight and we ran away from the table to see it. *You* have to see those native Jamaica bands to hear them. . . . As I said before no woman appears with the players, though there is a woman's part in the dancing. That part is taken by a man especially trained for that" (14; emphasis added). In *Mules and Men* Hurston does not address her reader in the second person, nor does she emphasize her trespassing on male territory when she attends storytelling sessions on the porch. Perhaps in unfamiliar territory, outside her native Eatonville, she is less sure that she can overcome her inferior female role.

Also in *Tell My Horse,* the narrator's position as sympathetic listener is mediated. As a black American, Hurston makes it clear that she does not necessarily share or agree with Jamaican and Haitian values, particularly those concerning the treatment of women. A frequent criticism of *Tell My Horse* is that Hurston abandons her cultural relativism for a kind of female chauvinism.[9] In chapter 5, "Women in the Caribbean," the author makes generalizations about the low status of women in the two cultures and compares their situation unfavorably with American women. Gwendolyn Mikell points out that as a black woman anthropologist, Hurston's life experiences caused her to intertwine an outsider's and insider's viewpoint. Even though "we may wish to accuse her of patronization," Mikell explains, "the skill with which she unmasked these social sensitivities reminds us that, as an intellectual, she was the contradictory product of the class-and-race conscious American society of the 1930's" (222). Though the author may seem ethnocentric here, I believe Hurston is defending her own tenuous status as social scientist by distancing herself from the cultural practices she observes. Furthermore, blending outsider and insider perspectives enables her to mediate between objective and subjective viewpoints without privileging either. Her criticisms of Caribbean culture in chapter 5 are counterbalanced by an equally honest appraisal of the context from which she operates. She addresses her audience at the beginning of the chapter as "Miss America, World's champion woman" (57), a lighthearted but critical epithet which indicts herself as well as her readers as snobs.

In representing "data" to an educated, and most probably, white audience, Hurston had to confront skepticism and even hostility toward her depictions of unfamiliar "primitive" cultural practices, especially native religions. She developed fictional strategies for valorizing African American hoodoo and Haitian voodoo.

(Later we will see Austin using similar strategies for Native American mysticism.) Hurston surrounds her discussions of New Orleans' hoodoo with an aura of mystery. She explains in *Mules and Men* that hoodoo is more a "suppressed religion" than a foolish superstition. "It is not the accepted theology of the Nation," she states, "and so believers conceal their faith. . . . The profound silence of the initiated remains what it is" (185). Likewise, in *Tell My Horse,* part 3, "Voodoo in Haiti," is devoted to a description of voodoo loa (gods) and ceremonies. Hurston compares voodoo rites with Catholicism and shows how the two have become amalgamated in Haitian culture (230–31). She explains that it is a religion of "the mysterious source of life," but "the symbolism is not better understood than that of other religions and consequently is taken too literally" (113). In *Mules and Men,* narrator Zora travels to New Orleans to become initiated herself into this secret faith, then gives her eye-witness account of her experiences. The strategy of withholding then giving information, telling the reader of the secrecy of the rites then only partially revealing them through personal reportage allows readers to experience the confusion of being immersed in a different culture. Throughout part 2 of *Mules and Men,* the narrator alternates between describing hoodoo rituals such as those she learns under hoodoo doctor Luke Turner (198–202) and omitting discussion of them: "I studied under Turner five months and learned all of the Leveau routines," she states, but does not tell what they are, for, she claims, "in this book all of the works of any doctor cannot be given" (202).

Before revealing her experiences with Kitty Brown, another New Orleans hoodoo doctor, the narrator cites several conjure stories not only to "illustrate the attitude of Negroes of the Deep South" (231) but also to testify to the effectiveness of Kitty's spells. All the evidence in this section of the book is circumstantial—the narrator does not give proof or offer any additional explanation or analysis of the phenomena. Letting other eyewitnesses testify first, the narrator can both claim and disclaim the efficacy of hoodoo—and the accumulation of testimonies prepares her audience for her own eyewitness account. As on the porches of Eatonville and Polk County, the narrator again mediates a position between educated observer and curious participant in order to dispel her audience's skepticism.

In *Tell My Horse* Hurston extends her strategy to confront the audience's disbelief in voodoo. First, she insists that the religion is too complex and comprehensive to explain in one book: "This work does not pretend to give a full account of either voodoo or voodoo gods. It would require several volumes. . . . Voodoo in Haiti has gathered about itself more detail of gods and rites than the Catholic church has in Rome" (131). Then, like the narrator in *Mules and Men,* she corroborates her observations of zombies with personal testimonies, "but without using actual names to avoid embarrassing the families of the victims" (192-94). Third, she narrates her own witnessing of a zombie in a hospital and verifies the account with a photograph. Throughout the text, photos of voodoo ceremonies and dances are interspersed, giving the book a kind of travelogue appearance. Hurston can assert that she was actually present at these events with the pictures to prove it.

Finally, the author uses another, more subtle means of challenging the reader's skepticism which she embeds within the narrative itself. The reader identifies with Hurston as narrator/character in her travel adventure as she first remains doubtful about the existence of voodoo. At one point in the book, she explains how she is assured by upper-class Haitians that zombies are only a myth (181). Soon after, of course, she observes one, and the word of her educated hosts is in doubt. Later in the book, before she goes to visit a bocor, or voodoo priest, her yard boy, Joseph, is frightened by what he tells her is the "cochon gris," a secret society he claims wants to eat his baby. When another upper-class Haitian visits Hurston, he learns what Joseph has told her, and Hurston overhears him berating Joseph for "tell[ing] a foreigner, who might go off and say bad things about Haiti such things" (203). The scene closes with the visitor and Hurston assuring each other that they understand "figures of speech," and the reader is left to wonder whether, again, the upper-class Haitians are trying to hide something from the narrator. Sure enough, in the next few pages Hurston describes her horrifying experience at a secret society meeting. Throughout the narrative, Hurston is dissuaded by her hosts from pursuing information about voodoo or the cochon gris, which only makes her—and the reader—more curious and determined in the search.

Another way Hurston reveals the complexity of the "primitive" cultures she documents is to foreground oral expression in her narratives, implicitly questioning the perceived superiority of written literature. In *Mules and Men,* we see a blurring between oral and written language in the construction of the narrative frame. The "conflict" of the plot, the competition among tale tellers, dramatizes the African American practice of "the dozens," or what Henry Louis Gates defines as "that age-old black ritual of graceful insult" (293). The tales often reflect the nature of the "talking game" on the porch. For example, in chapter 2, the men and women of Eatonville compete for linguistic primacy. The sexual battle on the porch is replayed in the tales. One storyteller, Gene, asserts, "her tongue is all de weapon a woman got" (30), prompting Mathilda to tell "why women always take advantage of men" with the well-known "keys to the kingdom" folktale. In this tale, woman might control man's access to the bedroom, the kitchen, and the cradle with the keys the Devil teaches her to use, but her power is strictly limited to the domestic sphere. Furthermore, Hurston makes the next performance in the chapter a song by Jack that describes one man courting three women. Although the narrator of the song might be "in hell" with "that pretty Johnson gal" in the last verse, he has still enjoyed the attentions of three different lovers with impunity. It seems that even in the content of the tales they tell, the women lose.

But the tale-telling sessions also reveal women subtly resisting the patriarchal culture. The chapter ends in a dialogue and exchange of insults between a brother and sister, which the sister wins. She has the last word while he, finally overcome by all the coon-dick has drunk, "mumbl[es] down in to his shirt and [goes] to sleep" (37). In this particular tale-telling session, as in others throughout the book, Hurston's literary construction mirrors and comments upon the verbal gaming the narrator observes, revealing complex linguistic practices of oral expression, as well as documenting the relative roles and status shared between the sexes.

The overall narrative structure of *Tell My Horse* appears deceptively simpler than Hurston's earlier ethnography, since it is mostly straightforward, first-person travelogue. But here as well, the author incorporates orality into the written account of her observations. She does this by breaking codes of standard ethnography—she includes her own opinions and reactions to the cultures in a kind of breezy, conversational style that defies objective reportage.[10] With her side comments and matter-of-fact generalizations, she might be a precursor to today's roaming television commentators. More significant, Hurston introduces postmodern ethnographic techniques after discarding Boasian models. She includes dialogues and scenes in *Tell My Horse* which reveal her interference in the cultures she observes. In Jamaica she insists upon going on a wild boar hunt (31) and even builds a stove for her hosts who have never owned one (23). Surely these actions would be considered unauthorized influence by ethnographers of the modern period. But Hurston includes the interaction and dialogues she engages in with her hosts to reveal not only the mutual exchange of cultural information, but also her self-reflexive stance. *Tell My Horse* becomes part diary in addition to travelogue, political commentary, and ethnographic description. This loosely structured, mixed genre represents a different way of transmitting oral data by replicating the ethnographer's reactions instead of censoring them for an illusory, "objective" style.[11]

By validating the "primitive" cultures she studies, Hurston implicitly questions Western cultural practices which deny supernatural experiences in favor of rational, objective knowledge—and, thus, her narratives begin to challenge the validity of Boasian ethnography itself. In the last two chapters of *Tell My Horse,* Hurston visits Dr. Reser, a white American man who has become a revered voodoo priest throughout Haiti. He is loved and trusted by the Haitians because he acts as their friend, not their superior (247). He tells Hurston about his belief in voodoo gods from "several instances of miraculous cures, warning, foretelling of events and prophecies" (256). Then he describes to her his experiences of being possessed:

> Incident piled on incident. A new personality burned up the one that had eaten supper with us. His blue-gray eyes glowed, but at the same time they drew far back into his head as if they went inside to gaze on things kept in a secret place. After awhile he began to speak. He told of marvelous revelations of the Brave Guedé cult. And as he spoke, he moved farther and farther from known land and into the territory of myths and mists. Before our very eyes, he walked out of his Nordic body and changed. Whatever the stuff of which the soul of Haiti is made, he was that. (257)

Here Hurston not only illustrates the doctor's willingness and ability to experience mysticism but also the relative nature of culture itself. Under Franz Boas, Hurston had helped to prove that race and culture were not synonymous. In this scene Reser becomes Haitian by fully accepting his adopted society's cultural practices: his "race" is culturally constructed.

Nevertheless, despite Hurston's eager participation in Jamaican and Haitian culture, she does not take the final step of becoming part of the culture as Dr. Reser does. In *Tell My Horse* and in *Mules and Men,* she maintains the status of outside observer, interested and sympathetic, but still removed. Both books close with folktales—or primary ethnographic data—(*Tell My Horse* ends with Dr. Reser's tale, "God and the Pintards") and Hurston affirms her position as cultural interpreter: "But the most important reason why I never tried to get my information second-hand out of Dr. Reser was because I consider myself amply equipped to go out in the field and get it myself" (252). So although throughout her narrative she questions accepted ethnographic techniques and challenges assumptions of objectivity, she still represents herself as a fieldworker in the end, a consummate outsider-insider.

While not celebrated as an ethnic or ethnographic author like Hurston, Mary Austin, nonetheless, uses ethnographic methods in her fiction. An autodidact, she immersed herself in Native American culture through participating in its rituals and studying its literature. She familiarized herself with anthropological terminology and methods. Like Hurston's *Mules and Men* and *Tell My Horse,* Austin's first two collections of short fiction, *The Land of Little Rain* (1903) and *Lost Borders* (1909) depict the relationship between narrator and tale as a function of the participant-observer relationship. It is important to note that Austin, while sympathetic and knowledgeable about Native American culture, was nevertheless Caucasian and thus unable to participate or validate her experiences as completely as Hurston could in studying her own Eatonville neighbors for *Mules and Men.*[12] To overcome the handicap of her outsider status, Austin often poses as witness and listener. She does so not only in individual narratives like "The Land" and "The Woman at the Eighteen Mile," but also to introduce collections of tales. *The Basket Woman* (1904), subtitled *Fanciful Tales for Children,* establishes the author as listener in the preface: "I know that the story of the Coyote-Spirit is true because the Basket Woman told it to me, and evidently believed it. She said she had seen Coyote-Spirits herself in Saline Valley and at Fish Lake. I know that the story of the Crooked Fir is true, because if you come up the Kearsarge trail with me I can show you the very tree where the White Bark Pine stood; for I was one of the party that took it on its travels over the mountain: and the rest of the stories are all as true as these" (vi–vii). By establishing a relationship with her "subjects" through listening and watching, Austin attempts to shift the emphasis away from her own ethnicity; still, her anxiety about an authentic voice is evident. Contrary to Hurston, whose shifting viewpoints often playfully tease the skeptical audience (as in the Sis Cat tale), Austin's multivocal narratives become a means of validating the original sources of the author/narrator's information.

Austin's stories often contain multiple layers of narration through hearsay and gossip. Like Hurston's Zora, Austin's narrators call into question the "truth" of the "data" presented, but instead of challenging the accuracy of the tales themselves by calling them "lies," they withhold crucial information from the audience or claim incomplete or contradictory knowledge. By doing so, Austin hopes to tempt her readers into the mystery of her tale in the same way that Hurston teases her audience by conflating narrator and character "Zora."

In "The Walking Woman," the last story in *Lost Borders,* the narrator learns of the elusive wandering woman about whom she writes "by report" when she stops at various places on her travels. She wants to meet the walking woman in person, to verify for herself whether or not she is comely or if she limps. In this story and in others, the narrator pursues a "trail" of hearsay in order to find her plot and confirm the truth behind it. In "The Woman at the Eighteen Mile," a story earlier in the collection, the narrator confesses, "[F]rom the moment of hearing of the finding of Lang's body at Dead Man's Spring, I knew I had struck upon the trail of the story" (203). Often the story the narrator wants to tell is not the typical male adventure of a lost explorer or a discovery of a mine in the desert; instead, as in "The Walking Woman" and "The Woman at the Eighteen Mile," it is a portrait of a mysterious individual, whose life may not be glamorous but whose survival on the harsh desert landscape is remarkable. Following trails to stories becomes the overall plot structure or frame of Austin's story collections. Through these shifting and mediating points of view, Austin foregrounds the act of collecting their story material as much as the tales themselves.

Like Hurston, Austin reveals the unreliability of her narrator. We see this strategy especially in the opening story of *Lost Borders,* "The Land." The narrator recounts an incident in which a friend brings her a potsherd and tells her that she "ought to find a story about [it] somewhere" (158). She replies that she will rather invent a story about it, which she proceeds to do. Later, after telling the story and publishing it in a magazine, strangers approach her and confirm its truth. The narrator then admits, "By this time, you understand, I had begun to believe the story myself" (158). This revelation reverses the narrative act: life imitates fiction instead of fiction deriving from life. The audience's trust in the narrator is lost if the very nature of the tale telling is called into question at the beginning of the book.

Hurston's careful depiction of hoodoo as an arcane but not ersatz religion affirms her stance as cultural relativist. Austin, likewise, celebrates Amerindian cultural practices and mysticism through her invocations of the mysterious influences of the desert and her depictions of wise Native American women. In the preface to *The Land of Little Rain* she writes: "I confess to a great liking for the Indian fashion of name-giving: every man known by that phrase which best expresses him to whoso names him. . . . For if I love a lake known by the name of a man who discovered it, which endears itself by reason of the close-locked pines it nourishes about its borders, you may look in my account to find it so described. But if the Indians have been there before me, you shall have their name, which is always beautifully fit and does not originate in the poor human desire for perpetuity" (3). Naming instead of possessing land is a repeated motif in Austin's short fiction. "Not the law, but the land sets the limit," the narrator asserts in "The Land of Little Rain" (9). The desert is associated with Amerindian culture and figured as impenetrable by Austin. Her characters are often overcome by "desertness" which moves them beyond the boundaries of "civilization" or white man's culture. In "The Land," the interaction of two cultures is again emphasized by the dichotomy between law and nature. Out there where "the law and landmarks fail together . . . almost anything might happen" (156). Actually, beyond the borders is where Austin gathers her stories. But the land that Indians inhabit, the desert, is also treacherous, for it claims both lives and souls. While celebrating its beauty, the narrator also cautions against its power. Austin's narrative strategy, like Hurston's, invites readers to identify with the mysterious allure of the landscape and the people who inhabit it while simultaneously undercutting their own bias of cultural superiority.

In her stories about Native American women, particularly "The Basket Woman," Austin makes implicit cultural comparisons in order to authenticate Amerindian culture. Seyavi, the basket woman, has "set her wit to fend for herself and her young son" (*The Land of Little Rain* 93) after the death of her mate, and she does so by selling baskets. The narrator compares Seyavi's art of basket making to white woman's hairstyling: "In our kind of society, when a woman ceases to alter the fashion of her hair, you guess that she has passed the crisis of her experience. . . . The Indian woman gets nearly the same personal note in the pattern of her baskets" (95). The irony here is unmistakable; Austin elevates Native American art by recontextualizing it in familiar terms that trivialize white culture as a result.

The narrator describes Seyavi's basket designs, which have "a touch beyond cleverness" (95), and explains how when Seyavi cuts "willows for baskets the soul of the weather [goes] into the wood" (96), something readers can only understand by owning one of her creations. At the end of the story we are given what might seem to be a pitiful picture of Seyavi, old and blind, sitting by the fire in the "campoodie" sharing gossip with her three other blind companions. But in this description is also a tribute to her "spiritual ichor" (98) as well as to the Indian way of life which allows her dignity to the end. Seyavi remains part of the campoodie, and if her only privacy is in her blanket, she still "sits by the unlit hearth of her tribe and digests her life, nourishing her spirit against the time of spirit's need" (99).

Throughout Austin's fiction, in fact, the figure of the Indian basket maker functions as a kind of *chisera,* or wise woman, for the narrator. In *The Basket Woman* Austin introduces her as the real narrator of the text who retains primary authority over it; the author is only a recorder of the stories she is told. As for Hurston, who learns secrets of hoodoo from Kitty Brown, Austin's narrators are initiated into the mysteries of Native American culture through women.

Austin's stories also reflect the literary techniques of the culture she observes.

In *The American Rhythm,* she describes the effects of her study of Amerindian speech on her writing. It has "given to [her] literary style its best thing, a selective economy of phrase, and its worst, a habit of doubling an idea back into its verbal envelope" (390). Here, I believe she is explaining the structure of her stories as "trails" without traditional plot development. The motifs of landscape imagery in individual stories coupled with the reappearance of characters like the basket woman and the pocket-hunter constitute the "doubling back," a Native American literary technique Paula Gunn Allen discusses in "The Sacred Hoop." One instance of recurrence can be noticed by juxtaposing Austin's first two collections of stories, *The Land of Little Rain* and *Lost Borders.* The first story in each describes the desert in essentially identical terms. In both, the land is first invoked from the outsider's perspective as a wasteland then revealed from the native view as mysterious and powerful. Another motif reinforcing what Allen calls the "mystical and psychic" in Native American thought is Austin's image of the wise woman, who though not always Native American, seems to subscribe to Indian cultural values. In *The Land of Little Rain* this character is represented by Seyavi, the basket maker, and in *Lost Borders* she is transfigured into the walking woman and the woman at the eighteen mile. Such motifs in themselves are not peculiar to Native American literary techniques, but their mystic quality underlines the cryptic aspects of the culture the author describes.

Austin's highly descriptive language conforms to her own study of Native American poetic form, which uses the "glyph" or "type of Amerindian song which is lyric in its emotional quality and yet cannot be expressed by the simple lyric cry" as its primary form (*American Rhythm* 53–54). The lyricism of Austin's narrative with its sometimes diffuse and even transcendental imagery simulates the form of the glyph. Both the glyph and the "inter-communicative silences" the narrator describes in "The Walking Woman" highlight aspects of Native American mysticism.

Austin's narrative frame also demonstrates the transference of tales from spoken to written form. *One Smoke Stories* (1934), the author's final collection of short fiction, is a group of tales literally meant to be told during the length of time it takes to smoke a ceremonial cigarette. Genre is determined by the combination of content plus culture, not the other way around. For instance, she explains in the introduction, "one-smoke stories are common to all who live in the area: the form is so admirably conceived for oral telling that all anecdote in the Indian country tends to fall into that shape, which accounts for my including in this collection tales of other peoples than Indians" (xiii–xiv). The author develops her theory of the origins of genre further in *The American Rhythm,* when she explains the effects of landscape and environment on literary form.

Like Hurston in *Tell My Horse,* Austin questions scientific objectivity and affirms the relative nature of culture in her fiction without rejecting her own position as interpreter of it. "White Wisdom," a tale in *One Smoke Stories,* epitomizes the author's ethnographic fiction. The story is narrated by a Ute Indian, an outsider to his audience of Navahos, yet like the author herself, no stranger, but another "tribesman" who has sympathetic reasons for sharing his "telling" (182). White "wisdom," as to be expected, is treachery for the Indians. Dan Kearny, the protagonist, is a supposed mixed-blood who never fits completely into either white or Ute culture. Ultimately his offer of marriage is rejected by a white woman and he accepts his Indian name of "Twice-Bitten." But while the story makes clear how white culture threatens Amerindian survival, it does not affirm Indian culture unequivocally, and thus avoids reverse ethnocentrism. Instead, the wisdom of the tale is represented through the foreknowledge of the *chisera,* the narrator's mother, who divines all along that Dan is not Ute at all by blood, for his parents were both white. The twist at the end of the story is not this revelation, however, but rather that Dan's ethnic origin is irrelevant. He has lived as a Ute most of his life; therefore, he has become one. Like Hurston's Dr. Reser in *Tell My Horse,* Austin's character illustrates the relative nature of the culture. One's race or membership in a particular culture is not biologically determined.

Finally, despite her deep, personal involvement with Native American mysticism, as an author, Austin, like Hurston, remains apart from the culture she records in order to maintain the delicate balance between her subject and her audience. As adopted outsiders, Dr. Reser and Dan Kearny represent the extreme of assimilation into another culture. Posing as ethnographer/narrators in the text, Austin and Hurston circumvent the complete subjectivity of cultural immersion experienced by their characters.

Thus incorporating oral and literary techniques from the cultures they studied, Zora Neale Hurston and Mary Austin developed original and complex literary forms. Their experiments with narrative form constitute part of a new tradition of writing by women regionalists in the modern period—ethnographic fiction. In addition to Hurston and Austin, many of their contemporaries were influenced to a greater or lesser degree by the developing social science of anthropology.[13] Tracing narrative strategies among these writers might help reveal how the reading public received and accepted ideas of cultural relativism. With new immigration restrictions and a rising tide of xenophobia occurring in the 1920s in the United States, the nation faced crucial decisions about whether to become a "melting pot" (cultural assimilation) or a "salad bowl" (cultural relativism and multiculturalism). Authors Hurston, Austin, and others through their ethnographic narratives questioned the ethnocentrism of their dominant Anglo-European culture. These questions have resurfaced in the 1980s and 1990s with a new generation of ethnic writers.

In fact, an important connection might be established between regional writers of the modern period and contemporary ethnic authors. Critics have explored Zora Neale Hurston's influence as a literary foremother for a generation of black women writers from Alice Walker to Toni Morrison, but they often overlook her narrative strategies in favor of her heroic female plots. Mary Austin is often recognized as a precursor for Willa Cather and her novels about the Southwest, but she is perhaps as much a model for Louise Erdrich and Barbara Kingsolver, who depict Native Americans interacting with white society. Today's ethnic authors can assume their audience is already familiar with multivocal narratives that question objective reportage and challenge ethnocentrism.

One example of the parallel between modernist and contemporary ethnographic literature is Gloria Naylor's *Mama Day* (1988), which explores the family and ancestry of an urban African American woman. In the first few pages of the novel, the narrator introduces the main characters and adds an anecdote about "Reema's boy," who leaves his rural home on the island of Willow Springs to become "educated":

> Look what happened when Reema's boy—the one with the pear-shaped head—came hauling himself back from one of those fancy colleges mainside, dragging his notebooks and tape recorder and a funny way of curling up his lip and clicking his teeth, all excited determined to put Willow Springs on the map. . . . And then when he went around asking us about 18 & 23, there weren't nothing to do but take pity on him as he rattled on about "ethnography," "unique speech patterns," "cultural preservation," and whatever else he seemed to be getting so much pleasure out of while talking into his little gray machine. (7)

One problem with Reema's boy, the narrator explains, is that he fails to listen to the people of Willow Springs to understand their stories, but instead arrives with predetermined categories of analysis. Naylor's introduction is a cautionary tale for would-be ethnic authors. Zora Neale Hurston and Mary Austin avoid the trap that Reema's boy falls into of treating their subjects as objects. Like Naylor's narrator, they know the pitfalls of appropriating the voice of the "other." Affirming cultural and narrative relativity, their ethnographic fiction not only charts a more complex territory in literary modernism but also illustrates a vital link between regional literature and postmodern multicultural texts.

Notes

1. See Manganaro's introductory chapter to *Modernist Anthropology: From Fieldwork to Text,* a collection of essays on modernist anthropology. He traces the cross-disciplinary influences between the humanities and social sciences to show how "anthropology vitally participated in the century's most important cultural and . . . literary movement" (Preface vi). Also included in this volume are essays considering Ruth Benedict's poetry and ethnography (Handler) and Margaret Mead's and Zora Neale Hurston's innovations in ethnographic reportage (Gordon).

2. See Torgovnick's chapter, "Defining the Primitive/Reimagining Modernity," in *Gone Primitive: Savage Intellects, Modern Lives,* for a discussion of the development of the Malinowski and Boas schools of anthropology and how cultural relativism affected Western assumptions about and ideas of the "primitive," that is, non-Western societies anthropologists often chose to study.

3. According to her biographer, Esther Stineman, Austin was a self-educated ethnologist; she sought out scholars in the field and corresponded with them (172). Austin was probably familiar with Boas's theories from her wide reading in Native American ethnography. In "Discovering America:

Mary Austin and Imagism," Ruppert confirms that in her contribution on aboriginal literature in the *Cambridge History of American Literature,* she quoted frequently from scientists such as Densmore, Fletcher, and Boas (255).

4. Later Hurston suffered for working outside accepted scientific methods. When she wanted to begin work for her Ph.D. in anthropology in 1935, her funding source, the Rosenwald Foundation, withdrew its support when it was discovered that she would spend only three semesters in classes before fieldwork. Edwin Embree, the foundation's president, felt she needed more "discipline" in learning ethnographic methods. See Hemenway (208–10).

5. For a relevant discussion of postmodern ethnography and its relation to feminist theory, see Mascia-Lees, Sharpe, and Cohen. They argue that unlike male anthropologists, feminists have been aware of the presence of the "other" for forty years. Only now are postmodern ethnographers (i.e., post-Boas) recognizing the need for the "other" to speak. Participant-observer anthropology, while concerned with the relationship of the dominant to the culture observed, nonetheless, still spoke from the position of the dominant (11).

6. I am indebted to Johnson for this critique of Hurston's outsider/insider status in *Mules and Men.*

7. See Willis's chapter on Hurston, "Wandering: Zora Neale Hurston's Search for Self and Method" (26–52). Willis explains how *Mules and Men* represents Hurston's "specifying," or verbal one-upmanship, in written form (31). She equates the author's "manners" in the Sis Cat tale with her aggressive writing strategy (29). Johnson and Boxwell also analyze this tale. Johnson concludes: "To turn one's own life into a trickster tale of which even the teller herself might be the dupe certainly goes far in deconstructing the possibility of representing the truth of identity" (289), while Boxwell uses the image of Sis Cat to underscore Hurston's self-representation as ethnographer in her text (613).

8. According to hooks, Hurston's strategy is to make her data more accessible by masking her true relationship to her academic mentors. Rather than operating under Boas's instructions, as she claims in the introduction to *Mules and Men,* in actuality she compelled him to support her study of African American folklore (137–38).

9. See, for instance, Hemenway, who considers *Tell My Horse* as Hurston's "poorest book, chiefly because of its form." He objects to naïve political analysis, her chauvinism, and her inclusion of legend instead of historical fact (248–49).

10. See Gordon for more on how Hurston departs from standard ethnographic genre in *Tell My Horse.*

11. This focus on self as both interpreter and creator of "data" resembles current postmodern ethnographic techniques more than modernist methods. See, for instance, Clifford.

12. See Rudnick and Ammons. Rudnick acknowledges Austin, Mabel Doge Luhan, and Alice Corbin Henderson's Anglo "patronizing" control over a subordinate culture but also affirms the positive exposure these artists gave Native American political and social issues (25). Ammons asks whether it is ever possible for "a member of a dominant group honestly to cross cultural boundaries," then answers her own question by saying that Austin came closer than most. She never assumed that she could completely understand or represent "Amerindian" art and culture (102).

13. Other writers I consider part of this tradition include Anzia Yezierska, Mildred Haun, and Sui Sin Far.

Works Cited

Allen, Paula Gunn. "The Sacred Hoop: A Contemporary Perspective." *Studies in American Indian Literature: Critical Essays and Course Designs.* Ed. Paula Gunn Allen. New York: MLA, 1983. 3–22.

Ammons, Elizabeth. "Form and Difference: Gertrude Stein and Mary Austin." *Conflicting Stories: America Women Writers at the Turn into the Twentieth Century.* New York: Oxford UP, 1992. 86–104.

Austin, Mary. *The American Rhythm: Studies and Reexpressions of Amerindian Songs.* New and enlarged ed. Boston: Houghton Mifflin, 1930.

———. *The Land of Little Rain.* 1903. Rpt. *Stories from the Country of Lost Borders.* 1–149.

———. *Lost Borders.* 1909. Rpt. *Stories from the Country of Lost Borders.* 151–263.

———. *The Basket Woman.* Boston: Houghton Mifflin, 1904. Rpt. New York: AMS, 1969.

———. *Stories from the Country of Lost Borders.* Ed. Marjorie Pryse. New Brunswick: Rutgers UP, 1987.

Boxwell, D. A. "'Sis Cat' as Ethnographer: Self-Presentation and Self-Inscription in Zora Neale Hurston's *Mules and Men*." *African-American Review* 26 (Winter 1992): 605–17.

Clifford, James. *The Predicament of Culture: Twentieth-Century Ethnography, Literature, and Art.* Cambridge: Harvard UP, 1988.

Gates, Henry Louis, Jr. "Afterward: Zora Neale Hurston: 'A Negro Way of Saying.'" *Mules and Men.* New York: Harper & Row, 1990. 287–97.

Gordon, Deborah. "The Politics of Ethnographic Authority: Race and Writing in the Ethnography of Margaret Mead and Zora Neale Hurston." Manganaro 146–62.

Hemenway, Robert E. *Zora Neale Hurston: A Literary Biography.* Urbana: U of Illinois P, 1977.

hooks, bell. "Saving Black Folk Culture: Zora Neale Hurston as Anthropologist and Writer." *Yearning: Race, Gender, and Cultural Politics.* Boston: South End, 1990. 135–43.

Hurston, Zora Neale. *Mules and Men.* 1935. Rpt. New York: Harper & Row, 1990.

———. *Tell My Horse.* 1938. Rpt. New York: Harper & Row, 1990.

Johnson, Barbara. "Thresholds of Difference: Structures of Address in Zora Neale Hurston." *Critical Inquiry* 12 (Autumn 1985): 278–89.

Manganaro, Marc, ed. *Modernist Anthropology: From Fieldwork to Text.* Princeton: Princeton UP, 1990.

Mascia-Lees, Frances, Patricia Sharpe, and Colleen Ballerino Cohen. "The Postmodernist Turn in Anthropology: Cautions from a Feminist Perspective." *Signs: Journal of Women in Culture and Society* 15 (Autumn 1989): 7–33.

Mikell, Gwendolyn. "When Horses Talk: Reflections on Zora Neale Hurston's Haitian Anthropology." *Phylon: The Atlanta University Review of Race and Culture* 43 (Sept. 1982): 218–30.

Naylor, Gloria. *Mama Day.* 1988. Rpt. New York: Vintage, 1989.

Rudnick, Lois. "Re-Naming the Land: Anglo Expatriate Women in the Southwest." *The Desert Is No Lady: Southwestern Landscapes in Women's Writing and Art.* Ed. Vera Norwood and Janice Monk. New Haven: Yale UP, 1987. 10–26.

Ruppert, James. "Discovering America: Mary Austin and Imagism." Ed. Paula Gunn Allen. *Studies in American Indian Literature: Critical Essays and Course Designs.* New York: MLA, 1983. 243–58.

Stineman, Esther Lanigan. *Mary Austin: Song of a Maverick.* New Haven: Yale UP, 1989.

Torgovnick, Marianna. *Gone Primitive: Savage Intellects, Modern Lives.* Chicago: U of Chicago P, 1990.

Willis, Susan. *Specifying: Black Women Writing the American Experience.* Madison: U of Wisconsin P, 1987.

Gendering Modernism: H.D., Imagism, and Masculinist Aesthetics

Michael Kaufmann

Modernism, it is said, "was unconsciously gendered as masculine" (Scott 2). The "male" bias of modernist aesthetic seems difficult to refute when the traditional roster of modernism has been composed largely of male writers—Eliot, Pound, Joyce, Yeats—with an occasional Moore or H.D. thrown in. Further, the modernist aesthetics of impersonality and objectivity correspond neatly to conventional conceptions of masculinity, and did work to exclude many women writers from serious consideration. The poetry and career of H.D., however, complicate the concept of a "masculinist" aesthetic for the first Anglo-American modernist poetry. H.D.'s poetry not only embodied the early principles of modernist poetry (as enumerated in the various imagist manifestos of Pound and Aldington) but actually enabled their formulation in the first place. Ironically, masculinist modernism's first poet was a woman.

It would be more accurate to cite a male bias to critics in their histories, accounts, and definitions of modernism that typically have obscured, until recently, women writers' contributions.[1] Later revisionist views, though, have similarly (but for opposite reasons) obscured H.D.'s contributions to the formulation of the first modernist poetics. The perceived need to define the work of female modernists as strictly countering that of male modernists itself sometimes obscures women writers' contributions to modernism—if their contribution happens to be to what some consider a masculinist version of modernism. Such, I would argue, is the case with Hilda Doolittle's early poetry. Caught in a double bind of literary history, H.D.'s central place in the origins of modernism remains largely unrecognized.[2]

Some commentators have noted how well H.D.'s early poetry, in its "reticence" and "brevity," fit "the hygiene Pound prescribed for a literature dedicated to 'Tennysonianess of speech'" (Collecott 9). The fit, as I will later detail, was more than accidental and not simply an illusion created by Pound's selective editorial decisions (in fact, he only occasionally made such decisions about her poetry; by H.D.'s own account, he merely submitted the poems she gave him [Doolittle, *End to Torment* 18]).

This shift that Pound had announced in poetics from favoring large sprawling epic form to praising the concision of the lyric marked a dramatic, but short-lived and little noted, revaluation of literary forms. Usually short lyric forms sit lowest on the scale of literary value, below the importance of the ode or epic. Imagism, the first modernist poetry, inverted completely the usual poetic hierarchy that estimates the value of a work "by its acreage" (as Pound would later describe it [Pound, "How I Began" 1]).[3] Further, such a reversal unexpectedly foregrounds a "feminine" form—since the more modest lyric has usually been considered appropriate for women poets—over a "masculine" one. Again the masculine nature of the first modernist poetics reveals a surprisingly feminine side.

However, the lyric form, with its open and direct emotional declaration, clashed with another cardinal rule of imagism—"the direct treatment of the subject." "We convey emotion," asserted Richard Aldington in a 1914 essay on imagism in the *Egoist*, "by presenting the object and circumstance of that emotion without comment. . . . No slop, no sentimentality" ("Modern Poetry and the Imagists" 202). Pound's principles, declared a few months earlier, stated a belief in "absolute rhythm (something that corresponds to the emotions)" and "technique as the test of a man's sincerity" (Pound, "A Retrospect" 9). Emotion must be "seen" but not "heard"; it must be expressed in the form of the poem rather than directly stated. If the lyric was to be serviceable for a new poetic, it had to be "toughened" up, shorn of its flowery tendencies and "softness." In the future, the lyric would be objective and "impersonal."

Though this prescribed toughening of the lyric would seem to weigh more heavily on women poets than male ones, just the opposite was true within the small group of imagists at the time—Pound, Richard Aldington, and Hilda Doolittle. While Pound and Aldington (in poems like "Middle-Aged" and "Au Vieux Jardin") lingered in a style uncomfortably close to the Georgian poetry they sought to distinguish themselves from, H.D. had already created a new style in "Priapus" (also titled "Orchard"), "Hermes of the Ways," and "Oread." "Middle-Aged," the first poem of his that Pound referred to as an "imagiste affair," begins unpromisingly with "Tis but a vague, invarious delight / As gold that rains about some buried king" (Pound, *Letters* 44; *Personae* II. 1–2). In addition to violating the imagist precepts on poetic diction, it openly declares its emotional content to the reader. Similarly, Aldington's "Au Vieux Jardin" (leaving aside the forced sophistication of the foreign-language title) declares itself. The speaker delights in water lilies and flagstones that set him "nighest to weeping."[4] Their other poems written around the same time suffer from the same open declarations of emotion they had proclaimed banished from poetry.

Perhaps this proves nothing other than that manifesto writers do not always follow their own precepts. That would be likely, though, only in the absence of H.D.'s work. At the time they are struggling to use the new poetics, she already is able to present her subject and to leave the reader to determine its emotional import rather than declaring it: "I saw the first pear / As it fell. / . . . Thou hast flayed us with thy blossoms (Doolittle, *Collected Poems* 28). Unlike her male counterparts, H.D.'s work illustrates the imagist aim (before there was an imagism) of "convey[ing] emotion by presenting the object and circumstance of that emotion without comment" (Aldington 202).

Neither Aldington nor Pound, however, was able to convey emotion without comment before H.D. showed them how. Pound's less well known account of his composition of "In a Station of the Metro" reveals his struggle to free himself from "sentiment." In this first telling of its composition, in the June 1913 issue of *T.P.'s Weekly,* the motivation for writing the poem is connected with reactions he had had to an earlier poem, "Piccadilly" (included in the 1909 edition of *Personae,* but dropped from all subsequent ones).[5] Pound says others dismissed the earlier poem as mere "sentiment" (Stock 1). The unnamed critics' comments on "sentiment" stung Pound enough to drop the poem from the "canon" of his own works and to excise emotional comment altogether from his later poem on a similar subject, "Metro," and even from poetry in general. Openly expressed sentiment, he discovered, had no place in poetry. In "Piccadilly" the speaker observes and laments the "beautiful, tragical faces" of the women passing by in the square (presumably prostitutes which the area was notorious for at the time), once "whole," now "sunken." The speaker openly declares his repulsion, calling them "vile" and emphasizes the pathos of the situation, asking who has forgotten them. In the next verse, he belies his Villon-like meditation on the transience of things mortal, asserting an inability to feel as much pity as he should. All of this in coyly poetic archaisms to boot—a far cry from the simple, direct presentation of image in "Metro."

Nowhere in this account, or in later ones, does he mention the example Doolittle's poetry provided for him in effecting the excision of open emotion. Counting back from the article's publication date of June 1913 (Pound said the poem took him a year to compose), one finds that Pound remembers beginning the poem near the time he usually recalled as first seeing Hilda Doolittle's poetry.

No doubt his experiences with the Poet's Club played a part in his moving away from direct expression, but by early summer 1912 he had had the benefit of Hulme's thinking for awhile and had produced nothing like "Metro," nor any imagist proclamations. Clearly, H.D.'s poetry helped him see a new way of writing poetry and solidified the definitions for a new poetic he had been considering.

In fact, the praise he had for H.D.'s poems when writing in 1912 to Harriet Monroe to arrange for their publication as the first "imagiste" works centers on their "objectivity." They would not embarrass him with "sentiment" (as his "Piccadilly" did). He could "show them in Paris without being ridiculed"; they were "objective— no slither . . . no excessive use of adjectives" (Monroe 264).[6]

"Metro" shows how much Pound had learned from Doolittle about effacing sentiment by excising adjectives since "Piccadilly." Pound hides the sentiment of his discovery of the petal-like women's faces shining in the dark of a subway station by omitting any adjective. The petals are not "delicate" nor are they "lovely" nor even "pink," any of which would make it easier to locate the speaker's feeling. Despite the impression of objectivity "Metro" imparts, the focus of the poem, even if it does not directly state it, is still primarily sentiment—and sentiment only different in being more positive than the sentiment found so objectionable in "Piccadilly" (wonder instead of disgust). The difference is that in "Metro" the feelings engendered by women's faces are occulted rather than expressed directly. Neither as a condensed panegyric on the beauty of women nor as a comparison of such beauty to that of flowers (or in this case flower parts) does the poem reveal itself as a particularly new insight. Pound's objectivity in this case is merely obscured or effaced sentiment.

The central situation of most of his poems during that period—a speaker observing women—might explain Pound's inability to achieve objectivity. Pound's poetry at the time took the form of social commentary that centered on women. "Women Before a Shop," "The Tea Shop," "Shop Girl," "Dans Un Omnibus de Londres" "Paganini's, November 8," and to a lesser extent "The Encounter" and "Tame Cat" all recount various observations of women in social, urban settings. The poems witness Pound's need to assert his presence as an observer to show both his social insight and artistic sensibility. That the central focus of the poems are female figures further suggests Pound's desire to control the feminine in the same way that descriptive "restraint" (the omission of adjectives in "Metro" for example) controls sentiment. Controlling sentiment, in other words, for Pound, equals controlling the female subject in his poetry—and vice versa, controlling the female subject brings sentiment under control. Leaving "himself" (that is, his speaker/surrogate) out of the poem would entail a loss of that control and defeat the purpose.

Because Pound places the speaker and his observations at the center of the poems, the images seem more decorative than things in themselves. In "Metro" the image of the petals on the bough simply depicts the loveliness of the women's faces in the underground. Similarly, "dawn enters like a gilded Pavlova" in "The Garret," in "Alba" the speaker's lover lies "as cool as the pale wet leaves of lily-of-the-valley," and in "The Encounter" a woman's fingers look "like the tissue of a Japanese paper napkin" (Pound, *Personae* II.5, 1, 4–5).

By contrast, H.D. does not use images to depict other things. She does not assert her own presence as an observer; rather, she emphasizes the qualities expressed in the subject. Her explorations show much greater impersonality. She focuses solely on the image itself, as is the case in her use of flowers—the sea rose, the sea lily, the sea violet. The flowers are not mere metaphors for the loveliness of women's faces, as they are in "Metro." Further, the flowers are not of interest for their beauty, as they conventionally are in poetry, but for other qualities they manifest—their endurance, their persistence, their strength. The "Sea Rose" is a "Harsh rose, / marred and with stint of petals," a "meagre flower." The sea rose is obviously no beauty rose, but somehow "more precious" (*Collected Poems* 5). The "Sea Lily" is "slashed and torn / but doubly rich" and "scales are dashed / from your stem, / sand cuts your petal, / furrows it with hard edge, / like flint" (*Collected Poems* 14). The "Sea Poppies" catch "root among wet pebbles / and drift flung by the sea / and grated shells" (*Collected Poems* 21), while the "Sea Violet" "lies fronting all the wind / . . . on the sand-bank" (25). Doolittle favors the harsh beauty of survival over the more conventional prettiness of Pound's images—such as his description of a woman walking "like a loose skein of silk blown against the wall" ("The Garden"). In true modernist form, H.D. asks to be "spare[d] . . . from loveliness" ("Orchard"), disdaining "beauty without strength" ("The Sheltered Garden"), while Pound focuses on typical poetic beauty. Where Pound only sees conventional prettiness, a fragile gaiety ("Be in me as the eternal moods / of the bleak wind, and not / As transient things are— / gaiety of flowers" [Pound, *Personae* II.1–3]), H.D., more careful in her observations, see flowers "fragile as agate" and "cut in rock" ("Sea Violet," "Garden"). Her poetry shows a much more direct and more subtle treatment of the thing than Pound's more generally "poetic" treatments—another reversal of expectation, since here the male modernist's poetry employs more poetic "prettiness." Mere poetry typically invited disdain from the male modernist—as H.D. recalled, Pound justified the cuts he made when editing by saying, "This is poetry."

The impersonality of H.D.'s poetry comes through in two ways. There is the way she addresses natural elements, such as sea and storm in poems like "Oread" and "Storm." The same might be said of "Orchard," "The Garden," and "Night." As with the flowers in her poems, H.D. explores the natural phenomena itself. A second way that H.D.'s poetry expressed the impersonality that Pound called for is in its speakers. In "Oread," for example, though H.D. takes on a persona, a mountain nymph (and not, interestingly, Pound's "Dryad"), her speaker invokes a collective response—"cover us with your pools of fir" (*Collected Poems* 55)—and focuses on the natural phenomenon itself rather than the cleverness of the speaker's reaction. This forms a contrast with Pound's speaker in "Metro." Though his speaker is unidentified and apparently absent, it is his mental leap between images that is insistently foregrounded. Pound in "Metro," as in his other poems, focuses on the speaker's perception. As Hugh Kenner points out when talking about the movement that formed around Pound as a whole, Pound is not interested "in getting the general look of the thing," but in the "process of cognition itself" (Kenner, *Ezra Pound* 73). Pound explores the perception, showing at the same time the speaker's powers of perception. Pound focuses on the process by which the emotion came to be, the *equation* as Pound referred to it; H.D. seeks to recreate the emotion itself.

Though objectivity and impersonality are not strictly male devices, then, each poet has a very different concept of them. For Pound, objectivity implies absence of direct emotional comment, the emotion of the scene derives from the situation described and additionally from the image used to describe it. The speaker, while unidentified, is very "visible" in the poem. For H.D., on the other hand, objectivity means impersonality, an almost absent "I," depicting and describing a scene. She portrays the emotion of the scene much more directly and vividly—without explicitly identifying it, though it still must be inferred from the scene. H.D.'s immersion in the poem, the submersion of her persona in the scene described, places less emphasis on the poet and on her powers of observation. Pound, on the other hand, calls attention to the poet/speaker's powers of observation. This difference may have also reinforced the lack of respect her early poetry received. It does not call attention to itself and its making of the image. Only the image itself is proffered.

That H.D. should so embody the imagist precepts is not news. Even at the time H.D. was recognized as the "peak of our achievement," "the purest of Imagists," but what some forget is why H.D.'s poems represent so well the imagist ideal: the ideal was created and formed around her poems (Ford 21, qtd. in Bryer 627). In other words, H.D. did not write her poems, as is implied, to suit Pound's and Aldington's ideals; their formulas, in large measure, grew out of H.D.'s poetic practice. They did not have as clear a notion of what their precepts implied in practice until H.D. showed it to them in her poetry. And while it is likely Pound put more thought into the theoretical definition of imagism, H.D. clearly understood better what sort of poetry he envisioned than he himself.

Critics have always acknowledged that H.D. had a part in imagism, but few have ever highlighted her as the first imagist poet or as providing the poetic examples for the precepts of imagism. She is viewed primarily as a follower and protégée. H.D.'s lack of recognition derives in large part from the fact that she was a woman (and therefore by definition a follower rather than an originator in earlier critical eyes), but it also derives from confusion and disagreement over imagism's importance and its early history. Tied to the difficulties with imagism's status is the hierarchy of poetic forms and the reversal of that hierarchy attempted by imagism, favoring the concise lyric over the sprawling epic (with attendant overtones of gendering of the forms). Finally, H.D. herself felt ambivalent over her imagist label and desired to escape it, which led her to downplay her role in imagism. In later years, imagism was something she was attempting to flee, not claim credit for.

An early critical dismissal of imagism shows in F. R. Leavis's *New Bearings in English Poetry*. Leavis described imagism (almost repeating Pound's own pronouncement on the matter in his obituary on Harold Monro) as "little more than a recognition that something was wrong with poetry" (73).[7] Writing a few years later, in 1937, T. S. Eliot sounded a similar note, declaring that "the accomplishment of the Imagist movement in verse seems to me, in retrospect, to have been critical rather than creative; and as criticism, very important." He further asseverated that "the only poet and critic who survived Imagism to develop in a larger way was Mr. Pound" (Eliot 668). In the thirties, then, imagism was something to have survived, and no one had—at least not in the estimation of one of modernism's more prominent writer/critics.

Following suit, Hugh Kenner asserted that the history of the imagist movement was "a red herring" and that it was better "to keep one's eyes on Pound's texts" (his critical pronouncements that is) (Kenner, *Ezra Pound* 58). Like Eliot, Kenner believed Pound was the only true survivor—perhaps the only one who was ever truly living. In his later reorientation of modernism strictly around Pound, the fact that H.D. could write imagist poems even before its formulation came into being seems only happy coincidence (Kenner claims Pound had done the same as well—though as I have shown this is not the case [Kenner, *Pound Era* 185]). It is easy to see with such advice how H.D.'s part in imagism was lost. Not only is imagism itself dismissed but the only figure of importance was held to be its primary manifesto writer.

The advice by Kenner, one of modernism's more influential critics, to follow strictly Pound's critical works has created two effects. First, the critical precepts themselves become evidence of the manifesto writer's poetic practice and not his poetry. Second, the public pronouncements by modernism's most vocal critical minds have become the primary shapers of thought on modernism and modernist literary history (one thinks immediately of Eliot's pronouncements on *Ulysses* and the resultant misinterpretations he caused). Hilda Doolittle, and most women modernists (Virginia Woolf was a notable exception), preferred not to be involved in the public critical skirmishes that seemed to have delighted the Pounds and the Eliots.[8] Hence they had to depend on others for describing and defining them to contemporary and later readers, which meant they sometimes did not get described or defined at all. Instead, it is the manifesto writers who are most often heard and most often remembered.

Even before critics dismissed imagism, Hilda Doolittle's part in it became obscured as the introduction of Amy Lowell into the group caused a rift and an ensuing struggle for "ownership" of the movement between Flint and Pound over T. E. Hulme's role in originating imagist principles. The public pronouncements vary in interesting ways from the private ones. Publicly, the dispute centered on which *man* can rightfully claim title to originating imagism, a pattern that continues in recent critical adjudications of the matter.[9] The debate should not only be whether Hulme or Pound should be credited with imagism, but why H.D.'s role in it has been all but lost.

Publicly, Pound praised H.D. as a prime practitioner of imagism, but he never credited her to the extent he did in private for her contribution in formulating imagism by example. Pound's public response to Flint's contention that Hulme started imagism generously acknowledges an even less likely inspiration in Ford Madox Ford, as "the critical LIGHT during the years immediately pre-war in London" (Kenner, *Ezra Pound* 307). Privately, however, Pound spoke of Hilda Doolittle as imagism's originator. Writing to Harriet Monroe in September 1915 (during the splintering within imagism), he claimed that the "whole affair [imagism] was started not very seriously chiefly to get H.D.'s poems a hearing" (qtd. in De Chasca 105). Pound's dismissive attitude derives from his pique at the loss of control over the imagist label with Amy Lowell's entry and financing of the imagist anthology. Later

Pound offered a less flippant account—imagism "was formulated almost in order to give emphasis to certain qualities that she [H.D.] possessed to a maximum degree" (qtd. in Pound, *Ezra Pound and Dorothy Shakespear* 343). Part of the problem lies in the very terms of the dispute that assumes a single mind must originate anything. Everything must be seen in terms of ownership and possession, and only one person must ultimately be the party responsible. It seems more clearly a very fruitful collaboration between Hulme's ideas on poetry meshing and galvanizing Pound's own. Yet just as clearly neither was able to put their ideas into practice—until H.D. showed Pound the means of doing so.[10] Only when he saw her poetry did he understand the full implications of his new prescription for poetry. Still, as generous as Pound often was in his private praise of H.D.'s importance in begetting imagism, he was unwilling to share public credit with her to any great extent.

H.D.'s obscured place in originating imagism is not solely, however, a male conspiracy of silence. Eager to shed her association later in her career, she continually downplayed her role in the movement in most public statements she made on the matter. She would later speak of her "'success'" as "small and rather specialized," adverting to both the short and limited nature of the praise she garnered—more personal than professional—and the "smallness" of the poetry (in literal terms that is) that her success rested on (Doolittle, *Tribute to Freud* 149). Her modest assessment belies her centrality to imagism. As Aldington said, "H.D. *was* imagism" both in her poetry and in her editorial and publishing roles (*Life for Life's Sake* 124). Indeed, she "appears as the chief-among-equals in the collecting of poems for the Imagist anthologies" and was almost solely responsible for the publication of the 1917 anthology (Pondrom, "Selected Letters" 580). Her pronouncements, though, come from a time when she desperately wanted to have no more part of imagism or being thought of as an imagist. Imagism became a burden she could not cast off. She could shuck all the work of arranging and editing the imagist anthology, which she had largely managed, but critics refused to allow her to give up her title of the "perfect Imagist" and explore the new epic style she favored.

Consequently, in the late fifties, when she eventually comes to tell the story of the beginning of imagism, H.D. depicts it mainly as something imposed on her. Significantly, she begins *End to Torment,* her account of the early London years, commenting on critical views of her work. "They speak of [chiselled] verse," she writes, said she "crystallize[d]" her poems (*End to Torment* 3). She speaks of feeling "frozen in the moment," ostensibly in a remembered moment from her early relationship with Pound, but clearly she feels frozen poetically as a result of critic's refusal to recognize any merit in her later poetry. They refuse her the right to create any verse but the "chiselled." No wonder her often noted description of the scene emphasizes Pound's naming of her and her poems and his slashing pencil (Doolittle, *End to Torment* 18). She felt stamped by Pound's title—H.D., imagiste. H.D. wanted to disavow her ties to imagism: twice she wrote to remind Harriet Monroe after the publication of her first poems that she thought the "'Imagiste' in the first series has sufficiently identified me." She preferred her work be signed "H.D. simply, cutting out the affectation" of the title (qtd. in Harmer 39). But once affixed, the label seemed "to have stuck somehow" (qtd. in Harmer 111).

Critical questions on H.D.'s talents, for all the praise her imagist work received, came surprisingly early. One hears in many of the early misgivings about H.D.'s talents critical suspicions toward lyric as a minor and "feminine" form. Ultimately, the hesitations bear marks of simple sexism, questioning a poetry which they (mis)read as too poetic. The reversal initially effected by imagism of favoring a "lesser" form over the epic turned out to be short-lived. Harold Monro in 1915 described H.D. as a "true Imagist" (that dread title again) but felt her poems were "fragile as sea shells" and feared clumsily crushing them. One readily detects the conventional suspicion of lyric, but also overtones of the male modernist suspicion of the feminine "poetical" (a wrong-headed analysis of H.D.'s work) expressed in the form of careful regard (the stated fear of his male clumsiness inadvertently smashing H.D.'s feminine fragility) (Monro 80). Amy Lowell in *Tendencies in Modern American Poetry* (1917) disparaged H.D.'s poetry similarly, revealing that the disapproval—and its sexist overtones—was not solely male: "'H.D.' is not a poet of great breadth of mood nor of many moods. All her effects are delicate rather than broad" (271). "The faults of such poetry," according to Lowell, "are not in its treatment, but in it very texture. This is a narrow art, it has no scope. . . . There is a certain thinness in the original conception, and only the lustre of its polish saves it" (279). The comments imply a certain lack of substance in H.D.'s work, apparently deriving from her subject matter, the flowers and other natural phenomena. Monro and Lowell mistakenly read the images as traditional tropes of poetic prettiness, when it is the flowers' resilience and not their prettiness that H.D. finds intriguing in them. The flowers appearing in *Sea Garden,* like the poems themselves, survive harsh conditions, even critics' clumsiness.

The criticism of H.D.'s poetry—which must have stung, especially considering the sources—can be read more as criticism of imagism in particular and of the lyric in general. The attempted reversal of the poetic hierarchy, placing the lyric above the epic, fell flat, and critics rushed to "correct" the mistakes as earlier practitioners of the lyric such as Eliot and Pound abandoned the lyric and moved toward more "substantial" forms.

In a paradox that characterized H.D.'s relationship with critics, their later misgivings about her work came both from their dismissal of imagism and its possibilities and from her decision to move away from the earlier imagist style that they had declared so limited and narrow. Once her poetry became epic in style (perhaps partly in response to such critical comment), critics faulted her for departing from her earlier style, deciding she should never have abandoned it. As critics became less and less satisfied with her work because of its stylistic departures from imagism, they came to regard her poetic skills less and less highly. The shift away from imagism in *Red Roses for Bronze* brought disappointed comments from the *Times Literary Supple-*

ment and the *Spectator*. The latter found her "attempts to handle contemporary experience relaxed the frozen intensity of her verse and thawed it into a rather inconclusive fluidity" (the very sort of description H.D. despairs of in *End to Torment* [D.H.V. 186]). Babette Deutsche faulted *The Walls Do Not Fall* for its abstraction and departure from imagism (18). Randall Jarrell sounded the final judgment, dismissing *Tribute to Angels* with the comment that imagism is a poetic upon which it is "hard to base a later style" (741). Her excellencies in lyric form typed her success as "modest" and "limited" one dominance had again shifted back to larger, epic forms, such as those employed in Eliot's *Waste Land* and Pound's *Cantos*. Regarded as a lesser poet, H.D. was then ignored for her part in fostering imagism, since a "minor" talent by definition could not teach anything to ones with eras named after them. Clearly H.D. could not "survive" imagism because critics would not allow her to survive it. They insisted her best work was imagist and at the same time declared the imagist poetic narrow (exactly why H.D. herself had decided to move to her later style). Either way she would only be allowed to be a minor poet, either one who overreached her "true" talents or, if she had followed critical advice, wrote in a narrow and now outmoded style.

Until the seventies critics repeated this same refrain finding that H.D.'s "place in modern poetry . . . [is] minor (Quinn 30). Her "range of subjects and the complexity of mind and feeling" do not equal "Yeats, Eliot and Auden" (31). In other words, since in their opinion H.D.'s epics do not match the importance of Eliot's or Pound's (a judgment now contested), she cannot be an important poet. Her success lies in more "modest" forms, where woman's poetic strengths are generally supposed to lie, as Susan Stanford Friedman notes (*Psyche Reborn* xi).

Since earlier male critics found women writers easy to overlook in any case, again it should not be so surprising that H.D.'s early centrality to modernist poetry has been obscured. However, in an unexpected way, later attempts to reassert her importance as a modernist poet have also effaced H.D.'s role in imagism, since they usually revalued her later poetry at the expense of her earlier career and works. Most recent criticism has focused primarily on her neglected later works (and rightly so), both in fiction and poetry, in hopes of defining a countertradition of female modernism to balance that of Eliot and Pound and Joyce (a modernism formerly presented as The Modernism), so that the early work again receives short shrift.[11] In the later reevaluations of H.D.'s career, the early work is viewed as "self-limiting" and even "trivial" (Walker 142; Grahn 27, 101). And when her earlier work and style is considered valuable, it is more as a stage that was necessary for H.D. to transcend.[12] Imagism, in this view, provided a technique that she could develop into her later epic style. One can see here the accepted hierarchy of poetic forms reasserting itself—one must get past the lyric and moves on to more "substantial" forms like the epic.

While serving as an important corrective to the earlier narrow conceptions of modernism based on the works of a few male writers, the attempt to define a separate modernism created by women poets and writers has sometimes perpetuated the conditions that obscured H.D.'s contributions to imagism in early critical opinions. Critics that value H.D.'s later work prefer to see imagism as a stage in which she merely passed through rather than as something she had a part in originating. In such a view it is not desirable to examine too closely her part in imagism because it ties her with the very tradition she later defined herself against ("I can't think that I must be POUND-ELIOT" [qtd. in Pearson, n.p.]). It is also a worthy attempt to assert a woman writer's successes outside the earlier limits of "approved" poetic forms for women poets—usually meaning the lyric. However, to read H.D.'s career and the poetic forms she employs developmentally reinforces precisely the prejudices that the revisionist views of her work and of literature seek to correct. Why, in other words, is it important that H.D.'s attempts at epic be more significant than her early lyrics (leaving aside H.D.'s own statements in the matter)? Why should she compete against the excellencies of her own work?

My intent is not to return H.D. to the "critical cage of imagism," but to try to release her from the double bind in which literary history and her own career has put her (Friedman, *Psyche Reborn* xi). It is H.D.'s "misfortune" to have been instrumental in creating two strains of modernism—first aesthetically in the form of imagism, and then in subject matter, when she rebuilt modernism anew in her later epics. Consequently, in the critical battle over the excellencies of one over the other H.D. will lose even if she "wins," but that too derives from the notion that there must always be winners and losers in these literary contests we feel the need to create.

Examining the particular instance of H.D. and her part in fostering imagism raises significant questions about female modernism and the way in which it has usually been defined primarily *against* male modernism rather than *in relation* to it. Clearly Hilda Doolittle did later seek desperately to define herself against the epic style of "Pound/Eliot" and to forge her own epic strain, yet in appreciating her later achievements, her earlier interaction with male modernism is often neglected.

In neglecting the full range of H.D.'s poetry, we lose a more complete understanding of both masculinist modernism and feminine modernism, and their contradictions. Differences still emerge, but they are not as stark or as simple as they might initially have seemed. One finds an impersonality and an objectivity in H.D.'s writing (as we do in Marianne Moore's) also found in male modernism, but one also notes a much different conception of what objectivity and impersonality entails. Pound's objectivity effaces the emotional content of the poem; H.D.'s releases it, submerging the personality of the speaker in the poem. Other women writers who might be said to have participated in developing techniques usually attributed to male modernism could be examined with similar fruitfulness—Dorothy Richardson's stream of consciousness narration and Mina Loy's futurism to name two. In the process, we are much more likely to find just how many modernisms there are.

Notes

1. Though I do not agree with all of their conclusions, Susan Gilbert and Susan Gubar in *No Man's Land* and *The War of the Words* and Bonnie Kime Scott in her anthology *The Gender of Modernism* uncover women writers previously overlooked by literary history. I differ, however, in seeing these women writers as not simply an alternative or reactionary tradition to masculinist modernism, though certainly in many cases they do form such a tradition.

2. Cyrena Pondrom's "H.D. and the Origins of Imagism" is a notable exception.

3. One witnesses the revaluation in Pound's grudging praise of Whitman in "A Pact," where he allows for Whitman's revolutionary "matter" but finds need for a finer and more finished carving, whittling away at Whitman's sprawling epic form in favor of a small and jewel-like verse.

4. *Poetry* 1 (Nov. 1912). Also in *Des Imagistes,* ed. Ezra Pound (1914; rpt. New York: Frank Shay, 1917), 11. Cyrena Pondrom shows in detail the ways in which H.D.'s poetic efforts easily surpassed Aldington's and Pound's in their embodiment of imagist principles ("H.D." 77–78).

5. In the article "How I Began," Pound says he waited three years for the words for "Piccadilly." He then goes one to say he waited a year after the experience in the Paris Metropolitain before finding the words for the poem, which he printed in the article. One can find "Piccadilly" most easily in Gesner.

6. "Slither" is Pound's code for excess of emotion. See, for example, his remark in "Prolegomana" (first printed in *Poetry Review,* Feb. 1913): "At least for myself, I want it [poetry] so, austere, direct, free from emotional slither" ("A Retrospect" 12).

7. Pound wrote, "You have a period of muddle, a few of the brightest lads have a vague idea that something is a bit wrong, and nobody quite knows the answer" (*Polite Essays* 7).

8. Lawrence Rainey notes her unusual (for a modernist) critical silence (106–7).

9. See Ethan Lewis, "This Hulme Business," who, along with earlier commentators on the subject (Herbert N. Schneidau, N. Christophe de Nagy, John T. Gage, and Hugh Kenner), take up Pound's cause in the matter. Alun R. Jones, Glenn Hughes, Stanley Coffman, and Sir Herbert Read side with Flint on Hulme's behalf. As one might expect, Hilda Doolittle's name is nowhere mentioned.

10. See Lewis's article for comment on Hulme's poetry.

11. I am thinking of important works such as Susan Stanford Friedman's *Psyche Reborn* and *Penelope's Web.* I am not faulting the concentration on Doolittle's later works, especially considering their neglected status at the time. I do think, though, that the attempt to reorient H.D. studies to her later work often brought a corresponding (and unnecessary) devaluation of her earlier work.

12. See Friedman and Alicia Ostriker, who, for instance, read H.D.'s career developmentally, seeing the later work as overcoming the limitations of the earlier poetry (*Psyche Reborn* 3–10; Ostriker 30–33). Eileen Gregory persuasively shows the devaluation of H.D.'s earlier work in recent studies of her later works (525).

Works Cited

Aldington, Richard. *Life for Life's Sake.* London: Cassell, 1968.

———. "Modern Poetry and the Imagists." *Egoist* 1 (1 June 1914): 202.

Bryer, Jackson R. "H.D.: A Note on Her Critical Reputation." *Contemporary Literature* 10 (Autumn 1969): 627–31.

Coffman, Stanley. *Imagism: A Chapter in the History of Modern Poetry.* Norman: U of Oklahoma P, 1951.

Collecott, Diana. "Remembering Oneself: The Reputation and Latter Poetry of H.D." *Critical Quarterly* 27 (Spring 1985): 7–22.

De Chasca, Edmund S. *John Gould Fletcher and Imagism.* Columbia: U of Missouri P, 1978.

Deutsch, Babette, "The Last of the Imagists." *New York Herald Tribune Weekly Book Review* 1 Oct. 1944, 18.

Eliot, T. S. "A Commentary." *Criterion* (July 1937): 666–70.

Ford, Ford Madox. "Those Were the Times." *An Imagist Anthology.* New York: Boni & Liveright, 1930.

Friedman, Susan Stanford. *Psyche Reborn: The Emergence of H.D.* Bloomington: Indiana UP, 1981.

————. *Penelope's Web: Gender, Modernity, H.D.'s Fiction.* Cambridge: Cambridge UP, 1990.

Gage, John T. *In the Arresting Eye: The Rhetoric of Imagism.* Baton Rouge: Louisiana State UP, 1981.

Gesner, George, ed. *An Anthology of American Poetry.* Boston: Avenel, 1983.

Gilbert, Sandra M., and Susan Gubar. *No Man's Land: The Place of the Woman Writer in the Twentieth Century.* Vol. 1. *The War of the Words.* New Haven: Yale UP, 1989.

Grahn, Judy. *The Highest Apple: Sappho and the Lesbian Poetic Tradition.* San Francisco: Spinster's Ink, 1985.

Gregory, Eileen. "Rose Cut in Rock: Sappho to H.D.'s *Sea Garden*." *Contemporary Literature* 27 (Winter 1986): 525–52.

Harmer, J. B. *Victory in Limbo: Imagism 1908–1917.* New York: St. Martin's Press, 1975.

H.D. [Doolittle, Hilda]. *End to Torment.* New York: New Directions, 1979.

————. *H.D.: The Collected Poems, 1912–44.* Ed. Louis L. Martz. New York: New Directions, 1983.

————. *Tribute to Freud.* New York: Pantheon, 1956.

Hughes, Glenn. *Imagism and the Imagists.* Stanford: Stanford UP, 1931.

Jarrell, Randall. "Verse Chronicle." *The Nation* 161. 29 Dec. 1945. 741–42.

Jones, Alun R. *The Life and Opinions of T. E. Hulme.* Boston: Beacon, 1960.

Kenner, Hugh. *The Poetry of Ezra Pound.* New York: New Directions, 1951.

————. *The Pound Era.* Berkeley: U of California P, 1971.

Leavis, F. R. *New Bearings in English Poetry: A Study of the Contemporary Situation.* London: Chatto & Windus, 1938.

Lewis, Ethan. "'This Hulme Business' Revisited; Or, of Sequence and Simultaneity." *Paideuma* 22 (Spring–Fall 1993): 255–65.

Lowell, Amy. *Tendencies in Modern American Poetry.* 1917. Rpt. New York: Macmillan, 1971.

Monro, Harold. "The Imagist Discussed." *Egoist* 2 (May 1915): 77–80.

Monroe, Harriet. *A Poet's Life: Seventy Years in a Changing World.* New York: Macmillan, 1938.

de Nagy, N. Christophe. *Ezra Pound's Poetics and Literary Tradition.* Bern: Francke, 1966.

Ostriker, Alicia Suskin. *Stealing the Language: The Emergence of Women's Poetry in America.* Boston: Beacon, 1986.

Pearson, Norman Holmes. "Introduction." *Hermetic Definition,* by Pearson. New York: New Directions, 1972. N.p.

Pondrom, Cyrena. "H.D. and the Origins of Imagism." *Paideuma* 4 (Spring 1985): 73–97.

————. "Selected Letters from H.D. to F. S. Flint: A Commentary on the Imagist Period." *Contemporary Literature* 10 (Autumn 1969): 10, 557–625.

Pound, Ezra. *Ezra Pound and Dorothy Shakespear: Their Letters 1909–1914*. London: Faber & Faber, 1985.

—————. *Letters of Ezra Pound, 1907–1941*. Ed. D. D. Paige. New York: Harcourt Brace, 1950.

—————. *Personae: The Collected Poems of Ezra Pound*. New York: New Directions, 1926.

—————. *Polite Essays*. New York: New Directions, 1940.

—————. "A Retrospect." *Literary Essays of Ezra Pound*. New York: New Directions, 1968.

—————. "This Hulme Business." Rpt. *The Poetry of Ezra Pound*. By Hugh Kenner. Norfolk, CT: New Directions, 1951. 307–9.

Quinn, Vincent. *Hilda Doolittle*. New York: Twayne, 1967.

Rainey, Lawrence. "Canon, Gender, and Text: The Case of H.D." In *Representing Modernist Texts: Editing as Interpretation*. Ed. George Bornstein. Ann Arbor: U of Michigan P, 1991.

Read, Sir Herbert. *The True Voice of Feeling*. London: Faber & Faber, 1953.

Schneidau, Herbert N. *Ezra Pound: The Image and the Real*. Baton Rouge: Louisiana State UP, 1969.

Scott, Bonnie Kime. *The Gender of Modernism*. Bloomington: Indiana UP, 1990.

Stock, Noel. *The Life of Ezra Pound*. New York: Pantheon, 1970.

v., D. H. "The Lunatic, the Lover, and the Poet." *The Spectator* 148. 6 Feb. 1932. 186–87.

Walker, Cheryl. *The Nightingale's Burden: Women Poets and American Culture before 1900*. Bloomington: Indiana UP, 1982.

∾ Is Mary Llewellyn an Invert? The Modernist Supertext of *The Well of Loneliness*

Loralee MacPike

Radclyffe Hall is not usually included in the canon of modernism. Although she wrote during the same period as Virginia Woolf, H.D., Djuna Barnes, Dorothy Richardson, and Gertrude Stein, critical appraisal of her work has not produced claims that she was consciously working within what Fredric Jameson has called the "hegemonic modernist categories of irony, complexity, ambiguity, dense temporality, and particularly, aesthetic and utopian monumentality" (195). Indeed, *The Well of Loneliness* explicitly eschews irony in favor of high seriousness, complexity in favor of a unified characterization of the outcast lesbian Stephen Gordon, ambiguity in favor of unremitting approval, temporality in favor of scenes of drama, and utopian monumentality in favor of a highly personalized plea for individual acceptance. Nor could Hall have done otherwise with Stephen Gordon, for her purpose in the novel was the decidedly unmodern one of making the unfamiliar familiar and thereby acceptable. Yet I would argue that *The Well* has a modernist supertext consonant in unexamined ways with Jameson's "hegemonic categories" of modernism and that, when viewed as modernist, it offers one of the clearest paradigms of fiction's role in constructing lesbian sexuality in the first third of our century.

It is possible to locate one of the geneses of our contemporary construction of lesbianism in the invention of female sexual identities which took place in the 1920s. Unfortunately, by 1928, when Hall published *The Well,* the sexological creation of the "mythic, mannish lesbian"[1] and its echo in Stephen Gordon had overdetermined the context of discussion of lesbian "nature" by the force of its unity. Irony and ambiguity disappeared; the hegemony of agreement that Stephen Gordon was *the* lesbian disallowed space for other manifestations of lesbianism. The result was critical argument over whether Stephen Gordon could be both "typical" and "positive,"[2] too frequent conflation of homosociality and homoeroticism with lesbianism rather than explorations of their overlapping differences,[3] and a replication of nineteenth-century sexologists' taxonomies as critics "decide" whether a certain fictional character "is" or "is not" a lesbian.[4]

The work of the past decade on women modernists[5] makes this a moment in history when it is productive to re-view and rethink texts like Hall's whose "meanings" may have seemed finally decided, static, and unmodern, and gender studies offers one focus for such rethinking. In an effort to step aside from the predeterminism of existing sexological theory and literary criticism, I want to look at and through the cracks in them, to shift the fault lines, to see what other patterns might emerge were we to ask different questions.

We have in women's modernist fiction, for example, no extended firsthand account of women like Mary Llewellyn, Stephen Gordon's love in *The Well of Loneliness*. She exists in the interstices of Stephen's life; she peeps from the case studies of turn-of-the-century sexologists' tomes; no author widely read today but Hall has offered enough of her dilemma to warrant a reconstruction of her nature. When she is examined critically, it is as an adjunct and contrast to Stephen, a comparison which casts her as what Havelock Ellis called a "pseudo-homosexual"—a woman who, although congenitally "normal," loved a woman rather than a man for a variety of emotional, psychological, social, demographic, or economic reasons which sexology carefully separated from her sexuality.[6] When they spoke in the abstract about "the female invert," sexologists differentiated women like Mary from "true inverts" both iconographically—they tended not to manifest the mannish body and behavior styles of the "mythic, mannish lesbian"—and by their eventual life choices, that is, marrying a man when marriage became possible. Hall backgrounds Mary in order to foreground Stephen, a fine choice for the novel Hall chose to write but one which denies Mary her own voice. Much like Virginia Woolf's Olivia and Chloe in *A Room of One's Own,* she is but a shadow. Reading the novel in 1975, Jane Rule saw the only possible causes of (Stephen's) inversion to be physiological and viewed Mary, who lacked such physiology, as Stephen's lover but most definitely not as a "lesbian." Most critics since then, when they speak of Mary at all, find her no more than Ellis's "'feminine' love-object," the normal counterpart to Stephen's "'masculine' invert" (Ruehl 20), or simply "Stephen's very feminine lover Mary" (Whitlock 564), although Newton does recognize that Ellis's and Hall's dilemma when confronted with a "feminine" invert led to obvious lacunae in analysis. As astute a critic as Catharine R. Stimpson dismisses Mary thus: "For God's scheme includes congenital heterosexuals as well as congenital inverts. Mary has, somewhat belatedly, realized she is one of them" (372). Blanche Wiesen Cook emphasizes Hall's adherence to Havelock Ellis's iconography of inversion which resulted in Stephen Gordon but passes over Mary entirely and discusses Valerie Seymour as "'a creature apart,'" in Stephen's words (734). There has been no place for Mary Llewellyn *as an invert* in contemporary lesbian criticism. Yet it is profitable to ask the question: Is Mary Llewellyn an invert? What sort of invert? How might her sexual orientation be defined across the grain of her culture's sexological theory, her novel's narrative structural exclusion, and our own ongoing critical neglect? If, as Ruehl suggests, Hall was writing to "[open] up a space for other lesbians to speak for themselves" (21), it is important to find ways to allow Mary's voice, whatever it may say, to be heard.

I find this question of more than passing interest because of the relation between Hall's work and the modernist desire to see and create anew, which framed Hall's literary output. As I have noted, *The Well* is hardly a modernist document. It is traditionally realistic in form, elegiacally Latinate in diction, and bounded by sexological and psychological theory in characterization. The "newness" of its presentation of Stephen Gordon as the prototypical invert/lesbian appears to be its major claim to inclusion in the canon of modernism, and this claim is shaky at best given the extent to which Stephen conforms to contemporary theories of the looks, interests, abilities, and constraints of inverts. I argue in this essay, however, that *The Well of Loneliness* is indeed modernist; and Mary Llewellyn is the foundation for my evidence. She is one of the forgotten critical fragments which reconstitute the classic—and exclusionary—definitions of modernism.[7] An examination of the type or phenomenon Mary Llewellyn represents shows one way the historical, sexological, and fictional/imaginative matrix of the second half of the 1920s en/visioned and structured the crossing of "female" and "invert" anew.

The first place to look for such a crossing is sexology, which has been credited with creating Stephen Gordon.[8] Turn-of-the-century sexologists are said to agree in theory on a visual and behavioral iconography of inversion which critics of *The Well* believe Hall assumed wholesale.[9] Blanche Wiesen Cook has deplored the fact that Hall's "reading of such woman-hating and homophobic sex theorists . . . influenced and severely limited her range of options" (733), but I think Hall did not limit herself to their theories. While both Hall and Stephen believed that their own sexuality was congenital and that they had masculine souls (in keeping with Richard von Krafft-Ebing, Karl Ulrichs, Havelock Ellis, Edward Carpenter, and even Freud),[10] I wish to show the extent to which both sexology and Hall herself simultaneously undermined this apparently unidimensional sexological invert. Sexologists tacitly undermine the rigidity of their theory by their case studies; Hall undermines it by the creation of a visible, historically based, often class-bound range of inverted essence and experience centered on Mary Llewellyn.[11]

Mary Llewellyn enters *The Well of Loneliness* as a fragile, untried nineteen-year old in Stephen's ambulance unit in France in the middle of World War I. There are unmistakably "feminine" aspects to Mary's appearance, character, and behavior. During the full two years of her war experience with Stephen, she never rises to the rank of driver but remains an assistant. She often clings to Stephen's arm, holds her hand, fingers her lapel, rests her cheek against Stephen's shoulder. She is virtually always shown as vulnerable (often asleep), and her supervisor fears she will not "stick it" (278). Stephen repeatedly calls her "you little child" (308) and thinks of her as "so little" (285). Mary has the usual array of female accomplishments—typing, darning, housekeeping—and longs "to do womanly tasks for Stephen" (323). Stephen thinks of her as "perfect woman"—not *a* perfect woman, but simply *perfect woman,* the model of womanliness. Stephen's homosexual playwright friend Jonathan Brockett calls her "a perfectly normal young woman" (346), and Martin Hallam sees her as both "normal" and "all woman" (423). An enamored Pedro on Orotava sees her as "beautiful" enough to "get a real man to love her" (315). Hall constructs the relationship between Mary and Stephen on the basis of Mary's femininity: she desires to darn Stephen's socks; she brings the comfort of flowers, goldfish, and birds to their house; she pours out her love to Stephen in comforting, motherly letters (338). But of course the most telling evidence of Mary's femininity is her departure with Martin.

By contrast, the true invert constructed by sexology was mannish in appearance and activities and had a "homosexual mentality" (Hirschfeld 191) which ruled out desire for or response to a man. In fact, however, this construction was qualified by the sexologists' case studies. Many of Krafft-Ebing's case studies involved women entirely feminine in appearance (passim), and a number of the inverts Ellis described were also indistinguishably feminine (*Studies* 223–44). Of Krafft-Ebing's fifteen case studies of female inverts, five married and bore children, one performed oral sex with a man, and one recorded that the invert who had seduced her into a homosexual life-style subsequently married and bore children. Hirschfeld said quite matter-of-factly that homosexuals may even "incline exclusively toward heterosexuals" as partners (200) and cited cases of women who married, bore children, and tolerated heterosexual coitus. Of Ellis's six case studies of female inverts, three expressed a willingness to marry a man (despite avowals that they did not feel sexual desire for men), a fourth admitted to minor sexual activity with a particular man,[12] one detailed a "strong physical compulsion"—to the extent of being "on the point of losing all control of myself"—toward a man she knew slightly, and in subsequent discussions Ellis mentioned two other inverted women who married and bore children (*Studies* 223–44, 261). Krafft-Ebing specified that some inverts married "because they wish[ed] to be provided for" (265) or were uninformed about the nature of their sexual preferences; but they were still inverts. Hirschfeld said that "[t]he negative attitude toward the opposite sex is an important, but in itself not a decisive, sign of homosexuality" (210).

This confusion between anxious rigidity of theory and open fluidity of observation is reflected at the very core of the argument about the "nature" of the female invert: what sort of woman would be attracted to an invert? "[T]here cannot be any adequate return of the affection in the absence of an actual or latent homosexual disposition," Ellis states flatly (*Studies* 285). Thus, a woman who would be attracted to Stephen Gordon, who would return her affection, would have to have a "homosexual disposition." According to this view, Mary Llewellyn would have to be of homosexual disposition, that is, an invert. Such a view is directly contradicted, however, by Ellis's statement that "[i]n inverted women [who presumably have a homosexual disposition] some degree of masculinity or boyishness is . . . prevalent, and it is not usually found in the women to whom they are attracted" (*Studies* 288). But if "the women to whom they are attracted" also have a "homosexual disposition" (as they must in order to return the attraction), then they too should be attracted to feminine women. Ellis's theory therefore creates, rather than answers, the question of the feminine woman who is attracted to a masculine woman; it explains such attraction as an indication of both true inversion, else she could not have felt the attraction in the first place, and true femininity, else she could not have had a response to her partner's masculinity. Any attempt to explain Mary, as it is possible to "explain" Stephen, on the basis of Hall's knowledge of or adherence to sexological theory founders. Out of sexology's need to create absolute categories, it focuses on the most obvious type of invert, the mannish lesbian, and achieves scientifically exact pretensions by excluding the Marys from the theory (although, helpfully, not from the case studies upon which the theory rests). The only consistent and invariable feature of the true invert which emerges from the sexological construction of her is her psychic makeup, which remains inverted regardless of her looks, sexual activity, or affectional preference.

Sexology's scientific pretensions led its practitioners to prefer theories which were coherent, even, as we see, at the expense of their accuracy. Hall too, in creating Stephen Gordon, valued—and used to advantage—the coherence which Stephen gained from her adherence to sexological iconography and to Hall's own lived experience. But Stephen's very coherence, as iconized by the differences which make Mary seem unlike Stephen and therefore not an invert, accentuates the spaces which both sexological theory and *The Well* actually *create*. The novel contains such extratheoretical spaces which scientific theory must lack; and it is in them that I locate Mary Llewellyn. For she is, I maintain, part of an emerging new icon which came to full fruition only in the 1980s[13] but was beginning to emerge from the case studies of the sexologists and the pages of fiction and autobiography which in the 1920s undertook the dimensionalization of the lesbian in particularly modernist ways.

Mary Llewellyn offers an excellent standpoint from which to begin deconstructing sexology's lesbian because she dis/covers the difference on which deconstruction rests. And when we look closely at her characterization and at what actually goes on between her and Stephen, not just at the end of their relationship but also at the beginning, we find three things. First, Mary exhibits surprisingly many behaviors attributed to true inverts even while she fails to conform to the visual or activity iconography of the sexologists (and of Stephen herself), and it is she who initiates virtually all the physical contact of their courtship. Second, Stephen's behavior discourages that contact and belittles Mary as a possible invert; this is a function of the particular form Stephen's inversion has taken, her knowledge of sexological theory, and her class and family background, rather than a function of Mary's sexual orientation. Mediating this conflict is Hall's narrative structure, which places Mary and Stephen discursively together, rather than separate. Within this framework, it is possible to reconstruct Mary Llewellyn as the new lesbian.

Much of Mary's apparent femininity is imbricated with her class rather than her sexual orientation. This is nowhere more clear than when she views Stephen's wardrobe and imagines herself "looking after" Stephen by darning her socks and sewing on her buttons. Her knowledge of "how to pick up a ladder as well as the Invisible Mending people" (322) comes both because in a less affluent household she would have had to conserve clothing and because in a lower-middle-class household she would have been much more strictly limited to female activities and skills, and she would have had no alternate visions of her activities or her role. And so Mary frets over the cost of Stephen's stockings and "long[s] to do womanly tasks" so that Stephen will be "well served"—and indeed Mary's conception of feminine loving is a picture of lower-middle-class service rooted in gendered tasks. Hall even constructs her love for Stephen as a function of her "perfect woman"–ness (314) to Stephen's masculinity.

But Hall problematizes such classed femininities by placing them in a context of behaviors which belie them, making femininity as meaningless an indicator of Mary's particular sexual orientation as appearance or sexual activity were for the sexologists' case studies. For Mary is far from a typical girl. She is not tiny, as Stephen perceives her, but is five feet five inches tall, above average for a woman in 1918. She has taught herself driving and auto mechanics in order to repair her cousin's car and chauffeur him to his patients. She is discontented with the narrowness of her life, and alone and unaided she secures a position in the ambulance unit and travels across the war zone to get to it. Being "neither so frail nor so timid as Mrs. Breakspeare had thought her" (285), she sticks it with the Breakspeare ambulance unit, avoiding the injuries and breakdowns suffered by apparently stronger women.

More tellingly, it is Mary who initiates virtually all the early physical contact between herself and Stephen. During the war she takes Stephen's hand as they walk; she says, "'I've always been waiting for you'" and begs not to be sent away (294). In agreeing that she can stay, Stephen merely acquiesces to a connection which Mary has constructed. Their first night in the house at 35 Rue Jacob is emblematic of the pattern which characterizes their whole relationship. The evening is fraught with sexual tension in which Mary is physically and narratively a full participant. She is the first to touch Stephen sensually. She initiates their first kiss, saying, "'[D]o you know that you've never kissed me?'" and avowing that she wants Stephen's kiss "'[m]ore than anything else in the world'" (299). As during the war, at Orotava Mary takes Stephen's hand (308) and wants "Stephen to take her in her arms" (310); when Stephen will not, Mary tentatively lays her head on Stephen's shoulder in a gesture which combines apparent femininity and overt homosexual contact. Stephen's inflexible resistance to Mary's overtures makes Mary believe her advances have "'all been a heart-breaking mistake'"—the mistake of thinking Stephen cared for her in the way her actions have demonstrated she cares for Stephen (311). And when

Stephen finally does show her carefully hidden emotions and at last gives Mary information about inversion, Mary immediately accepts inverted intimacy and loves Stephen "'just as you are'" (312). Once in Paris, she constantly seeks the physical reassurance of Stephen's love (316). Stephen's unspoken longings, visible only to the reader, are overmatched by Mary's actions, which are far more daring and explicit than any of Stephen's. Mary is the pursuer, Stephen the hesitant and fearful pursued.[14]

At the same time, it is important to note that Mary never makes a connection between herself and the pattern of inversion Stephen gives her. She never says or implies "I'm that way too." Mary crosses a line when she approaches Stephen sexually; she becomes a kind of invert which neither the sexologists nor Hall made room for. And because her concept of her sexual self differs from Stephen's, we are precluded by Hall's limited-omniscient narrative focus on Stephen from knowing what that sexual self is.

Hall is careful to maintain an equivocal balance between self-knowledge and innocence in Mary. She states that Mary knew little of "herself, of her ardent, courageous, impulsive nature" (284–85), but knew she was no longer "contented with her narrow life" (285). Hall's structuring of Mary's life—from the social, occupational, and emotional confines of a Welsh orphanhood to a wider sphere in which her physical bravery, her access to knowledge, and her emotional range can emerge—provides the grounding for what it may be possible to call the "discovery" of her nature: "And now as though drawn by some hidden attraction, as though stirred by some irresistible impulse, quite beyond the realms of her own understanding, Mary turned in all faith and all innocence to Stephen" (284). Her innocence, uncorrupted by a knowledge of sexology's dire constructions and predictions, allows an openness which is interpreted as incipient lesbianism even by the "narrow, conventional" Mrs. Breakspeare, who calls it "'an emotional friendship, such as I fancy Mary Llewellyn is on the verge of feeling for you'" (289). We know that Stephen understands the meaning of their physical contact, but Hall is explicit that Mary does not: "she herself was unconscious" of "something far more fundamental" which she is feeling (297), a statement which likens Mary to the young Stephen who felt passion for Angela Crossby without understanding its etiology. Hall portrays this impulse and its resultant coupling as fated—"written upon tablets of stone by some wise if relentless recording finger" (284). This statement implies something innate in Mary and Stephen which determines their attraction to one another. Such an innate "something" could only, in Hall's sexological taxonomy, be congenital inversion.

Hall sexualizes Mary's ardor by casting it in a setting redolent of sexuality. Orotava, the scene of their first physical union, is linked with both nature and antiquity. The Villa del Cipres is so old that no one knows its history. Its garden exhibits a "primitive urge towards all manner of procreation" (305). Even the frogs sing "prehistoric love songs" (307). Stephen's Morton, which both bred her as an invert and rejected her inverted self, is just such an ancestral cradle. Orotava's fecundity counters Stephen's fears about the sterility of any relationship she might form with Mary. It justifies her self-delusion that "she would give Mary such a love as would be complete in itself without children" (300); it is the first of their surrogate procreations. When they are at last united, their love is "primitive and age-old as Nature herself" and they are in "the grip of Creation, of Creation's terrific urge to create" even in "sterile channels" (313). Hall's choice to cast the consummation of Stephen and Mary's love in terms of frustrated heterosexuality is yet another crossover between a feminized Mary and "true inversion."

Mary's equal involvement is also linguistically constructed. Their first night in Paris, Mary's touch creates in both herself and Stephen a "strange sympathy" which "closed down on them *both*" so that they sat very still, "feeling that in *their* stillness lay safety" (297). At Orotava they linger on the terrace because "*they* dreaded [the] moments of parting" (308). As Stephen refuses Mary's invitations, "*they* would feel so terribly divided. *Their* days would be heavy with misunderstandings, *their* nights filled with doubts, . . . all things . . . less perfect because of *their* own frustration" (311). Words of love become incapable of "compass[ing] *their* meaning" (316). "Love had" equally "lifted *them* up as on wings of fire" (317).[15] Linguistically, Mary is an equal partner in these joys and doubts and meanings; her feelings are thus made as intense as Stephen's, a perfect mirror match of the true invert.

Beyond the narrow confines of her relationship with Stephen, Mary is arrayed in *The Well* with a wide range of visual invert styles. Most of the women in Valerie Seymour's salon are so feminine that only a discerning eye (350) or "trained ear" (351) could register traces of the sexologists' masculine (352). Jamie's lover Barbara, who has been with Jamie since "the days of their childhood" (353), is "all woman as far as one could detect" and thus mirrors Mary's pattern, yet Mary remarks to Stephen that Barbara and Jamie "'were like you and me'" (403), a pair of inverts. Valerie considers Mary and Barbara as much inverts as Stephen and Jamie (406).[16] The existence and life-style of this range of women show Hall's underlying conviction that "biology is not a reliable index of sexuality" (O'Rourke 84), despite Ellis's willed belief that it was.

There is thus a visible and visual place within Hall's fictional the homosexual community for the Valeries and Barbaras and Marys, whom the community is willing to accept despite the fact that occasionally one may leave to marry, an event which is ascribed as much to social pressure as to spurious inversion.[17] The sadness and the wildness which both Stephen and the feminized inverts exhibit grow less out of conflict over their sexuality than out of limited social opportunities, out of explicit homosexual oppression, and out of public ridicule, which indeed drove many women in the 1920s to create an appearance of heterosexual lives which was at odds not with their sexual orientation but with its social manifestations—and, not least, in Stephen and Mary's case out of despair at the loss of class and place to which inversion seemed to doom them.[18] Thus, to conflate an inability to withstand social pressure with innate sexuality—to argue that it is a congenital feature of true inverts

that they would never renounce the pains of their existence for peace or comfort—
is to deny the very thing Hall created Stephen Gordon to proclaim: that it is society's
beliefs and restraints which doom her, not her nature.

Stephen herself recognizes that not all inverts are made in her pattern. In speaking with Valerie, she muses about "the hard-working, honourable men and women
. . . lacking in courage to admit their inversion" (405) and thus "passing" by marrying members of the opposite sex. These people would be considered "normal" by
sexologists, yet Stephen believes in their inversion and finds her vocation in writing
for and to them. And while it is true, as Cook has said, that Hall does not foreground
Valerie's "essential connectedness with and empathy for" other people (734), which
Stephen is not able to achieve, the possibilities Valerie represents are clearly present
in the novel and are frequently showcased by Hall as direct alternatives to Stephen's
choices. And of course that is one of my points: that Hall *chose* in creating Stephen
to focus on a particular set of visual and social constructions of inversion, not in order
to proclaim only a single invert path, but in order to make a point beyond the mere
anatomy of inversion. Mary lies outside that construction and cannot be evaluated
within it. But Hall *did* create Mary as well as Stephen; Mary's obviously sexual relationship with Stephen quite literally constructs another invert within *The Well* who
offers a standpoint different from Stephen's (and from Hall's). If one of the goals of
modernism was to see things anew, Hall's creation of Mary Llewellyn *as an invert* is
stunningly modernist, so much so that it has required the current outburst of gender theorizing to see it.

If Mary's character presentation is framed by Hall's need to foreground Stephen's
particularized lesbianism rather than by sexological theory, her relationship with
Stephen is likewise framed by Stephen's class-based attempt to replicate the sanc-
tity and location of her parents' marriage, a typical Freudian family triangle, rather
than by Mary's sexuality per se.[19] In a fairly straightforward variation on Oedipal
development, Stephen models herself on her father in order to become a person who
could possess her mother. Such a psychic development enables her to "find her
manhood" in leaving Morton (which is the class locale of Stephen's Self) and claiming a career as spokeswoman for persecuted inverts.

At the same time, however, Steven's covert goal in *The Well* is to go home to
Morton. She locates her parents' sanctified marriage within its bounds, not just
geographically but also socially. In the 1920s Paris offered many lesbians a home,[20]
but it is one Stephen cannot accept because it is outside the class bounds which define "home" for her. The bar life, their few excursions into public places, even Valerie
Seymour's salon, lack Morton's ability to confer social acceptability. That is why
Martin's Aunt Sarah is so much more acceptable a countess than the one Valerie
produces because she, like Lady Massey, is a connection to Morton, while Valerie's
Countess de Kerguelen is as estranged as Stephen from the locale of her class background. And this class background is generational. Morton is a *family* estate; Sir Philip
and Lady Anna's marriage is sanctified by its place within a descent line which

Stephen, as an invert, is powerless to continue. In order to recreate her ideal with Mary, then, Stephen must find a locale and a generationality for it. And both are problematic for the invert.

Even more tellingly, class creates a barrier between Stephen and Mary which conditions Mary's experience of her sexuality. One reason Mary feels free to pursue Stephen is that her class background has made her unaware of the sexological knowledge which causes Stephen so much conflict. The inescapably middle-class nature of Mary's conception of intimate relationships collides with Stephen's upper-class life. Mary's idea of domesticity is to care for Stephen, but Stephen is so well tended by her servants that Mary has no function and, unable because of her class background to recognize other ways of being Stephen's "lady," she is left without resources in the face of the world's hostility to their relationship.[21] From the beginning of their acquaintance Mary is intensely curious about Stephen's life. She pores over pictures of Morton, of Sir Philip, of Lady Anna, of Puddle and Raftery[22]—all symbolic of Stephen's class standing. She loves to hear Stephen talk of her writing, "though Mary had not read either of her novels—there had never been a library subscription" (286). Her idea of her role in her relationship with Stephen is an ideal of domestic service, sewing on buttons and mending ladders in stockings whose price and source Stephen cannot even bother to remember. She lacks the training which would allow her to run a house of Stephen's class (340). Her contributions to their aesthetic life are carp in the fountain and several pairs of pigeons—and, of course, their dog and surrogate child David, who, already mature, follows Mary home and thus is not of their raising/creation. Although she hopes to type for Stephen, her typing turns out to be too slow, so she is deprived even of this New Womanish occupation which was, by 1928, the refuge of ill-educated but upwardly mobile girls. Even were Stephen able to bring Mary home to Morton, Mary would never be able to reign there as Lady Anna does. Stephen's partner conflicts with Stephen's class.

One result of this conflict is that Stephen can find no way to behave toward Mary except as father to child. She chooses Mary's reading "even as Sir Philip had once taught his daughter" (331), and she instructs Mary in the sexology she learned from her father's books. She believes it is her job to build a "harbour of refuge for Mary" (356); never once does she consider Mary capable of building her own happiness, of sharing in the building, or of choosing a path different from Stephen's. Her paternalism replicates her father's control—of actions, of knowledge, and thus of choices—and creates a gulf between her and Mary.

Mary's eventual "choice" to "love" Martin Hallam, which has been offered as a major proof of her primary heterosexuality, must be seen within this conception of Steven's need to become her father as the only way to manifest her inversion. Within the Stephen/Mary dyad, Stephen can offer Mary only her inverted identity but never a social locale, and her own need for such a locale conditions her ability to accept Mary's choice to relinquish it. Indeed, we have no idea whether Mary would long for Morton intrinsically were it not a part of Stephen. Because of her allegiance to the heterosexual model of her parents' marriage as the ideal coupling, Stephen reads Martin as able to offer Mary locale—a home and a society, a Martin/Morton.[23] Stephen's creation of this dichotomized struggle is a result of her inescapably class-based view of the nature and value of Martin's offering to Mary. Without allowing Mary to witness or participate, Stephen tests herself against Martin, challenging him on explicitly male woman-winning grounds; and in one way—for Mary initially chooses Stephen—she wins, thus truly becoming her father and possessing her mother. But the possession proves to be fruitless because it is played out in Stephen's idiosyncratic context of the nexus of heterosexual marriage and place as it reflects social acceptability. This has long been seen as the crux of the lesbian problem in *The Well.* Angela asks Stephen, "'Could you marry me?'" (150); Jonathan Brockett tells Stephen that "'if you were a man . . . Mary might even be going to have an infant'" (346). The heterosexual triangle works as a dialectic which creates its own antithesis because it has a place (the family home as a locale of lineage) to evolve in. The lesbian triangle Stephen has set up lacks such a place and therefore lacks a dialectic. In *The Well* the possibility of legal marriage and children is the focus of the tension and purpose created by triangulation. The family triangle always seeks to replicate itself, and in this novel it does so by locating the heterosexual family and its home as the source of evolution. The triangle of Stephen/Mary/Martin allows Stephen, with the aid of Martin/Philip, to place Mary in the role of child/Stephen and dispose of her into marriage and heterosexuality, without her knowledge or consent, so that she may reproduce the next generation of triangular dialectic which Stephen herself has refused to reproduce. This use of Mary enables Stephen to act out her unfilled feminine role even as she repeats, and thus justifies, her own exclusion from the romantic dyad of Philip/Anna which Mary and Martin reproduce.

Mary's part in this constructed triangle is ambiguous. She is "[r]eassured by the presence of Martin Hallam" (420) and enjoys the social pleasures the presence of a man makes possible—dinners where Stephen will not be stared at, for instance. When she ceases to be the object of negative public scrutiny, she is more content. Mary is "neither so courageous nor so defiant as she had imagined," and "like many another woman before her, she was well content to feel herself protected" (420). Martin sees her as "'not strong enough to fight the whole world'" (425) and "divine[s]" "a great weariness of spirit, a great longing to be at peace" (429). But defiance of public opinion is not the single necessary condition of inversion, as Hall makes very clear when she speaks about those noble people who pass as normal (405), and we must remember that Stephen enjoyed being protected from exactly the same scrutiny and ridicule by her father. It is in Martin's interest to see Mary as weak and needing protection, for protection is the only thing he has to offer her. And it is noteworthy that Mary's sense of protection does not lead to *her* desire to leave Stephen for Martin. That impetus comes solely from Stephen and is set against "the perfect companionship and understanding that constitutes the great strength" of Stephen and Mary's relationship (428). Mary clings to her love for Stephen "with every memory that Stephen had stirred; with every passion that Stephen had fostered; with every instinct of loyalty that Stephen had aroused" (431). Stephen herself feels "powerless" to destroy Mary's tenacious love. Even after Stephen's faked infidelity, Mary reiterates her love: "'All my life I've given'" (435). Surely this is not the behavior of a woman longing for heterosexuality!

Within this framework Mary's final parting from Stephen cannot, as has often been claimed, constitute simple and conclusive proof that she is not an invert. Her avowal—"'But for you, I could have loved Martin Hallam!'"—is ambiguous in the context of her ardent feelings for Stephen. "Could have loved" does not necessarily mean "do love." Instead, it points toward an area Hall does not explore but whose existence the sexologists chronicle conclusively—the vast history of lesbians who married in order to achieve fully social lives.[24] The novel suggests (but by no means proves) that Mary will be able to contract an emotionally intimate marriage with Martin; but it does so only after showing her as equally capable of contracting such a union with Stephen, and in fact developing her ability to be intimate within her relationship with Stephen. It is, I would argue, not *Hall* who rejects Mary as a suitable invert, but *Stephen*. Mary leaves Stephen in the end not because she has finally discovered, or regained, her innate heterosexuality, but because Stephen creates a situation which Mary's honor cannot tolerate. Stephen's deception and Martin's presence are both engineered to deprive Mary of any home or support and then to fill that gap not in Mary's way but in Stephen's. Her marriage to Martin, then, is not a real alternative (within the structure Hall's novel creates) either to her relationship with Stephen or to an inverted life-style. It is the result of dishonesty, betrayal, interference, manipulation, and Stephen's preconditioned conception of a triangulated family romance, none of which are inherent in inversion itself. As O'Rourke has noted, "[T]he passage of Mary from Stephen, and homosexuality, to Martin and heterosexuality is shown as anything but natural and inevitable" (79). Instead, it is conditioned by Stephen's character and her conception of her role as an invert. It tells us little about Mary.

One reason it must tell us so little lies in Hall's narrative structure, which reinforces Stephen's management of Mary's sexuality. Hall's choice of third-person limited omniscient narration places the reader in Stephen's mind. For the purpose of normalizing the invert, such a narrative structure is ideal. Its drawback is that it cannot foreground anyone but Stephen. Mary can appear only as Stephen's partner, never as herself. Therefore, we cannot know what she feels about inversion or about her own sexuality or choices. We understand Stephen's feelings, which are limited by what she has read and experienced. Stephen creates for herself a pattern of inversion which accepts (as neither all other characters in the novel *nor* Hall do) the taxonomy, the iconography, and the social fate the sexologists presented. She does this partly because it is all she knows about inversion and partly because the knowledge resonates with her own (very individual) feelings about herself as a classed and gendered person. It was in Hall's overall interest to make Stephen so, as part of her goal of normalizing inversion for a hostile readership. Mary's role is circumscribed by Hall's need to isolate Stephen so Stephen can transcend the limitations of her own inversion. Mary's inversion is necessarily absent in such a narrative structure.

The imperative of Stephen's particular inversion requires a Mary who can be sacrificed; the justification of Stephen's particular inversion requires that the sacrifice be viewed as benefiting Mary despite Mary's own convictions, so that Stephen is still seen as a "good" person. Mary must remain ambiguous in order that Stephen can create an inverted and classed self. Given such a necessity, the critic must reconstruct Mary, as I have tried to do here. Far from being a pseudohomosexual, she is someone new, creating a definition of lesbian beyond sexology's theorizing, Hall's intention, or Stephen's imagining. Mary is a member of a group we now know existed (and still exists) in sizable numbers: lesbians who for social reasons create heterosexual (or heterosexual-appearing) unions while retaining a primary attraction to, and often an emotional commitment to, women.[25] Mary's conflicting history suggests that she is one of them, but this does not mean she is not a true invert.

What then of the novel's incipient modernism? In a novel so traditional in form, so formal in diction, so relentlessly straightforward in aim, can it be said that Radclyffe Hall did more than simply write antiquated novels during a period in which literature had outstripped her mental capacities? My answer would be yes; for in writing Mary Llewellyn as well as Stephen Gordon, Hall was not so much "making it new" as beginning what one might call the metamodernist task of making visible what had not yet been seen and therefore could not yet be seen anew. Mary Llewellyn is constructed as a type of lesbian, but because she is constructed by different social discourses than those which helped shape Stephen Gordon, she is invisible when we look through the critical, scientific, or social lenses which see Stephen so clearly. It is more dangerous for Mary to be seen as a lesbian precisely because she blurs the boundaries which sexology and Stephen Gordon so emphatically maintain. What critic Sherrie Inness has said recently about the beautiful and feminine lesbian protagonist of Edouard Bourdet's *The Captive* is equally true of Mary Llewellyn: "If this feminine, desirable woman could be a lesbian, then many women, not only mannish women, could conceivably be categorized as lesbians" (317). And herein lay, of course, the danger sexology was eager to construct out of existence: the possibility that one really *couldn't* tell an invert from a heterosexual woman. For then all women might be inverts. And the world would crumble. This is the threat of the modernist impulse in fiction: it splits open the world. In Stephen Gordon's mannishly inverted visibility lies Hall's safety; a book "about" Mary Llewellyn *as a lesbian* would be inconceivable precisely because she has been constructed as What Does Not Exist.

On the other hand, if one of the features of modernism was what Houston Baker has recently cast as "an acknowledgement of radical uncertainty" (3), then *The Well of Loneliness* can be seen as a (perhaps unintentional) icon of modernism. For just as surely as Stephen Gordon creates a (false) certainty about inversion, Mary Llewellyn deconstructs that certainty and offers up the elements of a "new" construction—the lesbian.

Much work remains to be done to reconstruct the variety of women-loving women whose self-conceptions have been instrumental in the present-day social, political, and physical construction of lesbianism.[26] Both women and men, both homosexuals and heterosexuals, constructed literary inverts in the decades before and after Hall wrote *The Well of Loneliness*. Without regarding *The Well* as a modernist document per se, and without denying Hall's obvious allegiance to—and need for—sexological theory, it is still possible to "see anew" Hall's necessarily oblique accounts of different patterns of lesbian living and consciousness which cross Stephen's. Hall was enough of an artist that *The Well,* although not consciously modernist, yields to modernist readings which help reveal its as yet unexamined fullness.

Notes

1. For a thorough discussion of this term and its referent, see Newton.

2. See Stimpson; Cook; Newton.

3. See Zimmerman.

4. In the confusing world of multiple nomenclatures, I have chosen in this essay to distinguish between the modernist conception of female homosexuality, for which I use the terms *invert* and *inversion,* following sexological terminology, and my own interpretations of that conception, which I call *lesbian* and *lesbianism.*

5. For an overview of this work, see Scott and Benstock on modernism in general, Marcus on Virginia Woolf.

6. Ellis speaks of "pseudo-homosexuality" in both *The Psychology of Sex* (224, 223) and *Studies in the Psychology of Sex* (237). He also refers to "acquired" homosexuality; see *Psychology of Sex* (245). He may have adopted the terminology from Magnus Hirschfeld, who refers to "pseudohomosexuality" in *Sexual Anomalies* (238).

7. There have been contestations of modernism on other grounds which parallel and complement my own. See, for instance, Baker for a recuperation of the Harlem renaissance.

8. For a survey of relevant sexological theory, see MacPike.

9. See Klaich; Rule; Cook; Stimpson; and Newton.

10. Freud's view is mentioned by Ellis in "The Theory of Sexual Inversion," in *Studies in the Psychology of Sex* (302–24, 308).

11. Other modernist novelists undermine a unidimensional theory of lesbianism by the transtheoretical picture of inversion and variety of inverts they present in their works, a subject beyond the scope of this essay.

12. This woman subsequently said her dislike of marriage was caused by other people's desire to compel her to marry, implying that physical repugnance was not her main criterion for refusing to marry.

13. She is discussed in works such as Faderman; Griffin; and Jay and Glasgow.

14. Mary's unfettered courting behavior toward Stephen is all the more remarkable in the face of Stephen's cold and unemotional response. Stephen orders Mary around, talks down to her as if she were small, belittles her, and tries to repress her own emotions. When she touches Mary, it is on Mary's hair (285) rather than her skin, or when Mary is asleep (286). During the war she brushes off Mary's attempts to initiate emotional conversations by smiling falsely and denying all feeling (286), and she does so again at Orotava when Mary complains that Stephen won't let her get close by condescendingly deflecting her meaning: "'Aren't you near? It seems to me you're quite near!'" (308). When Mary explicitly asks to be kissed, Stephen gives her merely a chaste peck on the cheek. As her love grows and Mary's invitations become ever more explicit, Stephen grows harsher and ruder. Hall is very careful to show this harshness as a function of Stephen's love—she would save Mary from the social degradation she herself has experienced, which she imagines the invariable lot of all inverts. But this explanation is not available to Mary. Mary must proceed on the understanding that Stephen is not attracted to her, does not care for her, feels no desire for her. And still she persists. Stephen recognizes Mary's actions as a sexual invitation and realizes that "she had only to call" and Mary would be hers in a union she understands to be "perfectly natural" (299).

15. I have added emphasis to all quotations in this paragraph.

16. Hall also presents other patterns of inversion, most notably the iconographic invert who never has sexual contact with another woman and therefore does not qualify as a true invert in Ellis's or Krafft-Ebing's definitions. Puddle in *The Well* is one such character; another is Frances Reide in Hall's *Saturday Life*. Elizabeth Romney in *The Unlit Lamp* presents yet another pattern of inversion. As Hall says, "'What doctor can know the entire truth? . . . The whole truth is known only to the normal invert'" (*The Well* 390).

17. Cf. Pat's Arabella; but she first runs off with another woman and only later marries, a relation which Hall characterizes as strictly opportunistic.

18. Faderman provides the best survey to date of lesbian social life in the 1920s.

19. The intersection of inversion and the family triangle dynamic is explored more fully in MacPike (1994).

20. See Gilbert and Gubar; Fitch; Benstock. The dreadful temporariness of such a home is painfully demonstrated in Simon.

21. It is also worth asking to what extent Mary's class influenced her manifestation of inversion. Stephen's particularized inversion is shown by Hall to be both "natural" (i.e., inborn) and a scientific construct which Stephen acquires as a result of her reading and study—that is, of the activities of a young woman of her class.

22. In conjunction with Stephen's feelings for Raftery, Mary sobs uncontrollably when Stephen must shoot a badly wounded horse, thus appropriating (through sharing) one of Stephen's class-based emotions (292).

23. Martin's attraction to Mary is in fact an indication that she *is* a true invert, for Martin seems to be attracted to inverts and to inverts alone. There is an utter absence of other women in his life between young adulthood, when he feels passion for Stephen, and a decade later, when he falls in love with Mary. In that interim he both read and thought "a great deal about the subject" of inversion. According to Havelock Ellis, "The man who is passionately attracted to an inverted

woman is usually of rather a feminine type. For instance, in one case present to my mind he was of somewhat neurotic heredity, of slight physical development, not sexually attractive to women, and very domesticated in his manner of living; in short, a man who might easily have been passionately attracted to his own sex" (257). By some measures, then, Martin is excludable from the ranks of "ordinary men" attraction to whom is an indication of non-inversion. Perhaps unwittingly, Hall raises the whole question of what it might mean for a woman of *any* sexuality to be attracted to a man.

24. See Faderman 63–92 for a study of American lesbians, whose history and sensibility differed somewhat from those of British lesbians.

25. Outstanding fictional examples include Dorothy Richardson (*Pointed Roofs*, 1918) and Virginia Woolf (*To the Lighthouse*, 1925; *Mrs. Dalloway*, 1928).

26. I am myself working on the presentation of lesbianism in novels by women (e.g., Lehmann's *Dusty Answer*, Macaulay's *Dangerous Ages*, Clemence Dane's *Regiment of Women*) as opposed to those in novels by men (e.g., Compton MacKenzie's *Extraordinary Women*, Waugh's *Vile Bodies*).

Works Cited

Baker, Houston A., Jr. *Modernism and the Harlem Renaissance*. Chicago: U of Chicago P, 1983.

Benstock, Shari. *Women of the Left Bank: Paris 1900–1914*. Austin: U of Texas P, 1986.

Cook, Blanche Wiesen. "'Women Alone Stir My Imagination': Lesbianism and the Cultural Tradition." *Signs: A Journal of Women in Culture and Society* 4 (1979): 718–39.

Ellis, Havelock. *The Psychology of Sex*. 1933. New York: Emerson Books, 1936.

———. *Studies in the Psychology of Sex*. 1901. Philadelphia: F. A. Davis, 1930.

Faderman, Lillian. *Odd Girls and Twilight Lovers: A History of Lesbian Life in Twentieth-Century America*. New York: Columbia UP, 1991.

Fitch, Noel Riley. *Sylvia Beach and the Lost Generation: A History of Literary Paris in the Twenties and Thirties*. New York: Norton, 1983.

Gilbert, Sandra M., and Susan Gubar. *No Man's Land: The Place of the Woman Writer in the Twentieth Century*. Vol. 2, *Sexchanges*. New Haven: Yale UP, 1989.

Griffin, Gabriele. *Heavenly Love? Lesbian Images in Twentieth-Century Women's Writing*. Manchester: Manchester UP, 1993.

Hall, Radclyffe. *A Saturday Life*. New York: J. Cape and H. Smith, 1930.

———. *The Unlit Lamp*. London: Cassell, 1924.

———. *The Well of Loneliness*. 1928. New York: Anchor, 1990.

Hirschfeld, Magnus. *Sexual Anomalies: The Origins, Nature, and Treatment of Sexual Disorders*. 1948. New York: Emerson Books, 1956.

Inness, Sherrie. "Who's Afraid of Stephen Gordon?: The Lesbian in the United States Popular Imagination of the 1920s." *NWSA Journal* 4 (1992): 303–20.

Jameson, Fredric. "Periodizing the 60s." *The Ideologies of Theory: Essays 1971–1986*. Vol. 2, *The Syntax of History*. Minneapolis: U of Minnesota P, 1988.

Jay, Karla, and Joanne Glasgow. *Lesbian Texts and Contexts: Radical Revisions*. New York: New York UP, 1990.

Klaich, Dolores. *Woman Plus Woman*. 1974. Tallahassee: Naiad, 1989.

Krafft-Ebing, Richard von. *Psychopathia Sexualis*. 1886. New York: Stein and Day, 1965.

MacPike, Loralee. "The Geography of Radclyffe Hall's Lesbian Country." *Historical Reflections / Réflexions Historiques* 20 (1994): 217–42.

Marcus, Jane. "An Embarrassment of Riches." *Women's Review of Books* Mar. 1994: 17–18.

———. "Pathographies: The Virginia Woolf Soap Opera." *Signs: A Journal of Women in Culture and Society* 17 (1992): 806–19.

Newton, Esther. "The 'Mythic, Mannish Lesbian': Radclyffe Hall and the New Woman." *Signs: A Journal of Women in Culture and Society* 9 (1984): 555–75.

O'Rourke, Rebecca. *Reflections on* The Well of Loneliness. London: Routledge, 1989.

Ruehl, Sonja. "Inverts and Experts: Radclyffe Hall and the Lesbian Identity." *Feminism, Culture and Politics*. Ed. Rosalind Brunt and Caroline Rowan. London: Lawrence & Wishart, 1982. 15–36.

Rule, Jane. *Lesbian Images*. New York: Pocket Books, 1975.

Scott, Bonnie Kime. *The Gender of Modernism*. Bloomington: Indiana UP, 1990.

Simon, Linda. *The Biography of Alice B. Toklas*. 1977. Lincoln: U of Nebraska P, 1991.

Stimpson, Catharine R. "Zero Degree Deviancy: The Lesbian Novel in English." *Critical Inquiry* 8 (1981): 363–79.

Whitlock, Gillian. "'Everything Is Out of Place': Radclyffe Hall and the Lesbian Literary Tradition." *Feminist Studies* 13 (1987): 555–82.

Woolf, Virginia. *A Room of One's Own*. New York: Harcourt Brace, 1981.

Zimmerman, Bonnie. "Lesbians Like 'This' and 'That.'" *New Lesbian Criticism: Literary and Cultural Reading*. Ed. Sally Munt. New York: Columbia UP, 1990.

❧ The Hostess and the Seamstress: Virginia Woolf's Creation of a Domestic Modernism

Geneviève Sanchis Morgan

In 1924 Virginia Woolf was simultaneously writing *Mrs. Dalloway* and preparing a talk on fiction for the Cambridge Heretics Society, in what was to become "Mr. Bennett and Mrs. Brown." In both works Woolf grapples with the relationship between the artist and her audience; the way she chooses to describe this delicate relationship is through the metaphor of the hostess and the guest. In "Mr. Bennett and Mrs. Brown" she makes the comparison explicit:

> Both in life and in literature it is necessary to have some means of bridging the gulf between the hostess and her unknown guest on one hand, and the writer and his unknown reader on the other. The hostess bethinks herself of the weather, for generations of hostesses have established the fact that it is a subject of universal interest in which we all believe. She begins by saying that we are having a wretched May, and, having thus got into touch with her unknown guest, proceeds to matters of great interest. So it is in literature. The writer must get into touch with his reader by putting before him something which he recognizes, which therefore stimulates his imagination and makes him willing to co-operate in the far more difficult business of intimacy. (243)

The image of the hostess recurs in almost all of Woolf's works—*Night and Day, Mrs. Dalloway, To the Lighthouse, Orlando, Between the Acts,* and "A Sketch of the Past"— and each time the hostess functions as a metaphor for the female artist.

The two novels Woolf wrote in the mid- to late twenties, *Mrs. Dalloway* and *To the Lighthouse,* present her most thorough explorations of the mysterious figure of the hostess. Moreover, the strategic positioning of a children's story, *Nurse Lugton's*

Golden Thimble in the manuscript of *Mrs. Dalloway,* supports her enterprise. Through her recurrent depiction of domestic artists, figured alternately as the hostess and the seamstress, Woolf's works argue for a poetics of domesticity.

The predominance of the hostess in Woolf's writing is perhaps due to the rise of the three "Great Society Hostesses" who dominated London society in the 1920s. Woolf and her circle attended several of the soirees given by Lady Emerald Cunard, Lady Sybil Colefax, and Mrs. Nancy Corrigan. Staging lavish parties at which they carefully selected and assembled their guests, their entertainment, and their menus, these women made a profession out of entertaining, often hosting as many as six gatherings a week.

Woolf was very much aware of the society hostesses and the popularity of their ephemeral productions; indeed, she was fascinated by their gatherings and she eventually became good friends with Sybil Colefax, whom the Bloomsberries jokingly called "the Colebox." It was a given in society circles that although Sybil Colefax had no particular wit of her own, she had the ability to combine people in interesting ways, creating brilliant evening parties. Woolf pokes fun at Sibyl Colefax's lack of personal brilliance when she comments of a great society hostess in her 1929 novel, *Orlando,* that "for almost seventeen years she said nothing memorable and all went well" (128); Woolf seems to have been intrigued by the ability of women who were not learned, or beautiful, or obviously talented in the traditional sense, but were nonetheless able to create memorable parties. It is not surprising, then, that while Woolf recognizes Sybil Colefax's lack of personal style, she still lists her in the preface to *Orlando* as one of the people who has helped her write the book. How, one may wonder, did a society hostess who made no pretensions toward art and had no wit of her own help Woolf write her book? And why do such women figure so prominently in her works?

As Woolf's comparison of the artist and hostess in "Mr. Bennett and Mrs. Brown" demonstrates, she seems to have identified the logistics of writing with the practice of orchestrating a party: as she no doubt realized, in both situations the auteur arranges an illusion that depends upon a delicate blend of timing, situation, and character. The hostess pulls her guest into a world of her imagination, much as the novelist does with the reader. Of the society party the narrator of *Orlando* comments: "All of these groups of people lie under an enchantment. The hostess is our modern Sibyl. She is a witch who lays her guests under a spell. In this house they think themselves happy; in that witty; in a third profound. It is all an illusion (which is nothing against it, for illusions are the most valuable and necessary of all things, and she who can create one is among the world's greatest benefactors)" (128). It is no coincidence that Woolf calls the hostess "our modern Sibyl"—she seems to have learned much from "the Colebox." The prominence of the great society hostesses gave Woolf a way to conceptualize her art in the lexicon of the age. As a woman and a writer, Woolf struggled to find a means of taking part in her "age" without letting it subsume her work. The image of the hostess offered her a solution.

The similarities between contemporary accounts of the great society hostesses and Woolf's characterization of her hostess Clarissa Dalloway suggest that she had such women in mind when she was writing *Mrs. Dalloway*. Lady Cunard dominated the London scene from 1912 to 1950, and her guests remembered her primarily for her charm and her careful assemblage of interesting political, royal, and artistic characters. Partygoers describe her as "exud[ing] goodwill, [and] brightening the room and her guests" (Courtney 99). More important to the genesis of Woolf's hostess, however, Roderick Cameron remembers Lady Cunard's ability to mark the moment: "the moment she entered a room one was conscious of her presence. The diamond-like glitter of her wit was a tangible thing and she wore it like a jewel; it glowed round her like an aura round the moon, pale and phosphorescent [and] as exhilarating as the cold on a frosty night" (Masters 109). Woolf uses similar language and imagery to characterize Clarissa, who is "cold," "pale," and like "one diamond, one woman who sat in her drawing-room and made a meeting-point, a radiancy" (55). Clarissa, too, is known for her ability "to sum it all up in the moment as she passes" (264). Excelling in the art of conversation and having the ability to know "people almost by instinct" (11), Clarissa echoes George Moore's description of Lady Cunard as "an artist, as much a social observer as La Rochefoucauld, or Madame de Sevigne. . . . Her art lay in conversation, that most evanescent form, and there was no Boswell to record it" (Masters 111). Woolf's recognition that there was "no Boswell to record" the feats of the domestic artist, and her goal of describing the life of ordinary women gave birth to her depictions of the hostess and seamstress.

That Woolf saw the home as the locus of all great aesthetic, social, and political change is evident throughout her writings. In fact, in "Mr. Bennett and Mrs. Brown" she offers a respectable, threadbare, elderly woman as the symbol of an evolving "modern" sensibility, instead of the business man, the industrial worker, or even the "New Woman." Indeed, the essay's claim that "all human relations have shifted— those between masters and servants, husbands and wives, parents and children," goes one step further, pinpointing the domestic sphere as the locus of more obvious changes in "religion, conduct, politics, and literature" (27). In *Mrs. Dalloway* we can see Woolf adhering to her own literary theorizing; besides portraying a "Mrs. Brown" (Clarissa Dalloway, an upper-middle-class woman of no public distinction), the novel focuses on the shifting relations between "masters and servants, husbands and wives, parents and children," in precisely the order the essay lays out. Woolf's application of a modernist lens to an equally incongruous landscape is evident in her children's story, *Nurse Lugton's Golden Thimble*. Representing the domestic realm becomes a way for Woolf to figure herself as an artist, both historically and personally. Woolf's decision, recorded during the writing of *Mrs. Dalloway,* to "write anything I want to," illustrates her use of the cultural legacy left her by her literal mother, who also wrote children's stories, and her literary mothers, Jane Austen, Charlotte Brontë, and George Eliot (*Mrs. Dalloway* ms. 2). Approaching the domestic realm with an eye for stylistics, much as the hostess does, Woolf found a means of negotiating her precarious identity as both a woman and an artist.

By creating "modernist" works that not only depict the domestic realm, but are also products of this same realm, Woolf strategically rejects the public, male-identified sphere as the cradle of aesthetic vision. In relation to traditional definitions of modernity one thinks of Wyndham Lewis's dismissal of the Omega Workshops' wares as "pretty" and "mid-Victorian," as opposed to the creations of the all-male Vorticist movement.[1] Lewis's definition hearkens back to Baudelaire's 1863 essay "The Painter of Modern Life," in which he defines the modern as the depiction of the ephemeral, everyday life of the city streets.[2] As Christine Froula demonstrates, such a gendering of art based itself upon the ideology of separate spheres (an ideology espoused by Woolf's parents, Julia and Leslie Stephen): "insofar as women's priorities must be home, husband, and children, public culture becomes a male domain; and insofar as culture is a male domain, the woman artist or culture-maker becomes a contradiction in terms" (Homans 138). In their representations of the domestic realm, Woolf's polemics and fiction reflect and reject this cultural contradiction.

Consequently, when Woolf began practicing her art she was presented with something of a no-win situation—women were expected to represent what they knew best (if they depicted anything at all), yet if they depicted the domestic realm they were often disparaged as "trivial" or "sentimental" female artists.[3] Lewis, for example, complained that the work of Woolf and other Bloomsbury artists was too "pale" and feminized (138). In *Men Without Art* he wrote that Woolf "adapted Joyce and Proust and other such things for the salon," adding, "Venus has become an introverted matriarch" (1, 138). When Woolf confided to her friend Madge Vaughan that "my only defense is that I write things as I see them; and I am quite conscious all the time that it is a very narrow, and rather bloodless point of view," she demonstrated her familiarity with the disparaging labels applied to women's art (Garnett vii).

Like Lewis, Woolf characterizes her work in gender-specific terms: her writing lacks virility, it is anemic and "bloodless." Indeed, her description prefigures the "narrow" bed slept in by the menopausal Clarissa Dalloway. Even Lytton Strachey, a good friend of Woolf's, found fault with her choice of subject matter. She described his reaction to *Mrs. Dalloway*: "what he says is that there is a discrepancy between the ornament (extremely beautiful) and what happens (rather ordinary—or unimportant)" (*Moment's Liberty* 198). Nonetheless, her treatment of domestic subject matter in modernist terms challenges the politics of aesthetic vision that designate men as the sole possessors of the "modern" gaze. Woolf's celebration of her "narrow" point of view defies critics who would dismiss her experience of modern life in favor of those of Lewis and Strachey.

The concept of a "politics of vision" is extremely useful in exploring Woolf's vexed relationship to a gendered modernism. Griselda Pollack develops the concept, asserting that an artwork's subject matter actively structures and anticipates a viewer's class, ethnicity, and gender—in sum, the audience's political identity. Similarly, in her discussion of *La Nourrice* by Berthe Morisot, Linda Nochlin employs the concept to demonstrate how the subject of the picture, a wet nurse feeding Morisot's daughter, anticipates an upper-class, European, female viewer. In contrast, although Woolf finds that Proust, Hardy, Flaubert, and Conrad use their eyes "as novelists have never used them before," she notes that none "of these great writers stops for a moment to describe a crystal jar as if it were an end in itself" (*Moment's Liberty* 141). The projected audience of these male-authored works does not escape her notice. Unlike Morisot's painting, traditional modernist works such as T. S. Eliot's *Waste Land* construct a male subject-position through their portrayal of public figures and spaces—the bar, the banks of the Thames, the deserted city streets. As Woolf realized, traditional modernist vision was difficult to reconcile with the cultural realities of the female artist.

Consequently, to engage in a modernist aesthetic a woman is forced to enter into textual/sexual politics, for as Woolf claims in "The Artist and Politics," the artist's work must engage itself in political debates: "two causes of supreme importance to [the artist] are in peril; the first is his own survival; the other is the survival of his art" (*Collected Essays* 232). Many women whom we now acknowledge as modernists—Dorothy Richardson, Djuna Barnes, Katherine Mansfield—had to engage in and revise modernist notions in order to justify their inclusion in a male-identified movement. By creating works that imply a female subject-position, Woolf transgresses the traditional politics of vision and forges a new type of modernism responsive to the female artist.

While examining the manuscripts of *Mrs. Dalloway* housed in the British Museum (Add. MSS 51,044-46), Wallace Hildick discovered the text of a children's story interpolated in the pages of the longer work. After conferring with Leonard Woolf regarding the origins of the story (of which Leonard had no knowledge), Hildick unveiled his discovery in the *Times Literary Supplement* of 17 June 1965.[4] In an accompanying article, Hildick writes of the disorder of the heavily rewritten three-volume manuscript that envelops the story, and of the way a reader could easily be "misled into assuming that [the children's story] is yet another rejected passage" of *Mrs. Dalloway* (496). Apparently not intended for commercial publication, the children's story (entitled simply, "The") depicts an elderly servant embroidering a set of drawing-room curtains before the fire.[5] The design she stitches is exotic—elephants, monkeys, a queen on her palanquin—but the imagination and setting that give birth to it are markedly domestic. Written in the same style as its host text, there is no plot per se: the story simply focuses on the moment when the nanny falls asleep and the fancywork she is stitching comes alive. Searching for a name for the story that was to be published by the Hogarth Press the following year, Leonard Woolf settled on the title, *Nurse Lugton's Golden Thimble,* from a phrase that appears in the middle of the text: "over [the scene] burnt Nurse Lugton's Golden Thimble like a sun" (8). That the story has since escaped critical notice is not surprising; the fanciful children's tale seems oddly out of place on the research library shelves, surrounded as it is by an ever-increasing array of "serious" Woolf scholarship.

While Hildick admits that "the tale was certainly influenced by the much more important work," he asserts that the children's story "was otherwise an entirely separate undertaking" (496) and fails to notice the obvious interrelations between the two works. Similarly, in Leonard's foreword to *Nurse Lugton's Golden Thimble* he writes that "the story appears in the middle of the text but has nothing to do with it" (5). Indeed, the title of Hildick's review, "Virginia Woolf for Children?" illustrates his desire to separate Woolf's two endeavors—one academic, the other "simpler, more childlike"—without examining the potential relationship of the texts (496). However, the congruences between the two purportedly "separate" works suggest that they should be read side by side. On a structural, thematic, and semantic level, *Nurse Lugton's Golden Thimble* echoes its host text. An examination of the intersection of the two works reveals that Woolf's development as a writer and as a modernist was predicated on her negotiation of domestic material.

When charting the development of Woolf's fiction—her movement from her first, unfocused novel, *The Voyage Out,* through her subsequent Victorian novel of manners, *Night and Day,* and finally to her first sustained modernist work, *Jacob's Room*—one can see how in the *Nurse Lugton's Golden Thimble/ Mrs. Dalloway* nexus Woolf is negotiating the previous three novels' subjects and stylistics into her first mature work of fiction. In many ways, *Nurse Lugton's Golden Thimble* serves as a microcosm for *Mrs. Dalloway,* in which Woolf articulates her commitment to the social concerns that informed her second novel without foregoing her commitment to the stylistic concerns of the age. Written in 1924, the year Woolf was feverishly working on her first work to blend successfully both the realism of *Night and Day* and the intangibility of *Jacob's Room, Nurse Lugton's Golden Thimble* marks Woolf's discovery of her own distinct voice—the voice of a domestic modernist which she would subsequently develop in works such as *To the Lighthouse* and *Between the Acts.* It is not by coincidence that she articulated her newly found voice a year later in the now famous "Modern Fiction": the achievement of *Mrs. Dalloway* granted her the authority to speak from a modernist perspective. However, the importance of the children's story in the history of her career continues to escape critical comment.

When addressing the subject of a female literary tradition in *A Room of One's Own,* the narrator is hard pressed to produce even a handful of literary foremothers. The novelists she does cite, however—Jane Austen, the Brontë sisters, and George Eliot—represent almost exclusively the domestic realm. In publishing Julia Stephen's essays and children's stories, Diane Gillespie and Elizabeth Steele have provided an invaluable glimpse of another literary foremother, Woolf's own mother, Julia Stephen. Stephen's rather odd and at times even sadistic stories reveal another type of "domestic" fiction that Woolf grew up on. Although she does not mention her mother's stories in *A Room of One's Own* (she had already done so in *To the Lighthouse,* when she has Mrs. Ramsay transform the nursery boar's head into a fairyland), *Nurse Lugton's Golden Thimble* alludes to the problematic cultural inheritance left to Woolf by her literal and literary mothers.[6]

In many ways Woolf's rendition of the children's story can be read as an experiment with a genre she identified as her mother's. Stephen's stories are redolent with mischievous monkeys, bears, and exotic birds, and Woolf finds a means of incorporating this feature into her work.[7] In addition, *Nurse Lugton's Golden Thimble,* like Stephen's stories, relies on a suspension of disbelief, a fall into the unconscious or fantasy land Lewis Carroll made so popular in his Alice stories. Finally, like her mother's tales, Woolf wrote her children's stories for circulation only within her circle of family and friends: she wrote *Nurse Lugton's Golden Thimble* for her niece, Ann Stephen, and *The Widow and the Parrot* for Julian Bell's childhood newspaper. *Nurse Lugton's Golden Thimble* strays from Stephen's writing, however, in its modernist flavor—particularly in its rejection of plot and resistance to closure. Both mother and daughter reflect the spirit of their respective historical moments in their works: Stephen's tales are highly moralistic while Woolf's story is distinctly modernist. In assuming her mother's genre but not her style, Woolf finds a means of acknowledging a (domestic) tradition antithetical to a masculine-based modernism.

One of the reasons Woolf chose her mother's genre may be because she found it amenable to potentially objectionable content. As she points out in her essay on Lewis Carroll, the fantastic element (most often introduced through sleep) in children's fiction allows us "to see the world upside down" (*Moment's Liberty* 71). In fact, Woolf claims that many so-called children's stories are not for children at all:

> Down, down, down we fall into that terrifying, wildly inconsequent, yet perfectly logical world where time races, then stands still; where space stretches, then contracts. It is the world of sleep; it is also the world of dreams. Without any conscious effort dreams come; the white rabbit, the walrus, and the carpenter. . . . The two Alices are not books for children; they are the only books in which we become children. President Wilson, Queen Victoria, *The Times* leader writer, the late Lord Salisbury—it does not matter how old, how important, or how insignificant you are, you become a child again. To become a child is very literal; to find everything so strange that nothing is surprising. (*Moment's Liberty* 71)

That Woolf identifies the readers of Carroll's stories as influential political figures— a president, a queen, a prime minister—supports her claim that children's stories are not for children; it also explains her choice of the genre as the vehicle for her modernist revisions. That the writer of children's stories may without reproach turn "the world upside down" makes this genre a subversive and powerful one.

The headnote that graces the second manuscript notebook, the one which bears the bulk of the first draft of *Mrs. Dalloway* and the entirety of *Nurse Lugton's Golden Thimble,* supports the importance of the children's story in Woolf's development as a writer. The first words she wrote in this notebook read: "a delicious idea comes to me that I will write anything I want to write" (*Mrs. Dalloway* ms. 2). This curious inscription suggests that in the process of writing *Mrs. Dalloway* Woolf finally found a balance between her desire to document women's domestic experiences while continuing to experiment with the genre of fiction. Woolf's insistence on domestic subject matter as the basis both for *Mrs. Dalloway* and the children's story it contains underlines her decision to "write anything" she wanted to. Her discovery (articulated a year later) that "everything is the proper stuff of fiction" occurred during the writing of *Nurse Lugton's Golden Thimble* and *Mrs. Dalloway* ("Modern Fiction" 110).

In *Men Without Art* Lewis derisively notes Woolf's refusal to model her works on traditional modernist models. As a result of her "failure," he calls her a "poor lost Georgian would-be novelist" (137) and likens *Mrs. Dalloway* to an old maid (139). Lewis realized that by creating a modernist work based largely in the domestic realm Woolf challenged the public, male-identified sphere as the locus of modernist creations. As he no doubt recognized, Woolf's resistance to the gendered politics of modernism displays itself in her fascination with the domestic artist, a figure Lewis would certainly deem an oxymoron. While many critics have remarked on Woolf's commitment to telling the stories of women's lives, none has yet emphasized her insistence on balancing the details of the domestic realm with the rigors of a modernist aesthetic.

In writing such seemingly divergent works (a children's tale and a modernist novel) Woolf anticipates a female gaze on several levels. First, the children's story implies a female subject-position, for as the first section of *To the Lighthouse* illustrates, it is the mother who usually reads such stories to children. Moreover, the sight that greets the reader's eyes, an aged servant, would be familiar to most contemporary female readers, as would her occupation, sewing. Woolf also writes toward a female audience in *Mrs. Dalloway* when she chronicles Clarissa's varied preparations for her impending party—shopping, planning, arranging—commonplace activities for typical middle- and upper-class women.

At a deeper level, however, Woolf creates an internalized female gaze by according the "objects" of her (and our) vision, Nurse Lugton and Clarissa, subjectivity. Like Woolf, Nurse Lugton and Clarissa experience their own aesthetic vision, albeit in different media. In *Nurse Lugton's Golden Thimble* it is the relatively mundane act of decorating a curtain that generates the "story" for both the nanny and Woolf; the nanny's vision transforms the ordinary material of the curtain (and of the blank page) into a landscape for her imagination: "The stuff was blue stuff; a curtain for Ms. Gingham's fine big drawing-room window. . . . [T]he blue stuff turned into blue air, and the trees waved; you could hear the waves breaking on the lake; and see the people crossing the bridge to market. Immediately, the animals began to move" (7). In *Mrs. Dalloway* it is another act of domestic artistry that generates the story: in preparation for her party that evening Clarissa has the drawing-room doors removed from their hinges. The resulting noise recalls to Clarissa the events of Bourton that lie at the heart of the novel: "for so it had always seemed to her, when, with a little squeak of the hinges, which she could hear now, she had burst open the French windows and plunged at Bourton into the open air" (3). The preparations for the evening party—taking the doors off the hinges, selecting flowers, rearranging the furniture, mending her dress—provide Clarissa and Woolf with their visions. The emphasis the children's story and novel place on the transformative power of domestic creations is not coincidental.

Selecting domestic backgrounds for her twin stories proves another means that Woolf employs in structurally mirroring her works. Instead of the two backgrounds most often associated with high art—the painters frame and the blank page—in *Nurse Lugton's Golden Thimble* Woolf uses an ordinary curtain as her canvas. Much as Roger Fry's Omega artists did, the nanny applies her imaginative vision to her immediate surroundings, integrating art and life. Furthermore, in contrast to works such as *The Waste Land* and the *Cantos,* this phantasmagoric scene emerges from the nanny's domestic, supposedly circumscribed imagination, for the story tells us that "she had only poked at [such beasts] through the bars with her umbrella at the zoo!" (9). In keeping with her characterization of children's stories, in this tale Woolf turns the politics of vision on its head; the figure traditionally represented as caged and sightless, the female, is outside the cage, actively gazing and translating her gaze into art. When Nurse Lugton falls asleep, her imagination is free to break the pattern of aesthetic vision: "they were only patterns so long as old Nurse stitched. But directly she began to snore. . . . [T]he animals began to move" (7). In breaking from the pattern of art (both in her choice of canvas and in her appropriation of the aesthetic gaze) Nurse Lugton adheres to Woolf's much contested assertion in *A Room of One's Own* that the female artist needs to break the "sequence" of narrative; instead of serving as the object of fictions, women must impose their own visions on the curtain, page, and canvas.

Generating the story from inside the domestic sphere reminds the reader of the curious inversion of space that takes place in *A Room of One's Own* when the narrator claims that it is perhaps better for the female artist to be locked out of male tradition (envisioned as the Oxbridge library), than to be locked in. In a similar vein, *Nurse Lugton* illustrates how exclusion from regular public experience does not stunt the female artist's growth or invalidate her vision. Rather, it affords her a fresh view of her surroundings; being "locked out" of male experience is precisely what allows Woolf to forge her brand of modernism. Accordingly, the narrator of the children's story boldly tells us that "over [the scene] burnt Nurse Lugton's golden thimble like a sun" (8). Here the domestic thimble replaces the sun/son, proving that interior and exterior boundaries breakdown under the power of a fertile imagination.

Woolf's framing of Clarissa's party with a curtain similar to the one Nurse Lugton embroiders is another means by which she links the two works. In *Mrs. Dalloway* the "curtain with its flight of birds of Paradise" (258) signals the beginning of the party. In the children's story the animals on the drapes come alive while in the novel "it seemed [when the drapes moved] as if there were a flight of wings into the room" (256). Woolf's use of a curtain in both texts demonstrates the artistic nature of both Nurse Lugton's and Clarissa's productions; although they take place in domestic settings, they, like theatrical dramas, are artificial. Looking forward to *Between the*

Acts, where Woolf treats a conjugal dispute in dramatic terms ("Then the curtain rose. They spoke." [219]), Woolf often likens carefully arranged domestic settings to "room[s] on the stage" (*Night and Day* 41). Indeed, Woolf's comparison of the party to a play becomes evident when Clarissa thinks that "every time she gave a party she had this feeling of being something not herself, and that every one was unreal in one way; much more real in another. It was, she thought, partly their clothes, partly being taken out of their ordinary ways, partly the background" (259). The curtains and the proscenium arch created by the removal of doors serve as physical markers underscoring the domestic drama of *Mrs. Dalloway.* The obvious artifice of the party—the costumes, the character roles, the background—marks Clarissa's creation as an artwork.

Woolf's emphasis on the theatrical nature of Clarissa's production demonstrates the performative nature of the party; in fact, the interactive, partially staged "wedding" and the "who-dunnit" murder mystery are two contemporary manifestations of such performance art. Like contemporary performance art, Clarissa's party is an art of the moment in which nothing tangible remains after the performance. Moreover, both arts focus on process rather than on a final, tangible product. When Clarissa's party begins to succeed, she perceives it in the rhythm of voices and emotions, instead of in a stable, tactile, or visual indicator of her achievement. Although the format of each "performance" remains basically the same (the comedy routine, the theatrical performance), each act is unique in its existence in a particular moment, and in its potential for change and spontaneous growth. In both Clarissa's party and contemporary performance art, for instance, part of the artwork depends upon factors beyond the artist's control.

In *Orlando* the narrator comments on the ephemeral nature of the party: "It was the same always. Nothing remained the next day, yet the excitement of the moment was intense. Thus we are forced to conclude that society is one of those brews such as skilled housekeepers serve hot about Christmas time, whose flavour depends upon the proper mixing and stirring of a dozen different ingredients" (123). The hostess and the artist strive for the same thing—a unified design, a pleasant rhythm. That Woolf focused so much attention on the hostess implies that she learned some of her craft from such a figure.

Although the children's story and the novel celebrate domestic art in general, they both focus on sewing as the paradigm of such art. In *Nurse Lugton's Golden Thimble* the needle challenges the pen and paintbrush as the primary tools of artistic expression, much as Clarissa's sewing scissors do Peter Walsh's knife near the beginning of the novel. Whereas some novels rely upon the knife for adventure, Woolf's novels center most often around the sewing basket; in fact, Peter's ineffectual playing with his knife parodies traditional male models of experience. As a result, *Mrs. Dalloway* explores several types of sewing, particularly dress and hat making. Woolf foregrounds the tools of domestic production (the same tools Nurse Lugton uses) when she has Clarissa think, "[S]he would mend . . . . she would take her silks, her scissors, her—what was it?—her thimble, of course, down into the drawing-room" (55–56). In Clarissa's skillful hands domestic tools create an art akin to poetry. In fact, Woolf reserves some of the novel's most poetic language to describe Clarissa's sewing: "Her needle, drawing the silk smoothly to its gentle pause, collected the green folds together and attached them, very lightly, to the belt. So on a summer's day waves collect, overbalance, and fall; collect and fall; and the whole world seems to be saying 'that is all' more and more ponderously, until even the heart in the body which lies in the sun on the beach says too, That is all" (58–59). Like a carefully constructed poem, Clarissa's mending displays a sense of rhythm, repetition, and impersonal beauty. Moreover, as with other art works, Clarissa's action stimulates an emotional response.[8]

It is this same dress made by Sally Parker (whom Clarissa calls "a real artist" [58]) that later transforms the middle-aged Clarissa into a mermaid lollopping on the waves, a sight as fantastic as the animal-covered Nurse Lugton. Moreover, the dress marks another inversion of inner/outer space; the text tells us it gleams only indoors: "by artificial light the green shone, but lost its colour . . . in the sun" (55). Hence the novel prepares the reader early on for the replacement of the sun with Nurse Lugton's artificially bright thimble.

Rezia Warren represents the artistry inherent in another type of sewing: the decoration of hats. Unlike Clarissa, who practices her art at her leisure, Rezia is a hatmaker by profession. The two places we see Rezia executing her art, however, are homes—her family home in Italy, and her married home in London. Rezia's hat decoration parallels Clarissa's party preparations. While Clarissa prepares her dress for her party, Rezia changes bare hats into beribboned and beaded accessories, and like Clarissa's party, these hats hold the transformative power of turning frumpy housewives into fashionable women. As she bases much of the action of the first section of To the Lighthouse against the backdrop of Mrs. Ramsay's knitting of the brown stocking, in Mrs. Dalloway Woolf silhouettes Septimus's madness against Rezia's intermittent sewing, either in the present or in memory. And like Clarissa's sewing, Rezia's also generates visions: "Hat, child, Brighton, needle. She built it up; first one thing, then another, she built it up, sewing" (221). In bringing different pieces together into a unified whole, Rezia's sewing becomes a metaphor for the act of writing. Given the way Woolf "stitched" Mrs. Dalloway together from five separate stories dealing with Clarissa's party, it is not surprising that Woolf uses the metaphor of sewing so often in the novel.[9] Indeed, Woolf was responsible for actually stitching together and decorating the covers of many of the Hogarth Press's first publications: as a result, sewing and writing became logical analogues for one another.

Woolf's surrounding of the children's tale with sewing scenes demonstrates the way Nurse Lugton's Golden Thimble develops themes engaged in the longer piece. The scene directly preceding the children's story depicts Rezia sewing, much as Nurse Lugton does: "there she was, Rezia, familiar, in plain daylight, sewing" (Mrs. Dalloway ms. 102). The text attaches some importance to her activity, for Septimus repeatedly remarks upon it; he particularly notes the pursed lips "that women had while sewing," then thinks, "[W]hat was there terrible about it? He asked himself, alighting again and again[,] a first time, a third time, on her face, on her hand . . . she sat sewing" (*Mrs. Dalloway* ms. 103). The paranoia that overtakes Septimus (and writers like Lewis and Strachey), could be the image of the successful female artist, independently spinning her domestic fictions: after all, by using her fingers and her imagination Penelope was able singlehandedly to stave off a host of persistent suitors. Woolf's strategic placing of *Nurse Lugton's Golden Thimble* in the manuscript after scenes depicting Rezia's sewing validates the domestic artistry her heroines practice. Not surprisingly, the scene following the children's story returns to Rezia's sewing: Septimus continues to watch her decorate a hat to look like "a coverlet of flowers" (*Mrs. Dalloway* ms. 108). Anticipating the longer work, the children's story describes the drapes that cover Nurse Lugton's knees as "covered with roses and grass" (11). As the art of Rezia and Nurse Lugton demonstrates, domestic art has the power of transforming interiors into paradisiacal gardens. In the case of *Nurse Lugton's Golden Thimble,* paradise is complete with animals of every species, and of course, men and women.[10] If sewing is a metaphor for writing, or art making, then the nexus of the two stories implies that the key to changing reality lies within the grasp of the artist's needle and pen.

As is commonly noted, because it eschews traditional plot, *Mrs. Dalloway* creates meaning largely through juxtaposition. It is significant, then, that after comparing the activities of Rezia and Nurse Lugton the novel shifts to Clarissa's party. It is as if before turning to the important party scene Woolf reaffirmed her commitment to the representation of domestic artistry. While Hildick theorizes that *Nurse Lugton's Golden Thimble* represents simply a "break" from the rigors of representing Septimus's madness, the children's story shows itself to be an important negotiation of male and female subject positions. Woolf brackets Septimus's retreat into the memories of his homoerotic war relationships with visions of the domestic artist at work. Her successful negotiation of these positions allows her to write *Mrs. Dalloway* and her most famous work, *To the Lighthouse.*

The final party scenes continue the patterning of the two works, further suggesting their intertextuality. The repetition of diction and cadences is particularly striking; for example, the final phrase of *Mrs. Dalloway,* "for there she was," is presaged in the manuscript's comment regarding Rezia, "there she was" (102), while *Nurse Lugton's Golden Thimble* confers an equal significance on the animals' stillness, "there they stood" (7). Similarly, when Peter notices Clarissa at the top of the stairs he thinks, "[T]his was one of these moments[,] one of the Events" (*Mrs. Dalloway* ms. 113), while a deleted passage from the children's story describes the equally mystical moment when the stitching metamorphoses into living animals as "the animals had not moved until [the moment, which was the moment] Nurse Lugton snored for the fifth time" (*Mrs. Dalloway* ms. 104; Woolf's brackets). The similar language patterns Woolf uses to describe these different situations binds them together, implying the common transformative experience of the artwork.

That the reader grapples with the artistry of the party is understandable: even Clarissa has trouble articulating it. In trying to explain her commitment to her creations, Clarissa thinks, "[A]ll she could say was (and nobody could be expected to understand): They're an offering" (184). Woolf realized the perils of celebrating Clarissa's productions as art; as a result she did not want to be too obvious in her assertions. In the published version she tempered Clarissa's original musings that "life meant bringing together[.] An artist did the same thing presumably" (*Mrs. Dalloway* ms. 54), deleting the latter half of the statement. In a similar vein, she changed, "she did it because it was an offering. Just as somebody writes a book after all" (*Mrs. Dalloway* ms. 54, 55) to "an offering; for the sake of offering, perhaps" (185). Woolf's revisions diffuse her original celebration of domestic art and weaken the comparison to the literary arts. Nonetheless, the published version harbors traces of the original argument in places such as Clarissa's statement that her art was "an offering . . . for the sake of offering." In echoing the aesthetes' "art for art's sake," Woolf gets her message across, if only in shorthand notation. "Mr. Bennett and Mrs. Brown," however, does not soften the message: the essay compares "the hostess and her unknown guest on the one hand" to "the writer and his unknown reader on the other" (34).

As Woolf discerned, critics such as Lewis and Strachey viewed her use of domestic subject matter as evidence of her novelistic weakness. She anticipates these impending criticisms when she has Clarissa worry that her husband and Peter Walsh "criticized her very unfairly, laughed at her very unjustly, for her parties" (183). Although her first drafts make the connection between the domestic and other arts clear, phrases such as "life meant bringing together[.] An artist did the same thing presumably" gesture perhaps too self-reflexively toward Woolf, tying her literary endeavors dangerously close to those of the domestic artists she depicts. Yet she did not omit all comparisons. Borrowing a term from the writer's medium, Clarissa thinks of her party as an assertion of "one's little point of view" (255). As Clarissa's musings suggest, in figuring the domestic artist Woolf explores her own artistry, one that also depends on domestic fictions.

Her application of a modernist lens to *Mrs. Dalloway* and *Nurse Lugton's Golden Thimble* calls for a reevaluation of aesthetic hierarchies that alienate the female artist and audience. Woolf's fiction questions values that place traditionally recognized aesthetic creations above such plotless domestic artistry as produced by Nurse Lugton, Clarissa Dalloway, and Woolf herself. Thus Woolf's works structure a reader that will disagree with Mrs. Ramsay's assessment in *To the Lighthouse* that "of the two [Mr. Ramsay] was infinitely more important, and what she gave the world, in comparison with what he gave, negligible" (62). In a metafictional sense, then, Clarissa Dalloway the "perfect hostess" (10) and Nurse Lugton the needle-worker become tropes for Woolf the domestic modernist. As the stories' obvious self-reflexivity illustrates, the domestic realm is not only a space capable of aesthetic production (Nurse Lugton's drapery design and Clarissa's party), it is also a space that inherently lends itself to modernist forms of representation (the actual books Woolf creates). Thus by depicting the domestic artist in modernist terms, Woolf chronicles her own genesis; the historical evolution of the artist is largely aided by such self-representations.

Notes

1. Vorticism interpreted the modern as man, the machine, and their urban interaction. See Anscombe.

2. Both Frascina's *Modernity and Modernism: French Painting in the Nineteenth Century* and Janet Wolff's *Feminine Sentences* make convincing arguments regarding Baudelaire's instrumental role in the modern. See Macleod for a discussion of the roots of British modernism.

3. Woolf's worry that *To the Lighthouse* deals with too "sentimental" a theme echoes Vanessa Bell's comment that Ethel Sands's and Nan Hudson's art is too feminine, too "pretty." See Anscombe 15.

4. For the version edited by Hildick, see 495. Duncan Grant provided an illustrated border for the text as well as for the version published by the Hogarth Press the following year.

5. Using the letters and diaries for clues to the impetus for Woolf's writing of *Nurse Lugton's Golden Thimble,* Hildick finds that Ann Stephen, Woolf's niece, was visiting at the time. As a result, Hildick concludes Woolf wrote it to amuse her. Woolf's reading to her niece out of the *Mrs. Dalloway* notebook supports the view of the novel as an articulation of her emerging aesthetic.

6. I am borrowing the concept of the literal and the literary from Patricia Moran.

7. Julia Stephen's penchant for animal nicknames is evident in her naming of Woolf "Goat" and Bell "Dolphin."

8. Whether or not a work elicited an emotional response was one of the tests Clive Bell used in deciding whether a production constituted a work of art. See his influential *Art.*

9. The stories are collected under the title *Mrs. Dalloway's Party.*

10. Mrs. Hilbery's declaration that Clarissa has created an "enchanted garden" (291) alludes to another type of paradise.

Works Cited

Anscombe, Isabelle. *Omega and After.* London: Thames & Hudson, 1981.

Baudelaire, Charles. "The Painter of Modern Life." *Modern Art and Modernism: A Critical Anthology.* Ed. Francis Frascina. New York: Harper & Row, 1982.

Bell, Clive. *Art.* London: Chatto & Windus, 1949.

Courtney, Nicholas. *In Society: The Brideshead Years.* London: Pavilion, 1986.

Frascina, Frances, ed. *Modernity and Modernism: French Painting in the Nineteenth Century.* New Haven: Yale UP, 1993.

Garnett, Angelica. Preface. *Night and Day.* By Virginia Woolf. London: Hogarth, 1990.

Hildick, Wallace. "Virginia Woolf for Children?" *Times Literary Supplement* 17 June 1965.

Homans, Margaret, ed. *Virginia Woolf: A Collection of Critical Essays.* Englewood Cliffs: Prentice-Hall, 1993.

Lewis, Wyndham. *Men Without Art.* Santa Rosa, CA: Black Sparrow, 1987.

Macleod, Dianne Sachko. "The Dialectics of Modernism and English Art." *British Journal of Aesthetics* 35 (1995): 1–14.

Masters, Brian. *Great Society Hostesses.* London: Constable, 1982.

Moran, Patricia. "Virginia Woolf and the Scene of Writing." *Modern Fiction Studies* 38 (1992): 81–100.

Nochlin, Linda. "Morisot's Wet Nurse: The Construction of Work and Leisure in Impressionist Art." *Perspectives on Morisot.* Ed. T. J. Edelstein. New York: Hudson Hills, 1990.

Pollack, Griselda. "The Gaze and the Look: Women with Binoculars—A Question of Difference." *Dealing with Degas: Representations of Women and the Politics of Vision.* Ed. Griselda Pollack. Pandora, 1992.

Stephen, Julia. *Stories for Children, Essays for Adults.* Ed. Diane Gillespie. Syracuse: Syracuse UP, 1987.

Wolff, Janet. *Feminine Sentences: Essays on Women and Culture.* Berkeley: U of California P, 1990.

Woolf, Leonard. Foreword. *Nurse Lugton's Golden Thimble.* By Virginia Woolf. London: Hogarth, 1973.

Woolf, Virginia. "The Artist and Politics." *Collected Essays.* Vol. 2. London: Hogarth, 1966.

———. *Between the Acts.* London: Harcourt Brace Jovanovich, 1941.

———. "Modern Fiction." *Collected Essays.* Vol. 2. London: Hogarth, 1966.

———. *A Moment's Liberty: The Shorter Diary.* Ed. Anne Oliver Bell. London: Hogarth, 1990.

———. "Mr. Bennett and Mrs. Brown." *The Essentials of Fiction.* Ed. Michael Hoffman. London: Duke, 1988.

———. *Mrs. Dalloway.* London: Harcourt Brace Jovanovich, 1953.

———. *Mrs. Dalloway.* Ms. Add. MSS 51,044-46. British Museum, London.

———. *Mrs. Dalloway's Party.* Ed. Stella McNichol. London: Hogarth, 1973.

———. *Night and Day.* London: Hogarth, 1990.

———. *Nurse Lugton's Golden Thimble.* London: Hogarth, 1966.

———. *Orlando: A Biography.* New York: Harcourt, Brace, 1928.

———. *A Room of One's Own.* London: Harcourt Brace Jovanovich, 1957.

———. *To the Lighthouse.* London: Harcourt Brace Jovanovich, 1955.

Modernism, Single Motherhood, and the Discourse of Women's Liberation in Rebecca West's *The Judge*

Shirley Peterson

And the one doesn't stir without the other. But we do not move together. When the one of us comes into the world, the other goes underground. When the one carries life, the other dies.—Luce Irigaray, 1981

In 1922, a year delivering both T. S. Eliot's *The Waste Land* and James Joyce's *Ulysses*, feminist journalist and fiction writer Rebecca West published her second novel, *The Judge*. While it is standard to cite the former two works in defining modernist concerns and stylistic techniques, *The Judge* has been relegated to the realm of the obscure and derivative.[1] Perhaps more than any other novel of the period, however, *The Judge* depicts a commonly overlooked dimension of early twentieth-century women's history: the anxieties of female liberation. One might expect to find feminists at this historical moment basking in the afterglow of the limited suffrage granted by Parliament in 1918.[2] On the contrary, following early feminists' lengthy suffrage campaign, the discourse of women's liberation faltered. In other words, the rhetoric of emancipation so effectively marshaled in nineteenth-century tracts seems to have lost its momentum in the 1920s postwar culture, a culture weary of conflict, gender-based or otherwise. Thus, behind West's novel stands a gifted writer who honed her considerable skills on the rhetoric of women's liberation in the first decade of the twentieth century, yet by 1922 her narrative reveals a great deal about the ambiguities and contradictions of liberation.

By way of understanding the dilemma of newly "liberated" women, we might consider Edward Said's observation on the "anti-imperialist" poet William Butler Yeats, voice of a concurrent struggle against British imperialism in Ireland. Said imagines the celebrated poet of the Irish Renaissance poised between two histori-cal/political moments, which he terms "Nationalist" and "Liberationist." While Yeats led the artistic vanguard for "identity-based" nationalist politics of the early Irish Renaissance, he "situates himself at that juncture where the violence of change is unarguable but where the results of the violence beseech necessary, if not always sufficient, reason" (235). Yeats, Said continues, "stopped short of imagining full political liberation, but he gave us a major international achievement in cultural decolonization" (238).

Borrowing Said's model, we can make a similar observation about postsuffrage feminism in that the difficulty of shifting from "identity-based" struggle to authen-tic "liberation" marks this celebratory moment in the women's movement as well. Like Yeats, chief spokesman for the modern Irish literary revival, West (of Scots-Irish descent) flourished as a saber-toothed feminist in the heyday of the women's suffrage movement prior to World War I. During this period, West, among other feminist writers, waged a similar "identity-based" struggle based on gender rather than nationality. Ironically, even the partial political liberation women achieved in 1918 literally dumbfounded some of feminism's strongest voices. Poised at the beginning of a new era, they confronted opposing forces: on the one hand, a nos-talgia-laden heroic past populated by such commanding presences as Emmeline and Christabel Pankhurst and Millicent Garret Fawcett; on the other hand, a future dis-oriented and cut loose from its social and moral bearings in a postwar cultural waste-land.[3] From the latter perspective, the foremothers of the women's movement loomed as a formidable act to follow. It is in this context that West's novel about a devouring mother and her future daughter-in-law (and heir apparent) becomes an inviting allegory of the women's movement in its immediate postsuffrage phase as it sought a modern identity in the overwhelming shadow of presuffrage feminism.

When Rebecca West published *The Judge,* she was a single parent undergoing the final break with H. G. Wells, the father of her illegitimate child. Despite their ten-year liaison, Wells had remained married to his wife, Jane. Thus, the West-Wells relationship had been fraught with difficulties from its inception due as much to the extraordinary personalities involved as to the socially unacceptable circumstances of their affair. If Wells shocked and amused the Edwardian literati as the Lothario of turn-of-the-century England, society both celebrated and derided Rebecca West as the era's consummate "New Woman." She was brash, intellectually sharp, quick-witted, and an emblem of the modern sexual revolution. Yet as postmodernist femi-nists have witnessed again, sexual revolutions belie the fact that women rarely es-cape the web of cultural sanctions that curtail female sexuality.[4] Such revolutions usually envision utopias (e.g., those of H. G. Wells) wherein women are simply more available to men without the consequences of pregnancy and child care.

West had enjoyed early acclaim for her political and creative writing; however, with *The Judge* she produced what many readers then (as well as today) perceived as a very uneven and perplexing novel. Upon its publication, a peevish Wells wrote to West that *The Judge* was "an ill conceived sprawl of a book with a faked hero and a faked climax, an aimless waste of your powers" (Ray 123). Other, more objective, critics joined in the disapprobation, including Virginia Woolf who called the book "stout, generous" and "lively" but ultimately compared it to "an over-stuffed sausage" that she could not finish (*Letters* 542).

More recently, Bonnie Kime Scott defends the novel from a poststructuralist perspective as a modernist refiguring of binary oppositions. *The Judge,* she argues, goes beyond the typical male/female duality to consider older/younger generations of females which West links to "that fly youth and beauty." She contends that "West's case demonstrates the difficulty of rethinking basic heterosexual, patriarchal structures in the modernist era, and encourages a more expansive definition of modernist experimentation and feminist modernism" (170). Scott's analysis augments Said's model by emphasizing the roles of gender and generation in such political and literary restructuring. In this regard, the novel's main female characters, Ellen Melville and Marion Yaverland, occupy a central position in a debate that perhaps issues from a dark corner of modernist history that requires further illumination: the split between "old" and "new" feminists, particularly over the role of the maternal.[5]

Even seventy-five years after its publication, perhaps only one thing is clear about the novel: it does not follow West's original plan for a story about "a judge who collapsed in a brothel, recognizing in his seizure that the woman he is with is the wife of a man he sentenced for murder" (Glendenning 81). What began as an investigation into patriarchal authority, sexual exploitation of women, and female revenge becomes a study of two women, both perhaps versions of West herself, and by extension, embodiments of the contradictions surrounding the 1920s liberated woman. Ellen Melville recalls the young activist West with a zealous devotion to women's liberation and a firm belief in female solidarity as a means of achieving it;[6] Marion Yaverland is a generation older, a disillusioned unwed mother who has been hardened by the solitude and isolation that accompany female sexual deviance. Ellen and Marion speak from their respective places of innocence and experience, their stories intersecting in the (con)fusion of romantic and maternal love. The novel's love plot involves Ellen with Richard, Marion's illegitimate son. Interestingly, West casts this plot in the context of suffrage politics, then decenters the heterosexual romance in the novel's second part for an unusual version of the family romance, part gothic romance, part psychological drama, and part feminist polemic. In the novel's latter half, Marion emerges as the site of conflicting desires and realities related to the "liberated" woman.

The novel interweaves political and familial desires with sexual ones for which feminist psychoanalytic theory provides useful insight.[7] For instance, Jessica Benjamin argues that "typically the mother is not articulated as a sexual subject, one who actively desires something for herself—quite the contrary. The mother is a profoundly desexualized figure. And we must suspect that this desexualization is part of her more general lack of subjectivity in society as a whole. Just as the mother's power is not her own, but is intended to serve her child, so, in a larger sense, woman does not have the freedom to do as she wills; she is not the subject of her own desire" (88). The problem of female desire, according to Benjamin, within the historical/political discourse of female liberation can be expressed as "the need for a mother who *is* articulated as a sexual subject, who is an agent, who does express desire" (89). Consequently, the "outlawed" (single mother) Marion symbolizes conflation of maternal and sexual desires to Ellen, soon to be sanctioned as an "in-law" through marriage.

The first half of the novel follows conventional terms of realism in its depiction of Ellen's early development from innocence to experience, that is, female adulthood. This development unfolds notably within a matriarchal environment, fostering the community and interconnectedness characteristic of female social development (Benjamin 25). She lives with her mother in Edinburgh and tries to pattern herself after her other maternal role models, the suffragettes. She is fatherless, a state which intensifies her marginalization within patriarchy. But rather than seeking a husband to integrate herself back into the patriarchal realm, Ellen spends her time as a budding activist, "composing speeches which she knew she would always be too shy to deliver" (10). She relishes her leisure time spent in subversive talk of suffrage and socialism. The matriarchal idols of both her community and her imagination seem to compensate for her absent father and to mitigate the humiliation and condescension this New Woman endures in her capacity as typist for a patronizing attorney and his son. Her biggest complaint is boredom exacerbated by the gloominess and vague agitation of youth.

Ellen sublimates any growing sexual desire into quasi-erotic passions for other women, present and past. She worships the suffragettes and fantasizes about Edinburgh's most famous resident ancestor, Mary, Queen of Scots. She feels a strong bond to this tragic kinswoman, linked as she is in Ellen's mind to Hawthorne's Hester Prynne. In this way, Mary foreshadows the tragic Marion, who suffers similar condemnation for violating moral and class barriers by giving birth to Squire Harry's illegitimate son. Ellen's bond to Mary/Marion recalls the Virgin/Whore duality that underlies the competing discourses of female sexual liberation. For Ellen, Mary is an ideal enshrined in the grotto of childhood innocence in which liberated women are tragically heroic yet pure (much like the religiously inflected suffragists); when Ellen later meets Mary's counterpart in Marion, she undergoes a rite of passage in which she witnesses firsthand the dark underside of such illusions.

Ellen's initiation into the patriarchal realm comes in the alluring form of the heterosexual romance. Richard Yaverland embodies another of Ellen's fantasies: the romantic and exotic hero found in such romantic adventures as *Treasure Island,* by fellow Scotsman Robert Louis Stevenson. Richard arrives in Edinburgh from Rio de Janeiro, where he has spent the past thirteen years. When he seeks legal advice from the firm where Ellen works, she is immediately enthralled. She imagines he has "gold rings in his ears" and "a magical air, like the ghost of a drowned man risen for revelry." His voice resonates "with suppressed magic" as he relates tales of South America, making Ellen increasingly aware of her own provincialism (26–29). Richard delights in Ellen's natural adventurousness and charm, but privately he regards her as another biologically destined woman whose "body would imprison her in soft places: she would be allowed no adventures other than love, no achievements other than births" (33). Richard's oddly fatalistic, if sympathetic, attitude stems from his own genealogy, which denies him a place in the patriarchal order. This order does not acknowledge him as a legitimate heir to his biological father; thus, part of his appeal as the modern liberated male is that he has less invested than most men in the status quo.

The collision of the romantic and the political plots—vividly rendered when Richard's and Ellen's eyes meet at a suffrage rally—initiates Ellen's departure from the sheltered matriarchal world of childhood innocence toward the alluring, yet ominous, adult world of sexual politics. Conflict erupts immediately in the disjunction of political and romantic desires. Ellen's attraction to Richard violates her feminist conviction never to marry in order to devote herself to the Cause; yet she does concede that "[l]ove must be a great compensation to those who have not political ambitions" (40). With the Edinburgh suffrage rally as ironic backdrop to the romantic drama, the debate over women's equality aptly focuses on the political consequences of marriage for a woman, especially one devoted to the Cause.

At this point, West vents her own disillusionment with the suffragettes (strategically deflected through Richard's point of view), particularly with the Pankhursts. Richard supports the suffragettes; in fact, he genuinely admires Mrs. Ormiston, the novel's Emmeline Pankhurst and one of Ellen's (and West's)[8] greatest heroes. To Richard, Mrs. Ormiston has "an invincible quality" and a "tragically serious" appearance that reminds him of his mother (61). But Mrs. Ormiston and her three daughters also call to mind a band of traveling minstrels "giving the young that guarantee that life is really as fine as story-books say, which can only be given by contemporary heroism. Little Ellen Melville, on the other side of the hall, was lifting the most wonderful face all fierce and glowing with hero-worship" (62).

Through Richard, West offers a bifurcated view of the women's movement, both celebrating and deriding the impact that the suffragettes had had on young imaginations such as her own.[9] Richard's comparison of Mrs. Ormiston to Marion Yaverland implies that Ellen's hero-worship of the suffragettes is misplaced and that the real hero is Marion, who refuses on a fundamental level to live by patriarchy's rules. As Jane Marcus notes, "[F]eminist support of unwed mothers on principle, like Ellen Melville's response to the suffragettes' speeches, is not enough. Intellectual radicalism is safe indeed, compared with the social ostracism suffered by unmarried mothers" (Introduction 6). Of course, West herself had come to realize during a lonely and isolated pregnancy that there was still a great gap between the theory of women's sexual liberation and the reality of the unwed mother.

Ellen's radicalism takes a more theoretical than actual form at this point, indicated by her ignorance of the biological facts behind unwed motherhood. Furthermore, her innocence blinds her to her own power. In a veiled allusion to Christabel Pankhurst's antisex campaign, Richard (parroting West) reasons that Puritanism is not the answer to women's degradation; sensuality is (66). Sounding like a precursor to today's men's movement, Richard complains about men's sexual repression. After years of debased sexual experience with women who stand "at the edge of the primeval swamps" but never fully immerse themselves in the substance of life, he longs for the primeval mother, for the "oozy mud" of the sensual life that repels other men (135, 424). Thus inclined, his thoughts, along with his eyes, turn to Ellen, daughter of the Pentlands and spiritual daughter-in-law of both Marion and the primordial mud flats of Essex where she resides.

The death of Ellen's biological mother ends the first section of the novel and Ellen's childish romanticism gives way to horror. Mrs. Melville has been the "good mother" to Ellen, instilling values like nurturance and generosity, but she has also encouraged the more stereotypically male traits of independence and strong-mindedness in Ellen because she "liked to pretend her daughter was a son" (44). Mrs. Melville's poverty and disastrous marriage limit her imagination and vitality. Because she is still bitter over her husband's abandonment, the best advice this Scottish mother can offer Ellen is to avoid Irishmen. Like the suffragettes, Mrs. Melville offers Ellen nurturance and community but clearly a desexualized notion of female desire. The home Mrs. Melville provides, while secure enough, offers no hope for a better future while presenting every likelihood that Ellen will turn into a bitter old woman like herself. Thus, to borrow Benjamin's terms, Ellen must seek elsewhere "for a mother who is articulated as a sexual subject, who is an agent, who does express desire" (Benjamin 89). When she buries Mrs. Melville, along with her childhood, Ellen begins a journey, both physical and symbolic, toward new experience.[10] At Yaverland's End, Marion's home, Ellen confronts not only a formidable future mother-in-law but also a troublesome matriarch. If Mrs. Melville and the suffragettes have offered continuity and a bond among women, Ellen learns from the ostracized Marion how strenuously patriarchy seeks to divide the sexual woman from the mother woman.

At first Ellen finds Marion a very enigmatic person who confounds one's maternal expectations. Marion is as unlike Ellen's own mother as the Pentlands are to the Essex flatlands, and her eccentricities and self-absorption confuse and disturb Ellen. Nevertheless, more similarities exist between Ellen and Marion than initially seem possible. Certainly Richard's attraction to Ellen derives from his recognition of her tragic beauty, something he associates with his mother, the archetypal tragic figure in his life. Initially, he seems locked in an Oedipal struggle with the two women as he notes "grudgingly" that Ellen "was as beautiful as his mother" (117), while he bitterly recalls how his mother's beauty was sacrificed to his father's selfishness. Ellen's Oedipal function as mother replacement becomes apparent in their similar personalities. Just as Marion keeps to herself after her scandalous affair with Harry, Ellen has lived a solitary life in Edinburgh, preferring nature to people despite her involvement with the suffragettes and her job. Both women seem to belong more to nature than to culture.

Marion's initial kindness to Ellen quickly develops Gothic overtones of danger. For example, she offers Ellen her former bedroom, which Marion believes is "sacred to the spirit of young love" (286) because it was in its long wide window that Marion was first admired by Harry. But Marion also tells Ellen the room's tragic love story of William Yaverland, her great-grandfather. Jealous and suspicious of his wife, he had the large window installed so that, while bedridden, he could spy on her and the handsome overseer. Ironically, the archetypal rites of love and death that haunt this overdetermined space foreshadow the novel's tragic ending. The suspense and anxiety triggered by this room mark a generic shift in the novel from what might be described as nineteenth-century bourgeois realism to twentieth-century horror story with modernist strains of psychological disorientation.

Another aspect of the house seems an extension of Marion herself. To Ellen, Marion's sitting room resembles a lighthouse tower, exuding Marion's excessive and invasive nature: "Here in this room the inconceivable had happened and she recognised that there was present an excess of beauty and an excess of being. For indeed the room was too like a lighthouse in the way that all who sat within were forced to look out on the windy firmament and see the earth spread far below. . . . She had never before seen a room so freely ventilated by beauty, and yet she knew that she would find living on the ledge of this view quite intolerable" (240–41). The room's excessive beauty starkly contrasts with Ellen's dreary Edinburgh home, and yet she recoils from it, marked as it is as the site of illicit sexuality. By extension, she recoils from what she terms Marion's own excessive personality, a force that seems to overwhelm and suffocate Ellen. Ellen's revulsion has both psychological and political dimensions. From a psychological perspective, Marion's Kurtz-like darkness emanates from her spiritual and moral isolation, characterized in Conrad fashion as a complete absorption in the self. Her oppressive presence, like a pall on Ellen and Richard, obscures Ellen's vision of their future together: "Not even death would stop this woman's habit of excessive living" (248).

From a political perspective, Ellen and Marion become allegorical figures of the women's movement itself as it undergoes a generational change. A monolithic reminder of first-wave feminism, Marion's overpowering presence recalls the unyielding courage of the suffragettes and even Mary, Queen of Scots. In the face of these maternal monuments of the past, Ellen flounders within the consequent reconfiguration of romance, politics, and sex. Yet her vision is blocked by the mother figure whose very legacy seemed to promise so much.

Another, more positive, facet of this symbolic lighthouse suggests Marion as a kind of beacon or guiding light for Ellen. In fact, Ellen's only hope may also be her biggest fear: Marion's extinction. This contradiction has a psychological dimension that is often played out in the struggle of daughters against mothers for subjectivity and individuation. According to Julia Kristeva, identity depends on the reconciliation of these two: "A woman seldom (although not necessarily) experiences her passion (love and hatred) for another woman without having taken her own mother's place—without having herself become a mother, and especially without slowly learning to differentiate between same beings—as being face to face with her daughter forces her to do" (184). Ellen's psychological struggle with Marion stems from Ellen's need to differentiate herself from a "same" being and to define a separate identity. Although Ellen's desire for identity demands that she replace Marion in Richard's mind, this is not a simple Oedipal process from the female perspective. Ellen's identity depends on her recognition of the maternal "as like and different" (Benjamin 30). Whereas Richard's failed Oedipal struggle, his inability to reconcile the maternal with the paternal influences in his life, brings about his destruction, Ellen and Marion offer another reading of the story based on Kristeva's notion of the symbiotic mother/daughter relationship.[11]

As a role model for female agency, however, Marion remains problematic because she is both victim and agent, beneficent and forbidding. Harry's victimation of Marion is initially motivated by passion, and he is somewhat redeemed by a class system that prohibits their legitimate union. Consequently, but ironically, the more violent victimization comes at the hands of her own class in the form of the sadistic and opportunistic Peacey. At first he appears to offer Marion help in the guise of a platonic marriage but later rapes her, leaving her emotionally devastated: "[S]he wandered in the dark caverns of her mind. Her capacity for sexual love lay dead in her. She saw it as a lovely naked boy lying with blue lips and purple blood pouring from his side, where it had been jagged by the boar who still snuffled the fair body, sitting by with its haunches in a spring" (287). The grotesque details of this scene, imagined metaphorically as a fatal assault on the libido by the savage (working-class) beast, suggest that Marion's punishment for her erotic (and class) transgression is rape and the annihilation of sexual desire. Even her beloved Harry joins in the condemnation, blaming her when he learns of Peacey's betrayal: "Damn it all, . . . you were unique!" (292). Her uniqueness, it seems, is rooted in the class system and sexual economy in which female use and value are inversely related, and female sexual desire irrelevant. The offspring of these two encounters reflect the consequences women suffer for deviating from sanctioned sexual desire. Marion is not only condemned for the class transgression and excessive love that produce Richard but also further punished through Peacey's atavistic son Roger, an intolerant and moralistic evangelist who inspires maternal revulsion and brings the story to its tragic conclusion.

West mitigates Marion's victimization, however, by the distancing effect of time and by her current overpowering presence. While there is no question of her absolute devotion to Richard or to her desire to see him happily married to Ellen, she wields a fatalistic destructive force alluded to in her warning to Richard, echoed in the novel's title: "Every mother is a judge who sentences the children for the sins of the father" (346). As an unwed and unrepentant mother, Marion poses an enormous threat to patriarchy, and to that extent she becomes, like West herself, emblematic of the danger of unchecked female sexuality. Insofar as daughters are sentenced as well as sons, we might also see here a proverb for a generation of young women left to sort out the contradictions that suffrage politics did not resolve. Based as it was on a premise of desexualized moral superiority, the nineteenth-century women's movement could not afford to scrutinize the basis upon which they waged their war. Along with the vote, therefore, feminists handed down the patriarchal sexual code that ensured condemnation of the sexually deviant woman. West announces here that all the children of the modern period were indeed punished for the sins of the father, through a system of retribution orchestrated by the demonic mother as the left hand of patriarchy.[12]

In a reading of the novel's conclusion that links it to other modernist works, Yaverland's End becomes another version of the modern wasteland featuring Marion as a female counterpart of the depleted Fisher King. As such a figure, she bequeaths to Ellen the potential to restore fertility to a barren culture. West echoes another modernist theme by leaving her surviving characters in exile, literally and metaphorically. Marion effectively seals Ellen's fate in her suicide note. Written in the margin of her calendar as if to indicate the timeless and spaceless realm of single motherhood outside patriarchy, the note conveys the mantle of maternal suffering from mother to daughter: "This is the end. Death. Death. Death. This is the end. I must die. Give him to Ellen. I must die" (423). These words touch Ellen "at the core of her soul," and "[h]er flesh . . . now knew the sorrow appropriate to the destruction of Marion's wide, productive body" (423). Marion's physical demise corresponds to Ellen's transformation from daughter to mother figure. No longer threatened by Marion's overwhelming presence, Ellen sorrowfully embraces the memory of Marion, now elevated through death to the realm of eternal mother. For the first time, Ellen can say, "Richard, I love your mother!" (424).

The novel's melodramatic denouement fulfills Marion's destructive pronouncement on her sons as well as her legacy to Ellen. When Roger blames Marion's death on Richard and Ellen's immorality, Richard drives a knife into Roger's heart, figuratively silencing the provincial voice of morality that condemned his mother and himself. At the novel's conclusion, Richard and Ellen are exiles, having fled the authorities to Kerith Island, where they agree to consummate their union, since marriage seems now impossible. Not knowing, or caring, "whether it was a son or daughter that waited for her there," Ellen retreats with Richard to a cattleman's hut which in its resemblance to the Christian manger scene reinforces Ellen's maternal destiny.[13] This exile suggests imprisonment rather than escape as Ellen embarks on a journey similar to Marion's with possibly the same dismal outcome. Nevertheless, Ellen perceives it as her victory: "Though the night should engulf Richard and Marion, the triumph was not with the night. In throwing in her lot with them and with the human race which is perpetually defeated, she was nevertheless choosing the side of victory" (480).

Despite Ellen's defiantly heroic stand, conflicting emotions clearly underlie the novel's conclusion. The emotions partially stem from West's disappointment with the legacy of sexual liberation and her ambivalence about motherhood. The novel demonstrates that, like most myths, those about female sexuality and sexual behavior die hard. The empowering ideology of liberation, autonomy and independence brandished by the early women's movement as a social corrective to gender inequality was easily undermined by the specter of the single mother, a potent reminder for West's generation that authentic female liberation was elusive.

It is one of the enduring ironies of the early women's movement that as soon as women won political voice, they seemed to fall mute. Critics have described the 1920s as women's retreat into "rooms of their own" or into the realm of fantasy as a response to the failure of bourgeois realism to bring about the promise of feminism.[14] Nevertheless, I see this moment more as a discursive shift, quite natural not to the failure of feminism but to the reformulation of a modernist agenda that includes female desire in a matrix of competing and paradoxical discourses of liberation.

Since Virginia Woolf is usually implicated in such feminist appraisals of the period, we might by way of comparison turn briefly to her 1919 novel *Night and Day* to examine how her feminist protagonist Mary Datchet reimagines female liberation: "Two rooms are all I should want. . . . [O]ne for eating, one for sleeping. Oh, but I should like another, a large one at the top, and a little garden where one could grow flowers. A path—so—down to a river, or up to a wood, and the sea not very far off, so that one could hear the waves at night. Ships just vanishing on the horizon" (334). Mary cannot finish her fantasy, perhaps because she has yet to articulate her desires fully in her mind. But the image remains a hopeful one, this woman's room providing more of an expansive vantage point of possibilities than a retreat from them. Like West's Ellen, Mary is a suffragist whose bond to her elders is fraught with reservations about the "Cause." She regards Mrs. Seal part of the feminist old guard, an "odd priestess of humanity" whose blind devotion disturbs Mary (170). Mrs. Seal's goal is nothing if not focused, and she never speculates beyond victory for the suffrage movement; it has become an end in itself. That this limited view would not satisfy a new wave of modern feminists is not surprising, but its limitations have has been overlooked. This discursive shift within feminism marks one of the defining moments of twentieth-century modernism that continue to reshape its historical, political, and literary profile.

Notes

1. See, for instance, Peter Wolfe, who criticizes the novel's "compositional mode" for being "locked in the death-lock of the Jamesian manner" (41–42).

2. In 1918 the franchise was limited to women over thirty. In 1928 it was extended to adult women who occupied, or were the wives of men who occupied, premises of not less than five pounds annual value.

3. Historian Susan Kingsley Kent describes this postwar shift as regressive: "Prewar feminists had vigorously attacked the notion of separate spheres and the medical and scientific discourses about gender and sexuality upon which those spheres rested. Many feminists after World War I, by contrast, pursued a program that championed rather than challenged the prevailing ideas about masculinity and femininity appearing in the literature of psychoanalysis and sexology. In embracing radically new—and seemingly liberating—views of women as human beings with sexual identities, many feminists . . . accepted theories of sexual difference that helped to advance notions of separate spheres for men and women" (*Making Peace* 6).

4. See Butler, for example, on more current theorists of sexuality: "This utopian notion of a sexuality freed from heterosexual constructs . . . failed to acknowledge the ways in which power relations continue to construct sexuality for women even within the terms of a 'liberated' heterosexuality or lesbianism" (29).

5. See Kent, *Making Peace* (114–39).

6. See Jane Marcus, *The Young Rebecca,* for representative writings of this early West.

7. Also, as Kent argues in *Sex and Suffrage,* the desire for suffrage was inextricably linked to sexual desire.

8. See West's essay "A Reed of Steel" in Marcus, *The Young Rebecca* (243–62) in which she expresses her admiration for Mrs. Pankhurst.

9. To her, the suffragettes represent a revered but outdated mode of feminism, articulated in the familiar rhetoric of liberation, but no longer offering viable direction. Just twelve years younger than Christabel Pankhurst, West repudiates the arguments of Pankhurst and earlier feminists (e.g., Sarah Grand and Frances Swiney) who saw themselves as sexual victims of a system that sanctioned male immorality at women's expense. Political power, they argued, would provide the female body with access to the body politic, the only physical gratification required. Conversely, and sounding disturbingly like a prototype of Camille Paglia, West insists that women cast off this martyr role that had defined Victorian women's sexuality and transform sexuality into empowerment by refusing the conventions of morality that had typically kept them in the control of patriarchy.

10. The passage describing Ellen's departure from Edinburgh after her mother's death also recalls the exit of Adam and Eve from the Garden: "Through this grim landscape they stepped forward, silent and hand in hand, grieving because she [Ellen's mother] had lived without glory, she who was so much loved by them, whose life was going to be so glorious" (197). This moment ends Ellen's life of innocence, and the second part of the book begins her experience.

11. See also Luce Irigaray 67.

12. In Gilbert and Gubar's terms, this sense that male "heirs" had been displaced by "hers" was characteristic of post–World War I attitudes (280).

13. See Scott (179) for an elaboration of this image.

14. See Showalter, *A Literature of Their Own,* and Marcus, "A Wilderness of One's Own."

Works Cited

Benjamin, Jessica. *The Bonds of Love: Psychoanalysis, Feminism, and the Problem of Domination.* New York: Pantheon, 1988.

Butler, Judith. *Gender Trouble: Feminism and the Subversion of Identity.* New York: Routledge, 1990.

Gilbert, Sandra M., and Susan Gubar. *No Man's Land: The Place of the Woman Writer in the Twentieth Century.* Vol. 2, *Sexchanges.* New Haven: Yale UP, 1989.

Glendenning, Victoria. *Rebecca West: A Life.* London: Weidenfeld, 1987.

Irigaray, Luce. "And the One Doesn't Stir Without the Other." Trans. Helene Vivienne Wenzel. *Signs* 7.1 (1981): 60–67.

Kent, Susan Kingsley. *Making Peace: The Reconstruction of Gender in Interwar Britain.* Princeton: Princeton UP, 1993.

———. *Sex and Suffrage in Britain: 1860–1914.* Princeton: Princeton UP, 1987.

Kristeva, Julia. "Stabat Mater." *The Kristeva Reader.* Ed. Toril Moi. New York: Columbia UP, 1986.

Marcus, Jane. Introduction. West, *The Judge.*

———. "A Wilderness of One's Own: Feminist Fantasy Novels of the Twenties: Rebecca West and Sylvia Townsend Warner." *Women Writers and the City.* Ed. Susan Merrill Squier. Knoxville: U of Tennessee P, 1984. 134–60.

———, ed. *The Young Rebecca: Writings of Rebecca West 1911–1917.* New York: Viking, 1982.

Ray, Gordon. *H. G. Wells and Rebecca West.* New Haven: Yale UP, 1974.

Said, Edward. *Culture and Imperialism.* New York: Vintage, 1994.

Scott, Bonnie Kime. "Refiguring the Binary, Breaking the Cycle: Rebecca West as Feminist Modernist." *Twentieth Century Literature: A Scholarly and Critical Journal* 37.2 (1991): 169–91.

Showalter, Elaine. *A Literature of Their Own.* Princeton: Princeton UP, 1977.

West, Rebecca. *The Judge.* 1922. London: Virago, 1980.

Wolfe, Peter. *Rebecca West: Artist and Thinker.* Carbondale: Southern Illinois UP, 1971.

Woolf, Virginia. *The Letters of Virginia Woolf, Vol. II.* Ed. Nigel Nicolson and Joanne Trautman. New York: Harcourt, 1976.

———. *Night and Day.* 1920. New York: Harcourt, 1937.

Virginia Woolf as Modernist Foremother in Maureen Duffy's Play *A Nightingale in Bloomsbury Square*

Christine W. Sizemore

Marianne DeKoven argues that modernism's characteristic traits of "self-cancellation, unresolved contradiction [and] unsynthesized dialectic" (22) are a result of an early-twentieth-century ambivalence about the "possibility of radical social change [that] . . . was differently inflected for male and female modernists. Male modernists generally feared the loss of hegemony . . . while female modernists feared punishment for desiring that change" (4). Although she acknowledges that Virginia Woolf was an "exemplary exception" to many male modernists' repudiation of "revolutionary social change" (188), DeKoven still sees in Rachel Vinrace's death in *The Voyage Out and* in Rhoda's suicide in *The Waves* the female modernist's fear of punishment for desiring social change. If, as Woolf says of women writers in *A Room of One's Own*, "we think back through our mothers if we are women" (76), contemporary women writers must come to terms with this fear of punishment in their modernist literary foremothers.

Sandra Gilbert and Susan Gubar have described in detail in their "affiliation complex," the ambivalence with which modernist women writers faced their own empowering but potentially engulfing literary foremothers.[1] The anxiety modernist women writers experienced, however, was mitigated because "the inexorable logic [of] . . . the literary matrilineage ha[d] . . . been repeatedly erased, obscured, or fragmented." Modernist women writers could therefore "adopt" the literary foremother they found most "empowering" (Gilbert and Gubar 199–200). The situation for contemporary women writers is different. They cannot just adopt but must first come to terms with Virginia Woolf, "the first canonized twentieth-century woman writer" (Marcus, "Pathographies" 807).[2] The anxiety about Woolf as literary foremother is therefore greater than any modernist woman experienced about any previous influential woman writer.

A particularly vivid example of this anxiety about Woolf as a literary foremother occurs in a play by contemporary British lesbian writer, Maureen Duffy, who was born in 1933 to a working-class, single mother in East London and has published fourteen novels as well as several volumes of poetry. Duffy's play about Virginia Woolf's last hours, "A Nightingale in Bloomsbury Square," was written in 1972 and first produced in Hampstead in September 1973. In this play Duffy examines her own fears about Woolf's ability to engulf her as a writer, her concerns about Woolf's class, and her disappointments that Woolf was not more radical about social change, particularly in defense of lesbianism. As a lesbian Duffy explores the role of Woolf as literary foremother without letting that investigation turn into the reinforcement of the "binary, heterosexist framework" that Judith Butler fears psychoanalytic theories of "maternal identification" can promote (66). Duffy clearly engages psychoanalytic thought when she structures much of the play as a dialogue between Woolf and Freud. Since the play is set in the last hours of Woolf's life, it evokes DeKoven's theory about modernist women writers' fear of punishment, which is reenacted by the suicide from which even Woolf's lover, Vita Sackville-West, cannot dissuade her. The play reveals the issues behind Duffy's ambivalence about Woolf not only in its genre and structure but particularly in its language and imagery. Duffy often uses Woolf's own words as the basis of the play's language and imagery, but Duffy revises them to make issues of the body and sexuality more explicit than Woolf was able to do. Woolf admits in "Professions for Women" that she was unable to tell "the truth about my own experiences as a body" (153). Duffy revises Woolf to create a literary foremother who can do so.

Other contemporary British writers, such as Doris Lessing and Margaret Drabble,[3] were also ambivalent about Woolf as their canonized literary foremother, but their comments come in interviews and essays rather than literary pieces. American writers, such as May Sarton and Alice Walker, also felt Woolf's presence as literary foremother strongly, but both are less intense than Duffy. Sarton's admiration for Woolf is revealed in her 1953 elegy "Letter from Chicago."[4] Walker acknowledges Woolf's influence in *In Search of our Mother's Gardens,* but stresses how much harder it was for African American women to write than for "Shakespeare's sister." For Sarton and Walker, as Americans, the influence of Woolf as the canonized literary foremother is more diluted than it is for contemporary British women writers whose closeness to Woolf and ambivalence about her is dramatized in Maureen Duffy's play.

As a novelist, Maureen Duffy was brought early in her career to a confrontation with Woolf. By the time Duffy had written her fourth novel, *Paradox Players* in 1968, critics were already comparing her to Woolf, saying that Duffy's novels were like Woolf's in that both writers "have the knack of tuning the physical world precisely to the pitch of the characters' emotions" ("Cold and Gray" 104). Since in many ways

Duffy's novels exhibit the same "unresolved contradiction and unsynthesized dialectic" that DeKoven finds typical of modernist writing (22), Duffy had to find her precise distance from a literary foremother to whom she was perhaps becoming too close. Furthermore, as a working-class and lesbian[5] writer, Duffy felt ambivalence about Woolf's class and about Woolf's sexual orientation as it had been presented in the early 1970s.

Duffy's portrait of Woolf was influenced not only by her sense of rivalry with Woolf and her fear of being engulfed by her but also by the sources that were available to Duffy in 1972. In 1972 one of the most readily available sources about Woolf was Quentin Bell's biography, which was published the year Duffy was writing her play. Duffy clearly worked very closely with the Bell biography, using passages from it. She also went occasionally to specific passages in the then unpublished diaries and letters to expand on passages that Bell had quoted,[6] but her characterization of "Virginia" in the play is in part a result of her resistance to and reaction against Bell's portrait of Woolf as a frigid, upper-class woman.

As a lesbian writer, Duffy feels strongly about mother figures, as she demonstrated in her first novel, the autobiographical *That's How It Was* (1962). In her 1982 preface to that work Duffy says, "[T]he core of my first book, the relationship to the mother . . . I have mined repeatedly in later work" (xi). Catherine Stimpson also emphasizes the role of the mother in lesbian writing: a "mother waits at the heart of the labyrinth of some lesbian texts. . . . Finding her in herself and through a surrogate, the lesbian reenacts a daughter's desire for the woman to whom she was so linked, from whom she was then so severed" (256).[7] Jane Marcus argues that this same search for the mother figure is in Woolf's own writings: "Woolf, as the writing daughter, is also playing the role of lover and suitor to the lost mother" (*Patriarchy* 8). In her play Duffy portrays Woolf as the writing daughter working out feelings about both her parents. Vita Sackville-West, the third character in the play, represents Woolf's lesbian lover,[8] but the play focuses more on Woolf's anxieties about her parents and her writings than on her lesbian desires. Duffy herself is both drawn to Woolf and seems to resist aspects of Woolf that make Woolf seem too distant and upper class. Duffy mitigates these anxieties by revisioning and coarsening Woolf's imagery, thereby re-creating Woolf as an earthier literary foremother.

Duffy examines these issues and her relationship to Woolf not in a novel but in a drama. Although now Duffy is better known as a novelist, in the late sixties and early seventies she had written as many plays as novels.[9] Drama was also a more neutral genre in which to work out her complex feelings toward Woolf, since Woolf did not usually write dramas, and Duffy would be less likely to be compared to her in a different genre. Furthermore, drama, particularly drama in which the author uses the actual words and images of the literary foremother as Duffy does, is like D. W. Winnicott's "transitional" or "play" space, where a child can play independently in the knowledge that his or her mother is not far away. In this "transitional" space the child is in the mother's presence but is "alone," differentiated from the mother and not focused on her. In this space the child can create. The mother's presence gives the child a sense of protection and confidence, and the space allows the freedom for creation. The dramatization of the literary foremother allows the contemporary writer to come close to the literary foremother and establish a connection with her and yet remain in control.

Although the "play space" described so far sounds benign, Winnicott's concept actually includes room for negative feelings as well. The child needs room to express angry and destructive feelings (Winnicott 91) in order to achieve distance and separation from the mother. Psychoanalyst Jessica Benjamin explains that Winnicott's concept of "destruction" is part of the process of differentiation and "is best understood as a refusal . . . the mental experience of 'You do not exist for me,' whose favorable outcome is pleasure in the other's survival" (38). "Play space" can thus contain a variety of feelings both positive and negative. Likewise drama as play space offers the opportunity for the woman writer to explore her fear of and anxiety about the modernist literary foremother as well as an exuberant connection to the literary tradition set up by the foremother.[10] Precisely because drama was not the genre of the nineteenth-century or the modernist literary foremothers, it is a safe space in which the contemporary woman writer can create her own relationship with the literary foremother. The dramatist can portray the negative sides of the literary foremother, that is, try to destroy her, but the dramatist can also revise the literary foremother within the play space and allow her to survive as a powerful literary figure. It is the variety of feelings toward the literary foremother that gives power and intensity to the drama.[11]

Duffy's interest in psychoanalytic thought and on understanding Woolf as a literary foremother is demonstrated by Duffy's use of Freud as the chief antagonist for "Virginia," as Woolf is called in the play. Freud has a complex ambivalent role in the play in that he both stands for the male patriarchy and for Woolf's father Leslie Stephen, and yet also for that Freudian system which just might treat the modernist woman writer's fear of punishment and Woolf's own drive toward suicide. Freud is the one with whom Virginia works out several issues centered around creativity, madness, war, sexuality, and the relationship to and use of family members.

Woolf herself had an ambivalent relationship to Freud because although the Hogarth Press translated and published his works and her brother Adrian even became an analyst, she specifically refrained from reading his work until after his death. When she does start reading him in 1939, she notes in her diary that she is "gulping up Freud" (5:249), but her earlier comments on Freud, particularly her review "Freudian Fiction" and a letter to Mary McCarthy (*Letters* 3:134–35) were extremely negative (Kushen 40). Elizabeth Abel suggests that part of Woolf's anxiety about Freud was that Leonard Woolf in particular and English psychoanalytic groups in general focused on Freud's texts as literature (15–16). Duffy portrays this sense of Woolf's artistic rivalry with Freud clearly in the play. She implies that Woolf's refusal to read Freud earlier or to use his methods of treatment might stem from a fear that psychoanalysis would destroy the source of her creativity. Duffy's source for the idea is Alix Strachey's 1972 "recollection" of Virginia Woolf: "Virginia's imagination . . . was so interwoven with her fantasies . . . that if you stopped the madness you might have stopped the creativeness too. It seemed to me quite a reasonable judgment for Leonard to have made then [not to consult a psychoanalyst for Virginia]. . . . It may be preferable to be mad and be creative than to be treated by analysis and become ordinary" (Noble 117). Woolf herself comments on the literary value of madness in a June 22, 1930 letter to Ethel Smyth: "As an experience, madness is terrific, I can assure you, and not to be sniffed at; and in its lava I still find most of the things I write about. It shoots out of one everything shaped, final, not in mere driblets, as sanity does" (4:180).

In the play Duffy also suggests an Oedipal confrontation between Freud, in his father role, and Virginia, when Freud in the play says to Virginia, "[Y]ou have called to your father-confessor, myself, and your mother-lover [Vita] to lay those two old ghosts [of Woolf's parents]" (181). As a male "parent," Freud can hold off the anger of the mother figure whom Woolf has to kill because she is an "angel of the house." For the lesbian, however, who desires the mother, not the father, he becomes a rival, not a protector, and a threatening critic of lesbian orientation.

Although when first performed, "A Nightingale in Bloomsbury Square" was criticized for not having more dramatic structure,[12] a close reading of the play reveals that the play is a series of debates between Freud and Virginia and then between Vita and Virginia. These debates turn upon the symbol of a narcissus, the flower that Freud actually gave Woolf the one time she met him just before his death in 1939 of throat cancer (Bell 2:209; Woolf, *Diary* 5:202). Three times during the play Virginia asks Freud why he gave her a narcissus. Finally, she answers her own question.

The narcissus, although taken from a real life episode, has many psychoanalytic implications in its echoes of "narcissism." Both Freud and Heinz Kohut, a psychoanalyst and theorist about narcissism, link narcissism with homosexuality,[13] but in the play Duffy does not use the narcissus to discuss lesbian themes. Rather, the narcissus stands for the writer's need to be alone, a solitude that Duffy sees as sometimes painful but basically healthy. Duffy's views reflect Layton and Shapiro's attitude that although "many recent psychoanalytic theories also assert a strong link between creativity and narcissistic vulnerability . . . [the] prevalent view today holds creativity as a variation of a healthy manifestation of narcissism" (23).

Before the first mention of the narcissus, there is an introductory dialogue between Virginia and Freud in order for Virginia to establish herself as a fellow artist, not a potential patient. Even though Freud in the play is a very old man, described physically in the stage directions in Woolf's own words as a "screwed up shrunk very old man" (Duffy 170; Woolf, *Diary* 5:202), the dangers he poses as a doctor and psychoanalyst are real. The play opens just as Virginia is writing her suicide note. In the introductory exchanges with Freud, Virginia defends herself against charges of madness. Virginia criticizes doctors and the rest cure, and defiantly says to Freud,

"I'm not mad. I never was, have been and now I never will be" (170). Freud quotes from his 1898 paper "Sexuality in the Aetiology of the Neuroses" that the Woolfs published in 1924 in which he also criticizes the rest cure, but Virginia is not mollified. She quotes her 1924 description of the dominating Dr. Bradshaw from *Mrs. Dalloway*. These quotes establish the two characters as rival writers. Using the imagery of the play's title, Freud says, "So now we have quoted against each other like two nightingales singing out our territory in the darkened wood" (171). Virginia stands up to him: "You mustn't come into my thicket . . . as long as I keep on singing you can't cross my borders" (171). Using a vivid image of the destruction of a baby bird by the cutting open of an egg and the stirring up the yolk, Virginia says that Freud's methods of psychoanalysis would destroy her creativity. As a rival writer rather than patient, however, Virginia feels she can face him. Virginia says that Freud "seduced" Leonard into reviewing his books and took James Strachey and Adrian Stephen for his disciples, but she can resist him.

After Virginia establishes herself as a fellow writer, she asks Freud for the first time why he gave her a narcissus. Then some of the major themes of the play are introduced: the war, Leonard's and her plan for suicide if Hitler invades, her sorrow at her childlessness, and her writing. The first section of the play between the first question about the narcissus and its repetition focuses primarily on Woolf's marriage to Leonard and her lack of children. After Virginia asks Freud for the second time why he gave her the flower, the discussion of childlessness and writing becomes bolder; then the major theme of the second section is introduced: Virginia's relationships with her parents. To link the issues of writing, literary influence, and childbirth Duffy uses a phrase from *A Room of One's Own:* "masterpieces are not single and solitary births" (Woolf, *Room* 65). Duffy brings out both Woolf's pain about her childlessness and the difficulty of writing by amplifying Woolf's image of the Elizabethan tombstones with their kneeling children from *A Room of One's Own:* "A child doesn't have to be remade over and over as every book must be made. Every book is a birth and a death at once until at your own death they might sculpt them on your tomb in rows like the thirteen unlucky, died in infancy and at birth, kneeling children on Elizabethan monuments" (Duffy 177–78; *Room* 58). In the play Freud sympathizes, suggesting that his advice to Woolf on having children might have been different.[14]

One of the most important themes that is developed in the second section of the play involves Virginia's attitudes toward her parents. In order to present this issue, Duffy introduces the third character, Vita Sackville-West. In a neat transition from the themes of childbirth and writing, Virginia says to Freud that one of her books was not a difficult birth, *Orlando,* which began "as a joke" (Woolf, *Diary* 3:177) and was written in about six months. On cue, Vita, who was the model for Orlando, enters "in male evening dress like Dietrich in *Morocco*" (stage direction, 179). With Vita's presence, Virginia is able to analyze why she "killed" both parents. Echoing language from both *A Room of One's Own* and "Professions for Women," Virginia

explains that her mother is the "Angel of the House" whom she had to kill: "I mur-
dered the angel in the house. . . . I have never been mad, only guilty but no one
will, would believe me. . . . I killed her in order to write" (183–84). Virginia also
says that she "had become almost a son" (183) for her father, but like the "Manx cat,"[15]
she "couldn't create because [she] . . . had no tail" (Duffy 193; Woolf, *Room*, 11–
13). Virginia is the "son" who learned from the father about writing but who also
must kill "his" father-rival in order to write. Virginia sums up her relationship to
her parents toward the end of the play when she says, "Inside I was glad he was dead.
I killed them both you see. I wanted them dead" (192).

After Virginia briefly discusses several other themes with Vita, Virginia's fear of
Vita's "sapphic friends," her rivalry with Katherine Mansfield, and her fear of the
body, she asks the question about the narcissus for the third time. In this third section between the final question about the flower and Virginia's exit, Virginia answers
her own question. After restating the reasons why she needed to kill her parents,
Virginia suddenly turns to Freud and says, "I chose a room by myself. Is that the
meaning of your narcissus?" (191). Developing the theme of the solitary writer and
the sacrifices a writer must make, Virginia says, "I drive Leonard so far that in the
end he wishes me dead" (194), and to Vita she declares, "You left me, oh with ardent protestations but you left, to follow your husband to Persia like any harem wife.
. . . I am alone. I have always been alone." She says, "Your narcissus was just" (194).
Virginia had to reject her parents, Vita's love, and finally Freud's psychoanalysis in
order to write: "I would have been a case to you if I had gone to you for help. . . .
You would have made me an empty mould into which someone would have poured
the shape he wanted to turn out a decent pudding. Instead I have preferred to live
with the knowledge that I have killed both my parents in order to feed my own ego"
(196). Virginia accepts her guilt and her suffering, but not madness. At one point
early in the play, Virginia says to Freud, "I was only mad in patches" (177). Here
Duffy does acknowledge Woolf's episodes of depression and hearing voices, but
overall Duffy emphasizes Woolf's suffering not insanity. Duffy establishes the woman
writer's "room" of her own, separate from that of mother or father or husband or
even female lover. Independence for Virginia is costly; it involves pain and guilt and
loneliness, but it is the source of the woman writer's art, both Woolf's and Duffy's
own.

In a final monologue at the end of the play, Duffy allows Freud to explain his
influence on Woolf (and perhaps herself). Freud says, "[T]his lady rejected me but
she could not have written as she did without me" (202). Nonetheless, for Duffy,
the artist is still more important; Freud recognizes that "what the analyst does for
the individual the artist may do for society" (203). Duffy, like Woolf, could not have
written without Freud. She too uses Freudian imagery and Oedipal structures to
portray Virginia and her relationship to her parents, but by having the artist reform
society and the psychoanalyst only reform the individual, Duffy acknowledges that
Woolf is a greater influence than Freud. In these final lines Duffy manages to accept

Woolf as a literary foremother and distance herself from Woolf's fear of punishment. Virginia still walks out to commit suicide, but, having examined Woolf's pain, the contemporary writer can absorb Woolf's influence and sympathize with Woolf's suicide without feeling that a contemporary author must feel the same guilt that Woolf did.

Although Duffy accepted Woolf as a powerful literary foremother in her sympathetic characterization of Woolf in this play as someone who suffered some of the same pangs of creativity, loneliness, and childlessness that contemporary women writers also have suffered, she still had to work through her negative reaction to the issue of class in connection with Virginia Woolf. A contemporary working-class critic had the same reaction. Mary Childers notes that "although Woolf wrote persuasively about being an outsider, in relation to working-class women she was often on the outside looking down. There is ample room for hierarchy even on the margins" (87). Duffy uses several strategies in the play to try to come to terms with Woolf's class status. First Duffy brings in a real working-class voice. Then she re-visions Woolf in some of her analogies as more closely allied to the lower classes. Finally Duffy revises Woolf's own images.

Duffy's first task is to find a voice of the working-class woman connected with Woolf. Although Jane Marcus asserts that "a salient sub-text in every Virginia Woolf novel is the voice of working class women, the heroic charwomen" (*Patriarchy* 138), Duffy makes no use of any of these figures from Woolf's novels. Alex Zwerdling says that although Woolf taught working-class men and women and sympathized with many of Leonard's socialist views, there are few members of the "lower orders" in her novels and when "they do appear, they are often given a generic identity, their individual characteristics expunged" (96). Duffy instead takes a short passage from a real working-class woman, Woolf's own maid, Louie Mayer, and weaves it into the play to create the voice of a working-class woman. Duffy's character, Virginia, says toward the end of the play that Leonard's "tired; he's had enough. . . . I know his symptoms as well as he knows mine. Last time he left the veronal unlocked. . . . This time he's gone into the garden to be among growing things to plant. Soon he'll be planting me. When he asked Louie to give me a duster, I knew it had gone too far" (199). The reference to the unlocked veronal came from the Bell biography (2:16), but the reference to the duster comes from Louie Mayer's contribution to the 1972 volume *Recollections of Virginia Woolf*: "One morning, when I was tidying Mr Woolf's study, they both came into the room and Mr Woolf said, 'Louie, will you give Mrs Woolf a duster so that she can help you clean the room?' . . . [I]t seemed to be one of her bad days again, and he must have suggested that she might like to do something, perhaps help with the housework. I gave her a duster, but it seemed very strange. I had never known her want to do any housework with me before." Mayer goes on to recount that later that morning Woolf commits suicide (Noble 160). In Louie Mayer Duffy has found her own historical "charwoman" as a source.

In a second effort to revision Woolf's class, Duffy also has Virginia in the play contrast herself with Vita, making Vita the aristocrat and Virginia the worker: "The blood of the Sackvilles runs in your veins while in mine there runs printer's ink. I've slaved over my words like that skivvy in the garden over her washtub and pegs" (188). Although Woolf was sensitive about Vita's aristocratic heritage, this image is clearly not her own. In her introduction to Margaret Llewelyn Davies's book of writings by working-class members of the Women's Co-Operative Guild, Woolf writes: "after all the imagination is largely the child of the flesh. One could not be Mrs. Giles of Durham because one's body had never stood at the wash-tub" (xxi).[16] Woolf can not imagine a working-class woman like Mrs. Giles because Woolf herself had never stood at a washtub. Duffy, however, can, and "skivvy" is her word, not Woolf's.

Duffy's third reaction to Woolf's class in the play contains both Duffy's fear of Woolf as a potentially devouring and engulfing mother and a re-creation of Woolf into a stronger, earthier, less ladylike foremother. Duffy revises Woolf's own language from her diaries and essays, extending her imagery and often toughening and coarsening her language. Duffy particularly focuses on Woolf's imagery, first of appetite, teeth and food, and then of birds. For instance, a passage where Duffy clearly went to Woolf's diary in manuscript shows an intentional development of Woolf's images. In a diary passage from 1924, Woolf mentions that she and the assistant at Hogarth Press, have been "doing up Freud. . . . Thus one gets to know people, sucks the marrow out" (2:232). Abel refers to this passage as a "strikingly uncharacteristic figure of predation" and suggests that it reflects Woolf's hostility to Freud (15), but Duffy develops the phrase into an even more active and cannibalistic image when she has Virginia say, "I liked to go out and crack people's bones at parties, to taste the pith of them, gulp and cannibalize an evening of all of its oddity and excitement and salt every experience away until I need to take it out and unfurl it" (Duffy 176). Here is the dangerous, engulfing literary foremother.

A similar image pattern that reveals the violence of the potential engulfment links teeth with the bombing of London. The original association is Woolf's. In her 10 September 1940 entry, Woolf writes that she stood "by Jane Harrison's house. The house was still smouldering. . . . Scraps of cloth hanging to the bare walls at the side still standing. A looking glass I think swinging. Like a tooth knocked out—a clean cut" (*A Writer's Diary* 333; *Diary* 5:316). Duffy adds blood and intensifies the violence in her development of the image. In the play Virginia says, "London is maimed and gutted as if a butcher had turned dentist and torn the houses out of their sockets leaving bleeding holes" (181).

Duffy's Virginia seems voracious in her appetite for material for her novels, and imagery of food is intertwined with imagery of appetite and teeth. Patricia Moran argues that in the diaries and letters food imagery is used to portray "women who eat as sexually complicit with the fathers and male oppressors" (90). In the play Freud reminds Virginia that her father responded to her reading of books by saying, "'Gracious child how you gobble'" (Duffy 183). Later in the play Virginia says,

"I sucked . . . [Thoby, her brother's] body to a weightless ghost to feed my vision of him" (184). This imagery fits the image of the woman writer as devouring mother. Duffy builds a related image from Bell's description of one of Woolf's episodes of mental illness in 1913 in which he says Woolf "became convinced that her body was in some way monstrous. . . . [The] sordid belly demanding food" (Bell 2:15). Duffy combines this with Woolf's imagery in a letter thanking Vita for a pound of butter. Woolf writes: "[W]e discovered the butter in the envelope box. . . . I broke off a lump and ate it pure" (Bell 2:223). In the play Virginia says, "Oh the body Vita! . . . [T]he gorging demanding body. Now perversely when it's wrong to do so I want to glut my belly. That pound of butter you sent, I hacked a piece off and ate it raw" (185). The slight shift of diction from "broke off" to "hacked off" and from "pure" to "raw" reinforces the imagery of the cannibal and the butcher. In Woolf's letter to Vita and in her diary comment on 26 February 1941, that "[f]ood becomes an obsession" (5:357), the context seems more to be the rationing during the war and the difficulty of getting food, but Moran sees the same potentially dangerous aspects of food in Woolf's writing that Duffy does. Moran says that "because writing is associated with the greedy and demanding egotism of the male writer and father, Leslie Stephen, writing, like eating, becomes a murderous act directed against the mother. . . . The act of (woman) writing becomes the unacceptable act of (re)destroying the maternal body" (95). Duffy brings out the murderous potential of the food imagery, but for her the danger is not the woman writer who destroys the maternal body but rather the ravenous literary foremother who might well eat any literary children.

Duffy develops a similar motif of bird imagery, based on Bell and on Woolf's diaries, around the fear of male violence. Savage male beaks are ready to peck Virginia. Vanessa and Virginia become Procne and Philomela: "she the swallow and I the nightingale, both ravished by our brother, the rubber duck that spoiled our bath time" (199). The swallow and the nightingale are Woolf's images; Duffy adds a sinister rubber duck to allude to Virginia and Vanessa's abuse by their half-brother, George Duckworth.

Duffy not only revises Woolf's words to make Virginia to be much earthier and more direct in her language and style, but Duffy also makes her much more outspoken on issues of the body. Duffy makes Virginia very explicit in the linking of male sexuality and aggression and in her reaction of disgust to heterosexual sex. Duffy also highlights Virginia's lesbian feelings. At first Duffy ties Woolf's reticence on sexual matters to class when she has Virginia castigate herself for being "too lady-like" to write of women's sexuality as Joyce does (190). The extreme coarseness of Duffy's description of heterosexual sex, however, implies that Duffy is also working on another issue. She re-visions Woolf as a more outspoken lesbian by carefully interweaving Woolf's insights about the link between male sexuality and aggression to a strong revulsion for heterosexual sex. In "Thoughts on Peace in an Air Raid" Woolf says that men are driven by "ancient instincts, instincts fostered and cherished by education and tradition[,] . . . their fighting instinct, their subconscious Hitlerism" (156). In the play Virginia connects copulation and war: "It's about copulation isn't it. . . . [T]here they all are coupling in the grass with their mouths leached molten together and in the morning, now that war's come and all the pretences are shot to pieces, the bushes are blooming with underwear and silk stockings, and condoms like flat maggot white balloons after a party I was never invited to are littered on the grass under the trees or belly in the shallows, bluntnosed dead trout. Violence and lust. Bombs and buggery. Male aggression, the desire to possess and dominate" (177). Although Woolf mentions "buggery" in *Moments of Being* (194), the imagery of the used condoms is clearly Duffy's. Virginia is not the Woolf who was too ladylike to write of sex like Joyce, but an angry and different literary foremother who expresses Duffy's rage about the war and her own linking of male sexuality and war.

Toward the end of the play Virginia uses the same imagery linking heterosexual sex and death: "Hitlerism is simply male aggression made flesh. . . . All women can do is lie at home in their beds waiting for the pounce of a bomb, obscene sperm from the belly of an aircraft, that will generate death in their bodies. . . . [D]eath . . . my only faithful lover who has stalked me so long with his embrace of bone, the rape of the maggot burrowing between my thighs as once the singed white moths crept up my skirt to die in the hollow of my knee" (197–98). Although Duffy refers to Woolf's ideas about Hitlerism here and to Woolf's use of the moth in her essay on "The Death of the Moth," the imagery in the above passage takes its intensity and even its coarseness from Duffy's own war time experiences and perhaps some of the imagery of death and sexuality from John Donne, whose poetry Duffy is especially fond of. In these passages Duffy recreates a new Woolf who seems to speak with the "sinewy vigour and flexibility of the [East] London demotic" Duffy herself was "brought up on" ("Afterword," *The Microcosm* 290).

Duffy brings out Woolf's lesbianism more strongly in the play than Bell's biography or *A Writer's Diary*. Woolf's relationship with Vita is portrayed nostalgically as a beautiful but brief interlude by almost direct quotes from Woolf's diary and letters. Using a diary passage (3:52) quoted in full by Bell (2:117–18), Duffy has Vita say, "You wrote of me glowing in the grocer's at Sevenoaks on my pink legs like beach trees, wearing pearls like peacock's eggs" (190). Virginia also acknowledges lesbian desire for Madge Vaughan: "once, years ago, kissing Madge Vaughan on the terrace I felt it." Bell uses the word "pure" three times to describe this incident (1:61), but Duffy ignores him in this instance. To describe Virginia's feelings about Vita, Duffy turns to a letter Bell quotes to Vanessa (2:118): "and again one summer when you [Vita] came to stay with me and I boasted to Vanessa that the garden was full of lust and bees" (Duffy 195–96).

A reference to Katherine Mansfield shows greater complexity in Duffy's manipulation of Woolf's words to bring out lesbian themes. Duffy conflates three different references to Katherine Mansfield to create both jealousy and a more sexual allure between

Mansfield and Woolf. In a diary entry from 16 January 1923, Woolf recalls Mansfield after her death and mentions kisses that seem friendly rather than passionate: she "had her look of a Japanese doll. . . . Hers were beautiful eyes—rather doglike, brown . . . with a steady slow rather faithful and sad expression. . . . Her lips thin and hard. . . . She was inscrutable. Did she care for me? Sometimes she would say so—would kiss me— would look at me as if (is this sentiment?) her eyes would like always to be faithful" (2:226). Duffy combines this with much more critical passages. Quentin Bell describes John Middleton Murry, Mansfield's husband, as "president and oracle of the Underworld" (2:50). Earlier Bell describes Katherine Mansfield: she "dressed like a tart and behaved like a bitch" (2:37), and he quotes a 1917 diary entry in which Woolf says K. M. "stinks like a—well, civet cat that had taken to street walking" (2:45). A 1931 letter from Woolf to Vita repeats the idea: Katherine "could permeate one with her quality; and if one felt this cheap scent in it, it reeked in ones nostrils" (*Letters* 4:366). Duffy uses all these sources when Virginia says to Vita that Katherine "belonged to both underworlds, she and Murry, the literary demi-monde and the sexual. When she kissed me I caught the reek of civet like a cheap tart, and her lips were thin. She had the face of a Japanese schoolgirl, vulgar and inscrutable, but her eyes wanted to be faithful. Brown eyes always do" (185). Most of the words in this passage are Woolf's, but the intensity of the words reveals desire for Katherine, whereas Woolf's own words seem to emphasize criticism of Mansfield's class and dress.

"Nightingale in Bloomsbury Square" is intensely poetic in its strands of interwoven imagery and fascinating in its analysis of a writer's use of Woolf's life for literary material. It is a portrait of Woolf that some will dislike, and yet it shows a contemporary woman writer's intense engagement with Woolf's work. Duffy's play is powerful because it deals directly with the ambivalence that many contemporary women writers feel about Woolf as literary foremother. By using not only Freud himself but Freudian ideas, Duffy confronts the potentially engulfing mother figure and finds a space in which to relate to her. In her portrait of Woolf, Duffy expresses her own anger at Woolf for Woolf's limitations in expressing anger and desire. Duffy acknowledges Woolf's own guilt and "fear of punishment" for that which Woolf did express, but Duffy distances herself from that guilt and fear. Duffy celebrates what Woolf did achieve and sympathizes with her pain. Finally she recreates a new version of Woolf, one able to express herself in the "sinewy vigour . . . of the London demotic" ("Afterword" *The Microcosm* 290) that Duffy admires. In this revisioning of Woolf, Duffy is able to come to terms with Woolf's class status and Woolf's seeming reticence about sexuality that many contemporary women writers have complained about.[17]

Because Duffy works out her feelings about Woolf as literary foremother in the safe space of drama, she is then able to use modernist techniques in her ensuing novels. After Woolf, a number of female writers turned back to realism and eschewed the techniques of modernism as either too male or too separated from politics and issues of social change that women wanted to confront.[18] Duffy, however, is able to use Woolf's modernist techniques in her ensuing novels without feeling threatened by her influence. Once she has confronted Woolf in drama, Duffy appropriates the techniques of female modernism for her own use and adapts them to convey contemporary working-class and lesbian voices as well as the voice of the solitary artist.

Notes

1. I began my study of this play in a 1991 National Endowment for the Humanities seminar on feminism and modernism led by Susan Gubar. A small portion of this article focusing on narrative matrilineage was published in an earlier version as "A Portrait of Virginia Woolf in Maureen Duffy's Play, 'A Nightingale in Bloomsbury Square,'" *Virginia Woolf: Themes and Variations,* ed. Vara Neverow-Turk and Mark Hussey (New York: Pace UP, 1993), 205–15.

2. In her postmodernist view of Woolf, Caughie rejects the concept of "female literary experience" and Woolf as "the 'absent mother' of women writers" (4), but contemporary authors' many references to Woolf illustrate that they see themselves as indebted to her.

3. See my book *A Female Vision of the City* (5–7) and my article on Woolf and Lessing, "The 'Outsider-Within'" (60–62).

4. See Gilbert and Gubar's discussion of Woolf's influence on Sarton, 213–14.

5. In a 1973 interview Duffy says: "I only discovered my homosexuality because I fell in love with somebody, so I was never alone. . . . I never had any feeling of guilt. . . . It never seemed to me in the least unnatural or immoral or even, once I'd made the intellectual discovery, particularly unusual" (Barber 7–8).

6. *A Writer's Diary* was available in 1972, but the full diaries were not published until 1977. Although the original diaries had gone to the Berg collection in New York in 1970 (Anne O. Bell, "Editor's Preface," *The Diary of Virginia Woolf* 1:vii), photocopies existed at the University of Sussex which Duffy must have consulted.

7. Freud makes this link in his 1920 essay "The Psychogenesis of a Case of Homosexuality in a Woman" in which he says the "analysis revealed beyond all shadow of a doubt that the beloved lady was a substitute for—the mother" (*Sexuality and the Psychology of Love* 142–43.) Stimpson cautions that "lesbianism is far more than a matter of mother/daughter affairs, but the new texts suggest that one of its satisfactions is a return . . . to primal loves, when female/female . . . relationships structured the world (257).

8. Although Duffy created her portrayal of Vita based on Woolf's and Vita's letters, there has been a lot of recent scholarship on their relationship. See DeSalvo; Knopp; Meese, "When Virginia Looked at Vita"; and Marcus, *Patriarchy.*

9. Duffy initially preferred drama and poetry until she read Woolf and Joyce: "From eleven until just pre-university when I discovered Woolf and the two Joyces, James and Cary, my passion for literature was largely expressed through plays and poetry" ("Afterword" 290). Duffy had written six plays, of which "Rites" and "Solo" are the best known, and two volumes of poetry by the early 1970s.

10. Marianne Hirsch describes a similar pattern of the use of conflicting feelings in her term *oscilla-*

tion, which she describes as the narrative structure used by Woolf and other women writers in novels and essays. For her this oscillation reflects not only "oscillations between maternal and paternal attachments" but also "resistance against this course . . . the flight from womanhood. It applies to "women who bond and identify with women" as well as heterosexual women (102–3).

11. Power and intensity are precisely what are lacking in two other recent plays about Woolf that are uniformly positive about her. Edna O'Brien's "Virginia" (1981) concentrates on Woolf's relationship with her father, Leonard, and Vita Sackville-West, but says little about Woolf as a writer. Dianna MacLeod's *Two Together* (1988) focuses on Virginia and Vanessa as young women in Bloomsbury. These plays ignore any ambivalent feelings the writers might have about Woolf, and the resulting portraits portray Woolf merely as a "good enough [literary fore]mother," to use Winnicott's term, not an empowering writer who hands down a new tradition.

12. Drama critic Frank Marcus calls the play "an interrupted monologue, written with great sympathy and power" (128). Irving Wardle, who reviewed the play for the *Times* of London, felt the play lacked dramatic conflict and action. In the Hampstead production described by Wardle, Woolf was played by Sian Phillips, Freud by Richard Wilson, and Vita by Eleanor Brom. It was produced by Michael Rudman and set with a background of three enlarged book spines.

13. Freud in "On Narcissism" writes that "large amounts of libido of an essentially homosexual kind are drawn into the formation of the narcissistic ego ideal" (559). Kohut writes, "The intimate relationship between idealization and narcissism is attested to by the fact that homosexual libido is always predominantly involved" (246–47). Sackville-West writes Woolf that in *Orlando* Woolf "invented a new form of Narcissism,—I confess,—I am in love with Orlando" (quoted by Meese, "When Virginia Looked at Vita" 111), but Duffy does not explicitly use this letter.

14. Although in Duffy's view Freudianism does not require women artists to give up motherhood, Thomas Caramagno's theory that Woolf was manic-depressive might substantiate Leonard Woolf and Vanessa Bell's concern that having children could worsen Virginia Woolf's mental state since hormonal changes in pregnancy could influence manic-depression. Lithium therapy for manic-depression was not discovered until the 1940s.

15. Marcus discusses the use of the Manx cat to symbolize women. The missing tail is not only a symbol of the missing penis, Marcus points out, but also "a representation of women's missing tales in the men's college setting" (*Patriarchy* 173–74).

16. Elizabeth Meese notes that this essay and *Three Guineas* did earn the respect of the working-class American writer Tillie Olsen because of "Woolf's ability to recognize this unromanticized difference in the lives of working women, as well as her personal courage in speaking out against domination" (*Crossing the Double-Cross* 107).

17. Doris Lessing says, "I find [Woolf] . . . too much of a lady. . . . [Her work is] charming in a way[,] . . . but look what . . . [has been] left out" (Joyner 204–5). Although Margaret Drabble praises Woolf, she also complains: "There is something alienating about her hypersensitive, aesthetic manner. She seems to have insufficient contact with ordinary life—she didn't do enough washing up or something" (Stone 60).

18. DeKoven summarizes the numerous debates about the relationship between modernist aesthetic practices and politics in her first chapter.

Works Cited

Abel, Elizabeth. *Virginia Woolf and the Fictions of Psychoanalysis.* Chicago: U of Chicago P, 1989.

Barber, Dulan. "Maureen Duffy: Talking to Dulan Barber." *Transatlantic Review* 45 (Spring 1973): 5–16.

Bell, Quentin. *Virginia Woolf: A Biography.* 1972. London: Hogarth, 1990.

Benjamin, Jessica. *The Bonds of Love: Psychoanalysis, Feminism and the Problem of Domination.* New York: Pantheon, 1988.

Butler, Judith. *Gender Trouble: Feminism and the Subversion of Identity.* New York: Routledge, 1990.

Caramagno, Thomas C. *The Flight of the Mind: Virginia Woolf's Art and Manic-Depressive Illness.* Berkeley: U of California P, 1992.

Caughie, Pamela L. *Virginia Woolf and Postmodernism: Literature in Quest of Itself.* Urbana: U of Illinois P, 1991.

Childers, Mary M. "Virginia Woof on the Outside Looking Down: Reflections on the Class of Women." *Modern Fiction Studies* 38.1 (Spring 1992): 61–78.

"Cold and Grey." Rev. of *Paradox Players,* by Maureen Duffy. *Time* 13 Sept. 1968: 104.

DeKoven, Marianne. *Rich and Strange: Gender, History, Modernism.* Princeton: Princeton UP, 1991.

DeSalvo, Louise. "Lighting the Cave: The Relationship between Vita Sackville-West and Virginia Woolf." *Signs* 8.2 (1982): 195–214.

Duffy, Maureen. "Afterword." *The Microcosm.* By Duffy. 1966. London: Virago, 1989. N.p.

———. "A Nightingale in Bloomsbury Square." *Factions.* Ed. Giles Gordon and Alex Hamilton. London: Michael Joseph, 1974. 169–204.

———. *That's How It Was.* 1962. New York: Dial, 1984.

Freud, Sigmund. "On Narcissism: An Introduction." *The Freud Reader.* Ed. Peter Gay. New York: Norton, 1989. 545–62.

———. "The Psychogenesis of a Case of Homosexuality in a Woman." Trans. Barbara Low and R. Gabler. *Sexuality and the Psychology of Love.* New York: Collier, 1963.

———. "Sexuality in the Aetiology of the Neuroses (1898)." *Collected Papers.* Vol. 1. Trans. Joan Riviere. London: Hogarth, 1924. New York: Basic Books, 1959.

Gilbert, Sandra M., and Susan Gubar. *No Man's Land: The Place of the Woman Writer in the Twentieth Century.* Vol. 1, *The War of the Words.* New Haven: Yale UP, 1988.

Hirsch, Marianne. *The Mother/Daughter Plot: Narrative, Psycho-analysis, Feminism.* Bloomington: Indiana UP, 1989.

Joyner, Nancy Carol. "The Underside of the Butterfly: Lessing's Debt to Woolf." *Journal of Narrative Technique* 4.3 (1974): 204–11.

Knopp, Sherron E. "'If I Saw You Would You Kiss Me?': Sapphism and Subversiveness of Virginia Woolf's *Orlando.*" *PMLA* 103.1 (1988): 24–34.

Kohut, Heinz. "Forms and Transformations of Narcissism." *Journal of the American Psychoanalytic Association* 14 (1966): 243–72.

Kushen, Betty. "Virginia Woolf and Dr. Freud." *Literature and Psychology* 35.1–2 (1989): 37–45.

Layton, Lynne, and Barbara Shapiro, eds. *Narcissism and the Text: Studies in Literature and the Psychology of Self.* New York: New York UP, 1986.

Marcus, Frank. "Maureen Duffy." *Contemporary Dramatists.* 4th ed. Ed. D. L. Kirkpatrick. London: St. Jonas, 1988. 127–28.

Marcus, Jane. "Pathographies: The Virginia Woolf Soap Operas." *Signs* 17.4 (Summer 1992): 806–19.

———. *Virginia Woolf and the Languages of Patriarchy.* Bloomington: Indiana UP, 1987.

Meese, Elizabeth. *Crossing the Double-Cross: The Practice of Feminist Criticism.* Chapel Hill: U of North Carolina P, 1986.

———. "When Virginia Looked at Vita, What Did She See; Or, Lesbian: Feminist: Woman—What's the Differ(e/a)nce?" *Feminist Studies* 18.1 (1992): 99–117.

Moran, Patricia. "Virginia Woolf and the Scene of Writing." *Modern Fiction Studies* 38.1 (1992): 81–100.

Noble, Joan Russell, ed. *Recollections of Virginia Woolf.* London: Peter Owen, 1972. 154–63.

O'Brien, Edna. *Virginia.* New York: Harcourt Brace Jovanovich, 1985.

Sizemore, Christine W. *A Female Vision of the City: London in the Novels of Five British Women.* Knoxville: U of Tennessee P, 1989.

———. "The 'Outsider-Within': Virginia Woolf and Doris Lessing as Urban Novelists in *Mrs. Dalloway* and *The Four-Gated City.*" *Woolf and Lessing: Breaking the Mold.* Ed. Ruth Saxton and Jean Tobin. New York: St. Martin's, 1994. 59–72.

Stimpson, Catherine. "Zero Degree Deviancy: The Lesbian Novel in English." *Writing and Sexual Difference.* Ed. Elizabeth Abel. Chicago: U of Chicago P, 1982. 243–59.

Stone, Laurie. "Virginia Woolf: What Margaret Atwood, Edna O'Brien, Paul Theroux, Rita Mae Brown, and Other Writers Have Learned from Her." *Ms.* Nov. 1982: 59–60, 98.

Two Together. By Dianna MacLeod. Dir. Ellen McNally. Second Annual Conference on Virginia Woolf, New Haven, CT. 13 June 1992.

Wardle, Irving. Rev. of "A Nightingale in Bloomsbury Square," by Maureen Duffy. *Times* 19 Sept. 1973: 11.

Winnicott, D. W. *Playing and Reality.* New York: Basic Books, 1971.

Woolf, Virginia. *The Diary of Virginia Woolf.* Ed. Anne Oliver Bell. 5 vols. New York: Harcourt Brace Jovanovich, 1977–84.

———. "Freudian Fiction." Rev. of *An Imperfect Mother,* by J. D. Beresford. *Contemporary Writers.* Ed. Jean Guiguet. London: Hogarth, 1965.

———. "Introductory Letter to Margaret Llewelyn Davies." *Life as We Have Known It.* New York: Norton, 1931. xv–xxxix.

———. *The Letters of Virginia Woolf.* Ed. Nigel Nicholson with Joanne Troutmann. 6 vols. London: Hogarth, 1975–80.

———. *Moments of Being.* 2nd ed. Ed. Jeanne Schulkind. New York: Harcourt Brace Jovanovich, 1985.

———. "Professions for Women." *The Death of the Moth and Other Essays.* London: Hogarth, 1942. 149–54.

———. *A Room of One's Own.* 1929. New York: Harcourt Brace, Jovanovich, 1981.

———. "Thoughts on Peace in an Air Raid." *The Death of the Moth and Other Essays.* London: Hogarth, 1942. 154–57.

———. *A Writer's Diary.* Ed. Leonard Woolf. New York: Harcourt, Brace, 1953.

Zwerdling, Alex. *Virginia Woolf and the Real World.* Berkeley: U of California P, 1986.

∾ A Modernist Romance? Lytton Strachey and the Women of Bloomsbury

Julie Taddeo

Recent feminist scholarship has criticized modernism as a "masculine movement." While such women as Virginia Woolf, H.D., and Djuna Barnes represented an "alternative to the Pound era," critic Suzette Henke notes that modernism remained an exclusively male club motivated by a "phallocentric project" (325). Indeed, such moderns as Wyndham Lewis and Ezra Pound, founders of the short-lived Vorticist movement, seemed obsessed with virility, "hard, precise images," and a poetic language "as much like granite as it can be" (Henke 326). Suffragettes and aesthetes proved favorite targets of ridicule in the Vorticists' journal, *Blast* (327). As Sandra Gilbert and Susan Gubar argue, the modernist exhortation to "make it new" was not a gender-free statement. Male modernists like Pound associated modernity with masculinity, originality with the phallus, and the mind with an "upspurt of sperm" (Gilbert and Gubar, *Sexchanges* XI). Meanwhile, D. H. Lawrence advocated England's salvation through a "true phallic marriage" in which woman yielded "some sort of precedence to man." Lawrence especially disliked the members of the Bloomsbury Group, who rejected "the essential blood-contact between man and woman" (352). Bloomsbury, to his dismay, seized upon the images of androgyny, bisexuality, and hermaphroditism, instead.

Founded in 1906, the Bloomsbury Group had at its center Cambridge University graduates Lytton Strachey, John Maynard Keynes, Clive Bell, and Leonard Woolf, and sisters Virginia and Vanessa Stephen. On Thursday evenings the still unknown writers, artists, and intellectuals gathered for cocoa, whiskey, buns, and conversations on art, sex, and the meaning of "the good life." Recalling those early days of Bloomsbury, Leonard Woolf, like Pound, insisted that he and his friends were not part of a negative movement of destruction against the past: "We were out to construct something new. We were in the van of the builders of a new society which should be free, rational, civilized, and pursuing truth and beauty. It was all tremendously exhilarating" (*Sowing* 106). By the end of the Great War, the group's pacifism, bisexual affairs, art exhibits, and publications certainly had attracted international attention and recognition as part of a revolutionary cultural movement. Though the group avoided political activism, the members saw their personal relations and discussions as indicative of a "new society."

It was Strachey, Virginia Woolf added, who taught the young Edwardians to destroy "the barriers of reticence and reserve" and to escape the "masculine orgy" of their parents' generation ("Sex Talk" 22).[1] As a panacea to the sexual repression of the nineteenth century, Strachey recommended that the whole world "fuck and bugger and abuse themselves in public and generally misbehave to their hearts' content" (Levy 80).[2] Historians and literary critics have tended to accept Strachey's appraisal of the group as the "priests of a new civilisation."[3] For the men of Cambridge who had been well schooled in theories of masculine superiority and male romantic friendship, Bloomsbury represented the first opportunity for serious physical and intellectual interaction with women. Yet was Bloomsbury, as Carolyn Heilbrun argues, "the first actual example of the androgynous spirit in practice"? (115). Despite their bisexual love triangles and candid conversations about sex, the "Bloomsberries"[4] continued to operate within the Victorian ideological framework of gender difference and patriarchy. Particularly in Strachey's case, the construction of "something new" ultimately failed to include new ideas about and attitudes toward women.

Most studies of Strachey take for granted his literary and sexual contributions to modernism. Ulysses D'Aquila, for example, credits Strachey with debunking the Victorians and the art of biography in general with the 1918 publication of *Eminent Victorians* (134). Michael Holroyd's two-volume biography of Strachey details the writer's witticisms and homosexual love affairs as evidence of his rebellion against Victorian mores. But such studies offer little insight into the sexual politics of modernism. While Gilbert and Gubar's *No Man's Land* returns to Bloomsbury, it does so primarily to discuss Virginia Woolf and her relationship with male modernists *outside* the group. Woolf's literary reaction against T. S. Eliot and James Joyce provide valuable insight into her texts, but her longstanding friendship and professional rivalry with Strachey are equally revealing of Woolf's "flight from patriarchy." And while Eliot, Joyce, Pound, and Lawrence detested the "soft" men and homosexuals at the center of Bloomsbury, they shared more with their "unmanly" rivals than they dared realize. Strachey especially embodied what Gregory S. Jay notes in the case of Eliot: the urge to reassert masculine authority over such autonomous "New Women" as Woolf, Vanessa Bell, and his own sisters (236). As feminist critics now engage in the project of "rethinking modernism," Heilbrun's praise for the "revolutionary implications" of Strachey's works and "his vision of the dangers of sexual polarization" (136) also calls for reinterpretation.

Tall, bearded, long-haired, and frail, Strachey donned flamboyant colors, velvet cloaks, and earrings to appear before the public eye as androgyne par excellence. However, Strachey's attempts at transgressive sexual behavior did little to disrupt the "masculine symbolic order"[5] which critics of Bloomsbury such as Pound and Lawrence seemed determined to preserve. As Kari Weil suggests, androgyny's subversiveness is always undermined by its own reaffirmation of sexual polarization and the idea of the female as emotion and weakness and the male as intellect and virility (2). Furthermore, Strachey's journal entries and correspondence reveal that he was not as comfortable flaunting the rules and hierarchy of gender as he pretended. As the most vocal male voice of the group, Strachey regarded his female colleagues with a mixture of admiration, envy, and hostility. Women, he declared, belonged to that unreal, "phenomenal" realm of being and, therefore, were his intellectual, physical, and emotional inferiors. He recognized that his homosexuality placed him at the margins of bourgeois male superiority and at odds with the medical, legal, and moral definitions of "normal" male sexuality. His constructions of gender suggest his own crisis of masculinity; only through his social and literary relations with women was Strachey able to regain a position of power and authority allotted to other upper-middle-class men. Also, Strachey's encounters with female Bloomsbury, particularly his fifteen-year living arrangement with the artist Dora Carrington, illuminate the lingering Victorian definitions of gender which undermined the modernist sexual experiment.

In an essay delivered before his Bloomsbury colleagues in 1922, Lytton Strachey recalled the first three decades of his life. "69 Lancaster Gate" offered a picture of the "middle-class professional world of the Victorians, in which the old forms still lingered" (25). The essay paid particular attention to the household's female head, who shaped young Lytton's future interactions with and expectations of the opposite sex. With his older brothers away from home serving the Empire and his elderly father retired to his rooms, Lytton received his early education from his mother, Lady Strachey. Supervising his writing, reading, and diary keeping, Lady Strachey hoped to prepare her son for a university degree and imperial career. Lytton's poor health frequently interrupted this educational regime and forced Lady Strachey to send her son on long recuperative holidays from home. Like many Victorian bourgeois sons, Strachey regarded his mother with both adoration and contempt, and though she was his "sweet Angel" he seemed to thrive most when far from her heavenly domain. While at public school and university he received frequent visits from his mother, who feared that Lytton "does not manage himself properly when there is nobody to look after him and rout him out, and feed him with milk." As an adult, he thanked her for setting him on the path of success while secretly blaming her for his prolonged dependence and insecurity (he lived with her until his thirty-sixth year).

What Strachey resented most in his relations with his mother was the need for deception. At sixteen he read for the first time "with a rush of mingled pleasure and pain" Plato's *Symposium,* and recognized with "surprise, relief, and fear" that what he felt was "felt 2000 years ago in glorious Greece" (Diary entry 13 Nov. 1896, rpt. in Holroyd 1971, 82). In the company of his mother and older brothers, however, he was reminded of his "unnatural desires." While traveling, he sent postcards to "Dearest Mama," noting his unsuccessful searches for "good-looking women," though he did enjoy "the shops, the wine, and the food" (Strachey Papers, postcard 31 Dec. 1917). Intellectual matters took precedence over emotions in the Strachey family, and, according to Lytton, Lady Strachey, like all mothers, was incapable of understanding any of her children. "How terrible," he complained to Keynes, "to love so much and know so little" (Strachey-Keynes Letters 27 Feb. 1906).

Strachey's own ambivalence toward Lady Strachey influenced his fictional portrayal of the mother. The maternal figure rarely appears in Strachey's writings, but when she does she is either a babbling fool oblivious to her son's homosexuality or a castrating pursuer of political power. In his play about the Chinese Imperial Court during the Boxer Rebellion, for example, Strachey demonizes the mother. The Empress Dowager in *A Son of Heaven* (1913) usurps power from her weakling son and commands a troupe of eunuchs. Vain, power-hungry, and murderous, the Empress Dowager at one point proclaims, "Whoever dares to say I'm a woman, I'll have them cut in pieces. I'm a man, a man, a man." The son, however, cannot say the same for himself, and his discovery of maternal cruelty leaves him an emotional ruin. Ironically, Strachey's sisters produced this play in 1925 to raise funds for the London Society for Women's Service.

Whether or not Strachey fashioned his emasculating villainess after his own mother, he repeatedly lamented his inability to escape "her Ladyship." Fortunately, life with mother was eased by the presence of Strachey's unmarried sisters, Philippa, Pernel, and Marjorie. As New Women of the early twentieth century, the Strachey women eschewed marriage to pursue higher education, professional employment, and service to Mrs. Fawcett's suffrage campaign. In the absence of husbands, they offered their wifely devotion to Lytton's health and comfort. With them, Strachey shared a bond the siblings described as "a mystical sign without any beginning or end and means everything and nothing" (Philippa Strachey, Strachey Papers 1892). All too frequently the sisters pushed their own interests aside to rush to the bedside of their "Dear Husband." The loyalty and cohesion of the Strachey siblings, however, was disrupted by jealousies and rivalries. The sisters had a reputation for their "intellectual and political prowess" long before Lytton achieved fame as a writer.[6] He frequently avoided their suffrage rallies, secretly ridiculed feminists and all zealous female reformers, and even refused Pernel's request to guest lecture at Newnham College. He was particularly distraught when his university friends preferred the company of his sisters to that of his own.

It was at university that Strachey finally found what he always was to call "Paradise," or a haven from the all-female atmosphere of home. Against Lady Strachey's plan, he entered Cambridge instead of Oxford and in 1902 was elected to lifetime membership to the secret fraternal society of Apostles. Among such fellow "Brothers" as J. M. Keynes, G. E. Moore, and Leonard Woolf, Strachey embraced the Apostolic philosophy of "the good life," which extolled male beauty, love, and friendship. The Brothers voted to keep the women of Girton and Newnham Colleges out of their society, adhering to a belief in their own inherent intellectual and sexual superiority. They adopted the "Greek View of Life," which distinguished their elite, "real" world of spiritual, Platonic love and Cambridge from the larger "phenomenal" realm of politics, lust, the masses, and especially the opposite, "hollow" sex.[7] The exclusion of women and the maintenance of a homosocial setting was vital to the Apostles' construction of their own masculinity. As Eve Kosofsky Sedgwick notes, Victorian bourgeois men explored a range of forms and intensities of homosocial liaisons without admitting culturally defined "femininity" into them as a structuring term (21–22). Calling themselves "Higher Sodomites," the Apostles insisted that any contact with women would harm "the Apostolic character." Each week, Strachey or another Brother presented a paper on the Apostolic philosophy of manly love, while they chastised the "womanisers" at Oxford and attacked the "common buggers" (or "lower sodomites"), who perverted pure male friendship with desire.[8]

The Brothers were well aware of the dominant counterdiscourse on the dangers of all-male love. The 1885 Labouchère Amendment had criminalized all physical expressions of this love, and even such sympathetic treatments as Havelock Ellis's 1896 *Sexual Inversion* identified the homosexual as an "abnormality" (Weeks 63). Strachey responded by ridiculing the late Victorian sexologists who referred to homosexuals as a "third sex" or a form of pathological deviance. After all, he declared that he belonged to a category that reigned above the average man or woman. Yet at times Strachey doubted his masculinity and feared that the "crudities" of physical desire hindered his aspiration to the "Love of Souls."[9] Only with his "terribly intelligent" Brothers at Cambridge did Strachey hope to forge a spiritual, and sometimes physical, relationship. It was women, he believed, who were the "intermediate sex," bridging the gap that separated the lower and Higher Sodomite. Women offered not sexual or intellectual companionship, but the "special comforts" which other men simply could not provide.

Though absent from the meetings, women did play a large part in the Brothers' discussions. The young Apostles debated the pros and cons of marriage and proposed universal buggery as a solution to the "Woman Question." Curiously, Strachey's dictum to avoid slang and "coarse language" when discussing male sexuality did not apply to the topic of women. In fact, he deliberately selected such terms as "pussy" and "cunt" to imply the vulgarity of the female body. Overall, the Brothers tended to view the "phenomenal sex" within the Victorian paradigm of Angel/Whore, and it was the former with whom they were most comfortable. As Strachey noted, "[L]adies were as different from men as they were from prostitutes" (Strachey Papers n.d.).

Women were forbidden entry into the double-locked rooms of the society and denied knowledge of its secret codes and rituals. However, as Strachey and his Brothers gradually recognized, once outside Cambridge it was impossible to keep the phenomenal sex at the margins. Physical intimacy with women actually protected these men from corrupting their own "Higher" unions with each other. Women represented a "safety valve" whenever passion threatened to bring Brotherly Love to a "lower" level. Rupert Brooke, for example, championed the Higher Sodomy at the Apostles' weekly meetings but reacted with horror when Strachey's younger brother James attempted "copulation" (he embraced Brooke in his bedroom).[10] The two men resumed their friendship only after James seduced two of Brooke's girlfriends, Noel Olivier and Katherine Cox (Sherman 329–64). "Womanising" apparently was acceptable as long as it helped the Brothers avoid debasing their love for one another. Unfortunately, an actual "phenomenal marriage" usually resulted in boredom, a condition, according to Strachey, on par with that of the vegetable or the cow.[11] For those members of the society who insisted on physical unions with women, marriage to one another's sisters seemed the most obvious solution and even increased the bond of loyalty and cohesion between Brothers. While courting Virginia Stephen, Leonard Woolf wondered if he loved her because he was really in love with her brother Thoby, and if Clive Bell loved Thoby because he was in love with Vanessa Stephen (Lytton Strachey–Leonard Woolf Letters 13 July 1905)! Above all, women were the only ones who could provide these men with "a little rest, a little home life, a little comfort," as they now tried to make their marks as colonial civil servants, journalists, and academics.[12] And, on occasion, women even surprised the Brothers as intellectual rivals.

Once he went down from Cambridge and returned home to London, Strachey joined Keynes, Leonard Woolf, and Clive Bell for Thursday evenings in the company of Adrian Stephen and his sisters Vanessa and Virginia. At first, Strachey regarded the women as mere extensions of their other brother Thoby—the blonde Apollo known at Cambridge as the "Goth," and he referred to them collectively as the "Visigoths." After Thoby's sudden death in 1906, the sisters became the main attraction of the weekly "at homes" at the Gordon Square residence. The reputed beauty of the Stephen women did not go unnoticed by Strachey and his friends, who competed for the sisters' attention and flooded them with marriage proposals. For the first time the Apostles even discussed Plato and love and art with the opposite sex while Vanessa told bawdy jokes and Virginia quietly listened.

Strachey immediately formed a friendship with Virginia Stephen, whom he initially described to Leonard Woolf as "rather wonderful, quite witty, full of things to say, and absolutely out of rapport with reality" (Lytton Strachey–Leonard Woolf Letters 21 Dec. 1904), and the two agreed to formally correspond. In their letters they professed a shared love of literature as well as a hatred of their "repellent Victorian ancestors." To his surprise, Virginia also "seem[ed] to be a woman of sound and solid common sense" (L. Woolf and J. Strachey, eds., *Lytton Strachey and Virginia Woolf: Letters* 24 Aug. 1908). Despite this praise of the woman who read Greek,

Strachey primarily used his letters to Virginia to complain of his dim career pros-pects and "blank" future. He also posed as an interested suitor, flirting with Virginia and inviting her to "go off to the Farol Islands" with him. What began as a jest be-came a serious marriage proposal in 1909, following his cousin Duncan Grant's rejection of Strachey as a lover. Explaining his motivation to his brother James, Lytton wrote: "In my efforts to escape, I had a decided reverse. . . . I proposed to Virginia and was accepted. It was an awkward moment as you may imagine, espe-cially as I realised, the very minute it was happening, that the whole thing was re-pulsive to me" (Strachey Papers 9 Mar. 1909). Breathing a sigh of relief when Vir-ginia later confessed she was not in love with him, Strachey "was able to manage a fairly honourable retreat." After some consideration, he concluded that "the story is really rather amusing and singular," but he reminded James of "the immense se-crecy of the affair" (ibid.).

The timing of the proposal coincided with not only Grant's "betrayal" but also Leonard Woolf's own plan to ask Virginia to be his wife. Writing from his post as a civil servant in Ceylon, Woolf confided to Strachey that "the ghastly complications" of virginity and marriage "altogether appalled" him. However, marriage to Thoby's sister seemed his only hope "if [he was] ever to be saved" from his "degraded de-bauches." Envisioning his future with Virginia, Woolf concluded that "it is undoubt-edly the only way to happiness, to anything settled" and would save him from the "appalling alternatives [of] violent pleasures [and] the depths of depression" (Strachey-Woolf Letters 1 Feb. 1909). Shortly after receiving this letter, Strachey informed Woolf that he had "beat him to the punch" but miraculously escaped without even the horror of a kiss. Strachey did regret, however, that he could not force himself to marry Virginia: "I could have done it and could . . . have dominated and soared and at last made her completely mine" (19 Feb. 1909).

Perhaps her own fears of Strachey's need to dominate and soar compelled Vir-ginia Stephen to call off the proposal. Years later, she confided to her diary her re-lief that she had not entered into a "bloodless alliance" with Strachey: "Had I mar-ried Lytton I should never have written anything. . . . He checks and inhibits in the most curious way" (Bell, vol. 3: 14 Dec. 1929). This passage echoed her thoughts about her father on what would have been Sir Leslie Stephen's ninety-sixth birth-day: "His life would have entirely ended mine . . . no writing, no books; inconceiv-able" (Leonard Woolf, ed., *A Writer's Diary* 28 Nov. 1929). Virginia apparently sensed Strachey's patriarchal potential and preferred to regard him as a "female friend."

With the obstacle of romance removed, the two founders of the Bloomsbury group at 46 Gordon Square embarked on a primarily intellectual relationship. The relations between the two aspiring writers, however, gradually became riddled with jealousy—a violation of Bloomsbury's prohibition against professional and personal competition. Virginia, in particular, noted their very different and gendered oppor-tunities. After reading his poetry, she wrote to Strachey in 1908: "I want a fire and an armchair, silence, and hours of solitude. You enjoy all those things in your island." Meanwhile, her afternoons were wasted in the company of old women "who spoil my life" (L. Woolf and J. Strachey, eds., *Lytton Strachey and Virginia Woolf: Letters* 20 Nov. 1908). Strachey, she assumed, easily excelled in poetry, criticism, and belles-lettres, while "a painstaking woman who wishes to treat of life as she finds it, and to give voice to some of the perplexities of her sex, in plain English, has no chance at all" (28 Jan. 1909). Envy turned into anger when Virginia considered the elite Cambridge circle to which Strachey, her brother, and her husband continued to belong. She found it difficult to write to Lytton while he visited his alma mater: "It's all Cambridge—that detestable place, and the ap—s—les are so unreal, and their loves are so unreal. . . . When I think of it, I vomit—that's all—a green vomit, which gets into the ink and blisters the paper" (21 May 1912). Though Strachey enjoyed a dual membership in the society and Bloomsbury, a barrier existed between the two groups which even this woman "of good sense" could not cross. Excluded from the Brother's "real world," Woolf, to Strachey's surprise, refused to accept that privileged masculine domain as superior.

As the other original female member of Bloomsbury, Vanessa Stephen posed more of a romantic than intellectual threat to Strachey. After his disastrous marriage proposal to Virginia, he directed his attentions toward her older sister, and their intimacy was noted by relatives who declared the two to be in love. Regarding such a prospect, Strachey "roared with laughter" and "said that it certainly would be the proper thing." To Keynes, he confided, "I think she thinks really I am, and I feel I ought to be. But what is one to do?" (Strachey-Keynes Letters 30 Jan. 1907). He even tried to explain to Vanessa that his "real" affections were for Duncan Grant, but she did not "see the real jar of the whole thing." Vanessa's understanding was more acute than Strachey realized. In order to win his confidence, she downplayed what he perceived as her "feminine" traits. In her letters she discussed the pleasures of breathing in cigar smoke and bragged that she "felt [herself] becoming very like a male" (Strachey Papers 27 Aug. 1908). For costume parties she dressed in the attire of working-class youths and flirted with Lytton, who admitted that the outfits made him "pretty well gone under." At other times she teased him with her dreams in which Lytton was arrested in police raids of male brothels, and she even dared to request details of the male "beauties" at Cambridge. Their prolonged flirtation displeased Vanessa's husband, Clive Bell, whom Strachey assured, "You haven't any reason for alarm." Still, he refused to give Vanessa up entirely. "What I do want, and even hope for," Strachey explained to Bell, "is a continuance and increase of her friendship, and all those sympathetic satisfactions which I seem to perceive that she can give me. Is that too much?" Strachey regretted that "there are so few possible women that it would be a blow to be cut off there" (25 Oct. 1915).

Eventually, Vanessa's extramarital affair with Duncan Grant precipitated her expulsion from Strachey's category of worthy females. Resentment toward this rival for Grant's love increased after the birth of the couple's daughter. Visiting the new family on their farm in 1916, Strachey was struck by Vanessa's "dumb animality [which] came out more unmistakably than [he'd] ever known!" In his journal, Strachey asked, "Was it their married state that oppressed me?" He accused Vanessa of refusing him a moment alone with Grant, yet he also seemed eager to recapture the intimacy he once briefly shared with Vanessa himself. "I saw that the time had come to face Vanessa," he wrote. "Was she plain or beautiful? I could not decide. . . . How well I knew her!—and how little—how very little. . . . If I could only have flung myself into her arms! But I knew so well what would happen—her smile— her half-bewilderment, half-infinitely sensible acceptance—and her odd relapse" (26 June 1916). Instead, Strachey walked about the farm uncomfortably, annoyed that in the midst of all this domesticity he was not the center of attention. Vanessa, he believed, stood in the way of his love for Grant and posed an obstacle which he could not overcome. She offered domestic bliss and children, which, for the moment, Grant apparently preferred to Strachey's monologues on the beauty of the Higher Sodomy.

Outside of Bloomsbury, Strachey found other women with "confiding ways." Lady Ottoline Morrell, the wife of the liberal MP Philip Morrell, belonged to that breed of imperious overruling women like Florence Nightingale, Queen Victoria, and Lady Strachey whom Lytton both loved and hated. Strachey was attracted to what he considered Ottoline's "masculine" qualities (her tall physique and financial independence) as well as her "motherly instincts." Ottoline, in turn, saw in Strachey a little boy, "so well and full of fun and life and youth," but also "a solitary figure, seeking rather timidly and nervously for human adventures" (qtd. in Holroyd 504).

One such "adventure" which Ottoline facilitated was Strachey's desire to "change sexes."[13] Michael Holroyd observes that during Strachey's friendship with Ottoline, the writer exchanged his collar for a purple scarf, grew his hair long, and donned a yellow cape. Like "a couple of high-spirited, teen-age girls," Holroyd notes, Strachey and Ottoline were "all giggling and high heels and titillating gossip" (454). While Holroyd's description obviously is tainted by his own notions of "feminine" conduct, he relies on Ottoline's depiction of Strachey as a combination of rigid intellectual breeding and "feminine, nervous hysterical" behavior (463). Citing psychoanalyst Robert Stoller, Gilbert and Gubar attribute such appropriation of "female" costume and mannerisms to the male modernist's need to convert "humiliation to mastery." Strachey's occasional wearing of high heels and jewelry simply may have been a playful attempt at androgyny, or, as Stoller suggests, an attempt to become a "phallic woman"—to own the power of both sexes "in a single covertly but thrillingly male body" (*Sexchanges* 335). Since Strachey's "thrillingly male body" usually was troubled with illness, the new wardrobe perhaps allowed him to express what he considered his feminine side (his frailty and dependence on others) without renouncing completely his manliness. In his writings, Strachey's male subjects tend to own this power of both sexes, as well. When the women do, they appear as perverted man-haters, while men like the Earl of Essex remain beautiful and heroic: "The flaunting man of fashion whose codpiece proclaimed an astonishing virility, was he not also with his flowing hair and jewelled ears, effeminate?" (*Elizabeth and Essex* 9–10). When Strachey donned Ottoline's clothes, he temporarily transcended the limitations of his sex but still maintained his claim to patriarchy.

Though rumors spread linking Ottoline and Strachey as lovers, Strachey relied on the wealthy socialite primarily for emotional comfort during his unsuccessful pursuit of the artist Henry Lamb. Ottoline's worthiness as a confidante gradually declined, however, as she became more involved in her own love affairs, including a sexual interest in Lamb! In his letters to his Bloomsbury colleagues, Strachey spread rumors about Ottoline. The formerly "magnificent" and "sublime" woman became, in Strachey's eyes, "a syphilitic hag" and "a fearful Jezebel" (Strachey Papers 5 Nov. 1909).

Ottoline provided support and encouragement to Strachey during the years before he achieved the fame for which he hungered, but his need for female consolation remained even after his postwar literary success. What Strachey longed for, he told James, was someone who would fulfill his "occasional wish for a wife" without troubling him with her sexuality. In order for him to write and continue his search for male love, Strachey needed freedom from "wretched material circumstances," and he supposed a wife "would settle such affairs" for him. "Is this a fearful muddle?" he wondered (2 Oct. 1912).

The answer to his prayers finally appeared at a party hosted by Clive and Vanessa Bell in the autumn of 1915. Dora Carrington belonged to the younger generation of New Women who, like the older Strachey sisters, ardently supported female emancipation but rejected their celibate life-style. Carrington had fled her provincial middle-class home and the domineering mother whom she said imprisoned her "in a bird cage," and she at last found freedom in London. While an art student at the Slade, she deliberately fashioned her appearance and personality to erase signs of what she considered her "loathsome femininity" (Holroyd 637). She dropped her first name, wore trousers, and styled her hair after a Florentine pageboy, but her altered appearance did little to ease her sexual and artistic insecurities which ultimately bonded her to Strachey. Ignoring her friends' warnings that Strachey was "H-O-M-O-S-E-X-U-A-L," Carrington immediately fell in love with "that horrid old man with the beard" (Holroyd 634). For his part, Strachey was attracted to the art student's youth and boyishness as well as her eagerness to submit her will completely to his and place him at the center of her life. Despite her eventual marriage and subsequent love affairs, Carrington always put Lytton's health, comfort, and work before her own. Shortly after Strachey's death, in February 1932, she wrote to his sister Philippa: "You must *never* thank me for looking after Lytton—I know some people thought he was selfish, but it was I who was spoilt. He read to me every evening after dinner, he taught me all the values I have in life; he shared everything with me, all his thoughts and flaws and happinesses. Nobody will ever know how kind Lytton was to me, a Father and a complete friend. I was his debtor" (Strachey Papers Feb. 1932).

After their initial meeting, Strachey and Carrington began a correspondence, and through a loan from some Apostles, Strachey was able to propose an experiment. Anxious to escape his claustrophobic bedsit at Lady Strachey's, he rented a country cottage and asked Carrington to join him as his companion and caretaker. Eager to replace Lady Strachey as Lytton's sole protector, she readily agreed, but neither informed their mothers of the truth of their arrangement.[14] At their new home they divided the household chores: Carrington painted the rooms, supervised the servants, canned vegetables, and cooked special meals while Strachey paid the bills. Taking on the additional role of nursemaid, she provided eucalyptus oil and hot water bottles for Strachey's numerous colds. Whenever Strachey traveled, Carrington begged him for news of his "adventures" and in the same breath reminded him to change his socks and promised him shortbread upon his return. Signing her letters as "Your Chambermaid," she promised to remove all unnecessary details from Strachey's life, but made these details the focus of her own.

Before the couple settled into the routine of domestic bliss, Carrington and Strachey attempted a physical union. Despite previous flirtations with several male Slade students, Carrington had avoided intercourse, an act she said which "made [her] inside feel ashamed, unclean" (Garnett 17). While Carrington's "virginity complex" had provided fodder for Bloomsbury gossip and ridicule, she now offered her body to Strachey without hesitation. After all, they lived in such close proximity and sometimes shared a bed. Strachey also understood Carrington's sexual insecurities; since his youth he had described himself as hideous and unworthy of love, and he tended to pursue younger men whose rejections of his "lower" advances inevitably helped him adhere to his chaste notion of the Higher Sodomy. To his surprise, he admitted a physical attraction to Carrington, and the "next step" seemed inevitable. Carrington's diary, however, recorded her grief over the failed attempts at consummation: "He [Strachey] sat on the floor with me and clasped my hands in his and let me kiss his mouth, all enmeshed in the brittle beard, and my inside was as heavy as lead, as I knew how miserable it was going to be" (qtd. in Holroyd 683). Though he could not keep her as a mistress, Strachey insisted that there were "a great deal of many kinds of love." Still, Carrington regretted that she were not a youth "who could give [him] that peculiar extacy [sic]," and she knew that within Strachey's hierarchy of relations, those between men reigned supreme (Strachey Papers 23 Mar. 1917). Her frequent pleas for love often were mixed with regrets at "having confessed to you that I care so much." Years later in 1921 she continued to cry over "a savage cynical fate which had made it impossible for my love ever to be used by you" (14 May 1921).

Like the Strachey women, Carrington was expected to fit within that safe zone of sexless, "ministering angels."[15] She readily assumed the roles of chaste wife and mother to a man thirteen years her senior, but Carrington's physical presence did disturb Strachey. As he told James, he did not know what to make of these "creatures with cunts." These "modern young women" seemed to have something "hidden in them" which made him uneasy (31 May 1916). Fortunately, Carrington promised that neither her marriage nor her subsequent love affairs would diminish her devotion to her "Lord and Master." Children were forbidden admission to Strachey's cottage, and through birth control and abortion Carrington guaranteed that no "*petit peuple*" would ever upset the peaceful paradise she had created for him. Her lover, Gerald Brenan, observed Carrington's relations with Strachey with intense dismay (and jealousy), and he wondered at her ability to separate "the intellectual and the physical" (Gerzina 219). Brenan also noted that while Carrington may have escaped the "bird cage" of her mother's home, with Lytton she had "given up so many of [her] human qualities to become a tame little bird that flutters about the house and garden assisting, looking in, serving, inspiring" (Gerzina 229).

In Carrington's company Strachey felt safe, young, and loved. To augment the attractions of home, she converted their cottage into an extension of Cambridge— a haven for the younger Apostles who praised her cooking and Strachey's conversation. One Brother, James Doggart, told Strachey that Carrington reminded him of "the days of childhood as vividly as though he were still traversing them" (Strachey papers 30 Dec. 1921). In addition to arranging parties of young men, Carrington volunteered her beauty as a lure so that Strachey could admire her male pursuers. With Carrington's first lover, the artist Mark Gertler, Strachey flirted and shared books, and he mediated the couple's incessant arguing. In love with Carrington's next admirer, war veteran and Oxford graduate Reginald ("Ralph") Partridge, Strachey actively campaigned for the couple's marriage in 1921. Strachey did stipulate, though, that the marriage not upset the smooth management of the household or the focus of Carrington's allegiance, and Partridge soon became a welcome addition to the cottage, as gardener, chauffeur, and object of beauty. While Partridge boasted that the marriage bond would be in his favor, Carrington confided to Strachey that "the real difficulty is he (Ralph) likes me always to be with him and sometimes I prefer this life here. You are too good, so charming, that I'd like to serve you all my life" (10 May 1921). It was to Strachey, not her new husband, that Carrington ultimately promised that her heart "would in that sweet bondage die rather than try to gain its Liberty" (14 Feb. 1922).

Strachey reaped the most benefits from what he and Carrington called their new "triangular life" with Ralph. When abroad or at Cambridge, he sent letters to the newlyweds expressing his eagerness to return to his family "and all the comforts" of home. But the security of the triangle, unstable from its inception, collapsed under the strain of marital infidelities and Carrington's obsession with pleasing her "God," Strachey. By 1926, after several affairs, Partridge was living with the recent Cambridge graduate, Frances Marshall, in London and visiting the cottage on weekends. Both Carrington and Strachey implored the young woman to share Ralph with them, and Carrington proposed the part-time marriage, afraid that Strachey would lose interest in her once Ralph left permanently. She even wrote to Frances begging her to be "a little generous," since "the happiness of my relation with Lytton, ironically, is so bound up with Ralph, that that will be wrecked" (Garnett 332–33). After ten years together, though, she really had no cause for alarm, for Strachey's dependence began to equal her own. As Carrington became involved with other men and women, Strachey now wrote pleading letters for *her* return home. He felt lost and missed her "heavenly presence," but he also seemed envious of her increasing sexual activity as his own declined.

Early in her marriage, Carrington confided to a friend that her love for Lytton far exceeded her feelings for Ralph. "He [Strachey] might have made me his bootblack or taken me to Siberia, and I would have given up every friend I had to be with him," she declared (qtd. in Gerzina 187). Eventually, Carrington did give up her husband as well as her career to remain with Strachey. Despite this statement of self-enslavement, she feared at times that Strachey regarded her merely as an employee, and she angrily refused his offer of a pension. Aware that she neglected her art to tend house, Strachey proposed the pension in gratitude "for putting up with his befogged melancholies and helping him to face life" (Strachey Papers Nov. 1929). Curiously, despite his concerns for Carrington's financial independence, Strachey willed his cottage to Partridge, not Carrington.

In her biography of Carrington, Gretchen Gerzina asks the obvious question: Did life with Lytton Strachey cause Carrington to channel her talents into housekeeping and decoration? Gerzina seems untroubled that Carrington "made love the center of her life" as she destroyed her own canvasses and painting tiles (304). More important than her work, Carrington insisted (and convinced herself to believe), were the "vistas" that Strachey made for her. He gave her required reading lists and "a standard of sensible behavior which made it much easier to be reasonable" (Strachey Papers 4 Nov. 1929). She urged Strachey to treat her like one of those penwipers with "Use Me" embroidered on the cover, for, as she told him, "[t]hat's what I would like you to remember—that I am always your penwiper" (9 Sept. 1919). She even hoped that they might die at exactly the same moment, and when Strachey fell seriously ill, she attempted suicide, hoping to give her life for his. Shortly after Strachey's death in 1932, Carrington did kill herself. In her diary, Virginia Woolf blamed Lytton for Carrington's death: "I sometimes dislike him for it. He absorbed her, made her kill herself" (qtd. in Gerzina xxiv). But as Carrington's own final journal entry noted: "He first deceased, she for a little tried / to live without him, liked it not and died" (qtd. in Holroyd 1067).

Carrington and Strachey began their living arrangement as an experiment and perceived themselves as architects of a new sexual and social order. However, as Ruth Brandon argues in *The New Women and The Old Men,* the irony of post-Victorian modernity was the traditional form it assumed (251). Strachey's and Carrington's "marriage" was hardly the androgynous, radical union praised by Carolyn Heilbrun, who has compared the Bloomsberries to the sexual revolutionaries of the 1960s and 1970s. At the other end of the spectrum is a tendency to reduce this particular living arrangement to that of a misogynistic patriarch and his female domestic drudge. Aware of Strachey's expectations of women, Carrington willingly modified her artistic ambitions to become his "penwiper." By the age of thirty, she had decided that she "at last felt at peace with her lower self" and abandoned makeup to create an appearance more suitable to her house-bound life (Holroyd 870). "It was as though," observed one visitor to their cottage, "she had been worn to the bone by life and love" (870).

What compelled such New Women to subordinate their lives to the demands and convenience of men? Brandon argues that underlying the New Woman's quest for modernity was an overwhelming sense of guilt. Even the most advanced of thinkers refused to believe that women did not find their "deepest satisfaction" in family priorities (261). According to Elaine Showalter, one of Virginia Woolf's breakdowns followed Leonard's "decision" against children in the marriage. While her male colleagues frequently commented on her sister's fertility, Virginia was led to feel that, despite her own literary achievements, she had renounced a primary female role and destroyed her husband's opportunity to be a father (273). And Carrington, tormented by her "beastly femininity," nevertheless sought solace from her "moods" of depression in pickling, sewing, and tending Lytton's colds rather than in her art. In addition, Carrington's professional insecurities were fueled by her Bloomsbury colleagues. Roger Fry's "suggestion" that she give up her ambition of becoming a "serious artist" and turn to decorative art helped dissuade Carrington from exhibiting her paintings (Gerzina 68–69).

The Strachey-Carrington "ménage" raises the equally troubling question of why self-styled "New Men" accepted female subservience? Despite their claims to modernity, neither Strachey nor Carrington seemed capable of escaping Victorian gender codes which polarized the sexes and legitimized an attendant set of intellectual and emotional differences. The Apostolic definitions of masculinity and femininity which Strachey embraced at Cambridge and later applied to his relations with women were further extensions of these codes. Not even the odd women he encountered— the Stephen sisters, Lady Ottoline, or Carrington—succeeded in upsetting this gender system. Perhaps, then, as Gilbert and Gubar argue, the rise of the New Woman was not matched by the coming of a New Man at all (*Sexchanges* xii). Whether flamboyantly attired or bedridden like an "old maid,"[16] Strachey still harbored a desire for, not a release from, manliness; he longed to seduce and subdue insubordinate women whose intellect and talent matched his own.

Strachey's dilemma of coming to terms with his sexuality at a time of increasing legal and medical repression of male homosexuality also shaped his relations with women. Proclaiming himself one of Plato's descendants, Strachey was torn between his feelings of "colossal moral superiority" and guilt over what he sometimes called his "unnatural affections." Gregory S. Jay notes that male modernists like Eliot were engaged in a conflict between an embattled self and its threatening others: women, homosexuals, the lower classes, and savages (223). But in Strachey's case, he had *become* one of those threatening others—declared pathological and illegal by "experts" and pushed to the margins of masculinity. He therefore surrounded himself with admiring young men who praised his intellect and doting women who allowed him to play the role of patriarch. Unable to offer Strachey either the "peculiar extacy" of a lower sodomite or the spiritual love of a Brother, Carrington had no alternative models of behavior, other than those of wife, sister, mother, or nurse. Otherwise, she, like the women before her, risked losing her place within Strachey's small circle of privileged females.

While Strachey lived with Carrington he engaged in the most productive period of his literary career. His published biographies primarily documented the lives of powerful women: Florence Nightingale, Queen Victoria, Elizabeth I, all of whom challenged their assigned sphere of limited female action. Paul Fussell and other critics tend to regard Strachey's biographies as hilarious satires of British icons (Fussell 188). A feminist reading, however, suggests that these literary portraits were actually part of Strachey's need (perhaps unconscious) to strip these women of their political and sexual powers and restore the gender boundaries they had blurred. Strachey expressed his intention to peer beneath the women's heavy clothes, to look under their hoops, to discover the source of the "discordance" between the flesh and the "image of regality" (*Elizabeth and Essex* 9–10). Each unveiling revealed the women's dark secrets of sexual obsessions and fears and their internal battles between their masculine and feminine "elements." Strachey's literary version of the androgyne depicted a "grotesque anomaly"—in short, a female form with male drives. "Lascivious" Elizabeth, the "fiery steed" Victoria, and the tentacle-equipped Nightingale all channeled their unfulfilled sexual desires not into an urge to "do good" but into a quest for power (12). But the final victory belonged to their biographer. Strachey concluded his portraits with parting glances of senile, feeble, grandmotherly women with "the sting . . . taken out" (*Eminent Victorians* 172). They had finally received just punishment for loving power more than they loved men.

Carolyn Heilbrun claims that Strachey's "revolutionary" biographies reveal an understanding of "the androgynous mind" (149) that matched that of Virginia Woolf. That Strachey's *Elizabeth and Essex* and Woolf's *Orlando* were written during the same period (1928) suggests more of a professional rivalry than a friendly feminist collaboration, however. While Woolf tried to write a revisionary biography in which costume, not anatomy, is destiny (*Sexchanges* 344), Strachey wrote a biography in which anatomy is perversion. Regarding Elizabeth I, Strachey suggested a special cause for her neurotic condition: "Her sexual organisation was seriously warped"; a physical malformation as well as a "deeply seated repugnance to the crucial act of intercourse" marked the Queen with a "certain grotesque intensity" (*Elizabeth and Essex* 24–26). Strachey's attempts to understand the Queen's "virginity complex" resulted in, Woolf believed, a poor book unworthy of its author. After sharing her disappointed reaction to *Elizabeth and Essex* with Strachey, Woolf confided to her diary: "I felt . . . I had no longer anything to envy him for; and how dashing off Orlando I had done better than he had done; and how for the first time I think he thought of me as a writer, with some envy" (Bell, vol. 2: 234). Trying to understand a reason for his failure, she and Strachey both blamed his poor health and the suffocating praise of Carrington and his "young men."

The female subjects of Strachey's biographies represented composites. The intellect of Virginia, the sensuality of Ottoline and Vanessa, the domesticity of Carrington, the overbearing will of Lady Strachey, and the reformist zeal of the Strachey sisters all surfaced in the depictions of the female rulers and public servants. Ironically, it was Carrington's domestic assistance which freed Strachey to write and take literary revenge on all unconventional women. Claiming historical "objectivity," Strachey in fact rewrote these female lives, revealed his version of their "inner selves," and tore away the aura of mystery surrounding them.[17] Their unveiling was his triumph; he had, at last, succeeded in discovering what was "hidden in them."

Among Strachey's female acquaintances were some of the most creative and intelligent artists and writers of early-twentieth-century England. However, he seemed to prefer the company of women like Carrington, who placed his needs and thoughts above their own. On their fifteenth anniversary Carrington gratefully exclaimed to Strachey: "At last your labours toiling in the thick clay of my muddy brain have produced a blade of grass. For without such a diligent gardener, where would your most grateful Mopsa have been?" (Strachey Papers 22 July 1931). As a biographer Strachey exhibited equally thorough gardening skills, pruning famous women into "terrible creatures," domesticated queens, and lascivious old hags.

Nevertheless, this role of authority did not completely suit Strachey. His overwhelming desire to perceive and construct the feminine as powerless attests to his own crisis of identity. Strachey's frail health, delayed success, and his homosexuality jeopardized his claim to bourgeois masculine hegemony. He was often awkward in the role of patriarch expected of men of his social position. He shot at stags, surrounded himself with visual reminders of his virile father, and immersed himself in the all-male society of Cambridge and professional clubs whose members defined their masculinity by their class and gender exclusivity. At times, though, Strachey longed for a respite from this forced masculine posturing. He violated the Apostolic taboo to form intimacies with the "phenomenal sex" and even adopted some of its traits. He was, however, less sympathetic toward women who invaded male terrain. Though he wrote of the women who ruled Britannia, he was reluctant in his own relations with women to completely reverse roles, to let (as in the case of Florence Nightingale and Sidney Herbert) the "natural master" become the servant of the opposite sex (*Eminent Victorians* 151).

In the company of women Strachey longed for what he called an "immaculate" bond reminiscent of the days when he "rushed headlong to [his] mother and clasped her and kissed her with all [his] strength" (Strachey Papers 7 Apr. 1903). Long after leaving university, Strachey continued his search for that "ecstacy" of childhood, and with the women of Bloomsbury he attempted to "again love as much as that." His female colleagues, however, challenged Strachey's neat dichotomy of the "real" and the "phenomenal" and forced him to question his gendered concept of love, which excluded them from the higher emotional and intellectual life. Carrington especially attracted Strachey; her need to shock her elders, her relentless self-hatred, and her search for an ideal love uncomplicated by sex made her his mirror image. Together, this odd couple would renounce the conventional marriage and household of their parents' generation; they would discuss openly all matters, engage in an array of relationships, and their lives and art would reflect their "modern consciousness." Yet even for the Bloomsberries, inherited notions of gender interfered with their claims to modernity and their attempts to put ideals into practice. The retreat to the countryside may have saved them from the probing eyes of critics, enemies, and family, but how were they to transcend gender, to create an apatriarchal space? The Bloomsbury vision of a new sexual order remained, in the end, eminently Victorian.

Notes

I would like to thank the Society of Authors as agents of the Strachey Trust for permission to quote from the letters, essays, and journals of Lytton Strachey. I also am indebted to Sally Brown at the British Library for her assistance with the Strachey Papers, to librarians Jackie Cox at King's College and Elizabeth Ingalls at Sussex University, and to Michael Holroyd for encouraging yet another journey into Bloomsbury terrain.

1. In this Bloomsbury essay delivered in 1922, and published in Rosenbaum, Woolf described to her colleagues an early visit by Strachey in 1908:

> Suddenly the door opened and the long and sinister figure of Mr. Lytton Strachey stood on the threshold. He pointed his finger at a stain on Vanessa's white dress. "Semen?" he said. Can one really say it? I thought and burst out laughing. With that one word all barriers of reticence and reserve went down. . . . Sex permeated our conversation. The word bugger was never far from our lips. We discussed copulation with the same excitement and openness that we had discussed the nature of good. It is strange to think how reticent, how reserved we had been and for how long. (qtd. in Rosenbaum 22)

2. Lytton Strachey's advice to his Brothers in the Society of Apostles, "Will It Come Right in the End?" Paper delivered at Cambridge, 1908, reprinted in Levy.

3. Lytton Strachey referred to the mission of his elite circle of intellectuals in a letter to J. M. Keynes dated ?/1905 (King's College MSS, vol. 1).

4. As a term of self-identification, "Bloomsberries" was coined by Molly MacCarthy in 1910 or 1911. Her husband Desmond was an original, though peripheral, member of the group. According to Clive Bell, "the term, as she (Lady MacCarthy) used it, had a purely topographical import." See Clive Bell, *Old Friends: Personal Recollections,* cited in Rosenbaum (86).

5. I am borrowing this phrase from Fran Michel's article "Displacing Castration: *Nightwood, Ladies Almanack,* and Feminine Writing," *Contemporary Literature* 30.1 (1989): 48.

6. In a letter to her brother Lytton, dated 6 November 1895, Philippa Strachey recounted an inci-

dent at the Meteorological Council at which Sir Richard Strachey boasted of his daughters' "prowess" while the "old boys listened aghast" and murmured, "Oh yes, but everyone knows about the Strachey daughters!!!"

7. The "Greek View of Life" derives from Goldsworthy Lowes Dickinson's 1896 publication of the same name. The philosopher extolled the ancient Greeks' gendered system of work and love and declared pederastic friendships to be an "institution."

8. In a letter to Keynes dated 26 October 1905, Strachey referred to the "unforgivable sin" of "womanising," and by 1909 Keynes noted that Cambridge had become a "volcano" where "even the womanisers pretend to be sods lest they shouldn't be thought respectable."

9. Strachey's struggle with what he called his "lower" (physical) and "Higher" (spiritual) selves is revealed in his diaries and poetry written during his university years. At the meetings of the Apostles he boasted of the superior friendships and love affairs of the Higher Sodomites, but in private he expressed guilt over his "unnatural affections" and a fear that consummation of his desires would make him "unclean." In his fictional "Diary of an Athenian 400 B.C.," for example, Strachey defends the purity of "the Love of Souls" but admits that others may see him as unclean: "Remember that the thing itself may not be bad, though some make a bad use of it."

10. James Strachey wrote to his cousin Duncan Grant of this incident in a letter dated 1 September 1908. Surprised by Brooke's rejection, James cried, "Oh God! He's in love with a woman. Why did we think him a Sodomite? . . . Don't you see now *why* he's kept everything so infernally dark? He's ashamed—because it's a woman" (British Museum MSS ADD 60713).

11. Lytton Strachey debated the pros and cons of a "phenomenal marriage" in his Apostle paper "Does Absence Make the Heart Grow Fonder?" delivered to the Society on 19 November 1904.

12. Lytton Strachey to Duncan Grant, in a letter dated 5 February 1906, suggested one advantage of domesticity. Surrounded by his sisters and aunts, he wrote, "Sun, flowers, . . . and comparative comfort. . . . I think it may save me." Strachey's desire for the comforts of marriage was outweighed, however, by his passion for Duncan.

13. Strachey expressed this desire in a letter to Clive Bell dated 21 October 1909, in which he wrote: "What a pity one can't now and then change sexes!" Cited in Holroyd (454).

14. Lady Strachey did know about her son's new living arrangements but preferred to avoid any discussion of the matter. In her diary, Virginia Woolf recorded her conversation over tea with Lady Strachey, who "froze up and pretended not to know where it was. . . . Thinks they're ruined." See Bell, vol. 1, entry for 18 Jan. 1918.

15. Carrington boasted to Virginia Woolf that she was Strachey's "ministering angel" in a letter dated October 1918. However, she did note that taking care of Lytton often interfered with her own work: "How can I do woodblocks when for the last month . . . I've been a . . . hewer of wood and drawer of water."

16. Virginia Woolf described Strachey's life at his cottage Tidmarsh as "a little invalidish." While Carrington was absorbed in her household duties, Strachey, like an "old maid," seemed "obsessed with his health and comfort" (see Bell, vol. 1, entry for 16 June 1919).

17. Strachey's claim of "objectivity" is in his preface to *Eminent Victorians* (1918). This preface represents Strachey's "modernist manifesto" in which he attacks the traditional biography and proposes to write a new type of study in which he lays bare all the facts and reveals the "inner life" of his subjects.

Works Cited

Bell, Anne Olivier, ed. *The Diary of Virginia Woolf.* Vol. 1, *1915–1919*. London: Harcourt Brace Jovanovich, 1977.

———. *The Diary of Virginia Woolf.* Vol. 3, *1925–1930*. London: Harcourt Brace Jovanovich, 1980.

Brandon, Ruth. *The New Women and the Old Men: Love, Sex, and the Woman Question.* New York: Norton, 1990.

D'Aquila, Ulysses L. *Bloomsbury and Modernism.* New York: Peter Lang, 1989.

Dickinson, Goldworthy Lowes. *The Greek View of Life.* Ann Arbor: U of Michigan P, 1958.

Ellis, Havelock. *Studies in the Psychopathology of Sex.* Vol. 1, *Sexual Inversion.* New York: Random House, 1903.

Fussell, Paul. *The Great War and Modern Memory.* London: Oxford UP, 1975.

Garnett, David, ed. *Carrington: Letters and Extracts from Her Diaries.* London: Jonathan Cape, 1970.

Gerzina, Gretchen. *Carrington: A Life.* New York: Norton, 1989.

Gilbert, Sandra M., and Susan Gubar. *No Man's Land: The Place of the Woman Writer in the Twentieth Century.* Vol. 1, *The War of the Words.* New Haven: Yale UP, 1988.

———. *No Man's Land: The Place of the Woman Writer in the Twentieth Century.* Vol. 2, *Sexchanges.* New Haven: Yale UP, 1989.

Heilbrun, Carolyn. *Toward a Recognition of Androgyny.* New York: Knopf, 1973.

Henke, Suzette A. "(En)Gendering Modernism: Virginia Woolf and Djuna Barnes." *Rereading the New: A Backward Glance at Modernism.* Ed. Kevin J. H. Dettmar. Ann Arbor: U of Michigan P, 1992. 325–41.

Holroyd, Michael. *Lytton Strachey: A Biography.* London: Penguin, 1987.

———, ed. *Lytton Strachey by Himself: A Self-Portrait.* New York: Holt, Rinehart & Winston, 1971.

Jay, Gregory S. "Postmodernism in *The Waste Land:* Women, Mass Culture, and Others." *Rereading the New: A Backward Glance at Modernism.* Ed. Kevin J. H. Dettmar. Ann Arbor: U of Michigan P, 1992. 221–46.

Lawrence, D. H. "A Propos of *Lady Chatterley's Lover.*" New York: Bantam, 1983.

Levy, Paul, ed. *Lytton Strachey: The Really Interesting Question and Other Papers.* London: Weidenfeld & Nicolson, 1972.

Rosenbaum, S. P., ed. *The Bloomsbury Group: A Collection of Memoirs, Commentary and Criticism.* Toronto: U of Toronto P, 1975.

Sedgwick, Eve Kosofsky. *Between Men: English Literature and Male Homosocial Desire.* New York: Columbia UP, 1985.

Sherman, Murray H. "Lytton and James Strachey: Biography and Psychoanalysis." *Blood Brothers: Siblings as Writers.* Ed. Norman Kiel. New York: International Universities P, 1983. 329–64.

Showalter, Elaine. *A Literature of Their Own: British Women Novelists from Brontë to Lessing.* Princeton: Princeton UP, 1977.

Strachey, Lytton. "Diary of an Athenian, 400 B.C." London: British Museum MSS, unbound, n.d.

———. *Elizabeth and Essex: A Tragic History.* New York: Blue Ribbon Books, 1928.

———. *Eminent Victorians.* London: Folio, 1918.

———. Lytton Strachey–John Maynard Keynes Letters. Vols. 1–5. Cambridge: King's College Library.

————. Lytton Strachey–Leonard Woolf Letters. Sussex, England: Sussex University Library.

————. Queen Victoria. New York: Harcourt, Brace, 1921.

————. "A Son of Heaven." London: British Museum MSS, unbound, 1913.

————. The Strachey Papers. Including diaries, letters, Apostle essays, Bloomsbury essays, and Strachey-Carrington correspondence. London: British Museum.

————. "69 Lancaster Gate." 1922. Rpt. in Lytton Strachey by Himself. Ed. Michael Holroyd. New York: Holt, Rinehart & Winston, 1971. 16–28.

Weeks, Jeffrey. Coming Out: Homosexual Politics in Britain, from the Nineteenth Century to the Present. London: Quartet Books, 1977.

Weil, Kari. Androgyny and the Denial of Difference. Charlottesville: UP of Virginia, 1992.

Woolf, Leonard. Sowing: An Autobiography of the Years 1880–1904. London: Hogarth, 1960.

————, ed. A Writer's Diary: Being Extracts from the Diary of Virginia Woolf. London: Hogarth, 1954.

Woolf, Leonard, and James Strachey, eds. Lytton Strachey and Virginia Woolf: Letters. New York: Harcourt, Brace and Co., 1956.

Woolf, Virginia. "Sex Talk in Bloomsbury." The Bloomsbury Group: A Collection of Memoirs, Commentary and Criticism. Ed. S. P. Rosenbaum. Toronto: U of Toronto P, 1975.

ironic ("do be careful this time—get a good housekeeper"
ir relationship far more realistically ("what you want is to
, while you feel perfectly free to amuse yourself in every
.d is even ready to take him up on his suggestion that they
surprise. What He fails to comprehend is that She is also an
e that is not marked by her being his wife. At the end, they
. least never bored each other, and they have a truce, albeit

th *Enemies* and *Constancy* seem to us today, in their produc-
d conventional illusionism since they dramatized not a pos-
y, not even reality as it should be, whether in its melodra-
sions. Neither did they present a subjective view of reality,
later characterize expressionist theater. What they did was
reality itself—the Hapgoods' marriage in both *Enemies* and
odge and Jack Reed's tumultuous affair in *Constancy*. From
rs of the time, especially those of Dodge and Hutchins
it they were "true," as "truth" was available to the group of
mbers at the time.[11] Not only did the incidents recounted in
ents that were familiar to the audience, but the performers
ce and Hutchins Hapgood portrayed She and He in *Enemies*)
1. That intimacy of content and form undoubtedly accounted
ic environment. By being ultrarealistic, they in fact destroy
nd bridge the gap between audiences and performers. All
, supposedly personal experience, so that the boundary be-
lic also dissolves. Theater becomes an intimate exploration
he personal into the public in a way that changes its function
therapy and drama's movement from the general, that is, the
e concrete, that is, the idiosyncratic crisis.
ng, mainstream American theater and drama at the time of-
fare formulaic pieces intent on preserving an illusionistic
ealism of the type discussed here—a portrayal and explora-
familiar to the audience—did not participate in the popu-
oned canon. One can argue that Boyce merely wrote these
significant topic for purely utilitarian reasons. After all, the
ot exactly have a great pool of scripts to choose from. What-
ind *Enemies* and *Constancy*, however, they both accomplished
nce of illusionism. In a spectacular way, they collapsed the
thor/subject, character/object, and performer and epito-
unified work of art with a single source of creation, the Art-
embodied the main principles of the modernist New Stage-
tylization, synthesis and unification.[12]
artistic product is what was realized in Bryant's play, *The
dismissed by historians and rarely mentioned in criticism,[13]

"I Do Not Participate in Liberations": Female Dramatic and Theatrical Modernism in the 1910s and 1920s

Kornelia Tancheva

Until very recently, the conventional discussion of modernism in the American drama and theater in the 1910s and 1920s evolved in such a way that sooner or later Eugene O'Neill's name claimed the spotlight and his dramatic output mysteriously shrouded everybody else's work in a veil of embarrassed and embarrassing silence. Considering how few of O'Neill's male predecessors and contemporaries have been admitted to the modernist canon on an equal footing, it is hardly a shock to find out that for a long time women were grossly under- and misrepresented. What is more, sex and/or gender were explicitly brought to bear on their otherwise marginalized artistic production—for example, Susan Glaspell as Jig Cook's wife and assistant in his mission of organizing the Provincetown Players and as O'Neill's literary mother; Louise Bryant as Jack Reed's wife and O'Neill's mistress; Neith Boyce as Hutchins Hapgood's unfathomable counterpart in *Enemies*, incomplete and insufficient in herself, fulfilled only through the linguistic intervention of her husband; Edna St. Vincent Millay as the pretty-faced actress and Greenwich Village Muse; Sophie Treadwell as Elmer Rice's stylistic disciple. Djuna Barnes and Gertrude Stein proved so difficult to pigeonhole, especially in gender-specific categories, that they were totally absent from the traditional dramatic and theatrical canon.

Interestingly enough, many of the modernist women artists have gained significant critical appreciation for their contributions in other genres, especially fiction and poetry. Recent feminist revisions of the modernist canon have highlighted a female subtext of a stature commensurate to that of the "great" modernist "masters." It has alternatively been theorized as a subversion of patriarchal modernist structures and as a source of origin for "high" male modernism. Simultaneously, attention has been focused on the repression of women writers both in the construction of the dominant modernist paradigm and in the textual practices of the canonized modernists.[1] Stein and Barnes feature extensively here—they are currently considered exemplary representatives of *écriture féminine* and among the original sources of the modernist aesthetics.[2] In terms of dramatic output, however, it is only Glaspell and Treadwell that have successfully been incorporated in a feminist dramatic and theatrical canon while Barnes and Stein are rarely mentioned and Boyce, Millay, and Bryant hardly at all.[3] Whether it is a particular critical blindness or a perception of incompatibility among feminism, realism, and modernism in the theater, the fact remains that so far no consistent female subtext in modernist American drama and theater has been recovered.[4]

Here, I will consider works by three of those women playwrights only, Boyce's *Constancy* and *Enemies,* Bryant's *The Game,* and Barnes's *To the Dogs* in order to explore the diversity of female dramatic modernism and illustrate the contiguity of feminism, realism, and modernism in early-twentieth-century American drama and theater. Undoubtedly the analysis can be extended to include all the authors mentioned in the beginning with extremely gratifying results—Stein's works will be a perfect example of the destruction of familiar theatrical form, while Glaspell's of the mapping out of a specific space for female identity and subjectivity; Millay's and Treadwell's pieces can be seen as female interventions into "high" modernism. My selection is motivated as much by considerations of space, as by my desire to rescue Boyce and Bryant for a feminist discourse, and my understanding that Barnes's work is the epitome of the two tendencies I will be discussing.

In the process I will argue first, that modernism was not inconsistent with a female subject position and second, that theatrical realism as a mode of representation could accommodate both a strong feminist position and antinaturalistic modernist stylistic techniques. I will contend that these modernist women playwrights offered significant challenges and subversive strategies to the dominant dramatic and theatrical discourse and elaborated an idiosyncratic language and mise-en-scène, exploding the conventions of both traditional theater and modernist male drama. What is more, they also focused on the in-depth portrayal of female subjectivity by making women their primary interest and thus their dramas present forms of female identity construction within the very heart of modernism.

All these women stood in a rather ambiguous relation to both the mainstream and the experimental theater of the time. Boyce and Bryant entered the field accidentally, while Barnes's was to be a longer infatuation with somewhat disastrous effects. They were all associated with the Provincetown Players, one of the little theater groups, which produced *Constancy* (1915), *Enemies* (1916), *The Game* (1916), and three other plays by Barnes.[5] The emergence of independent theater groups willing to oppose the conventions of commercial Broadway[6] at the time was couched in the terms of delivering a long-promised salvation, through the conviction that "the theatre is a place for beauty, for design, for color, for imagination, for plays with spiritual content, for interpretation, for harmony of many parts, for a certain kind of poetry" (Moses 425).

The Provincetown Players v
American plays of high artistic
by a group of radical intellectua
were George (Jig) Cram Cool
productions in the summer of
they began to consider a mov
autumn of 1916, and for eight
can authors that were refused
mercial stage as part of their id
drama and theater.[8]

As part of this experimen
"modern" from the very begin
of the attention they paid to t
through a whole range of sty
impressionism. The degree to
pieces differed considerably.
intricately blended with natu

Nowhere more so than in
naturalistic, as is the action,
of the well-made play. Both d
and Rex in *Constancy,* He an
Rex has come back to reclai
of another woman. In her tu
grin, receives him as a friend
or of her love for him foreve
of infidelity of the soul and su
Finally, Rex departs furiousl
if it means she has stopped l
giveness] anyone ever gets"

He and She in *Enemies* are
delity." The husband feels ab
and her unwillingness to all

He: Our tastes and our vic
She: Our souls? Why shou

In a psychological analysis
done, it becomes clear that
necessarily correspond to h

She: You have wanted to
form you saw in your imag
plastic material. It models

Reserved and
[132]), she ass
censor and co
possible way"
separate—mu
artist and need
both agree they
an armed one.

As naturalist
tion context, th
sible or probabl
matic or politic
a technique that
transpose on the
Constancy and M
the numerous
Hapgood, it is c
artists and audier
the pieces follow
themselves (Neit
were implicated i
for an almost ther
theatrical illusion
together get to re
tween personal an
of privacy, openin
from entertainme
human principle,

Contextually sp
fered as their stan
picture of the wor
tion of an actual re
larly or critically sa
pieces on a person
Provincetowners o
ever the intentions
a structural transce
distinction betweer
mized the ideal of t
ist. In that sense the
craft—simplificatio

Theater as a unif
Game. It is very ofte

∽ "I Do Not Participate in Liberations": Female Dramatic and Theatrical Modernism in the 1910s and 1920s

Kornelia Tancheva

Until very recently, the conventional discussion of modernism in the American drama and theater in the 1910s and 1920s evolved in such a way that sooner or later Eugene O'Neill's name claimed the spotlight and his dramatic output mysteriously shrouded everybody else's work in a veil of embarrassed and embarrassing silence. Considering how few of O'Neill's male predecessors and contemporaries have been admitted to the modernist canon on an equal footing, it is hardly a shock to find out that for a long time women were grossly under- and misrepresented. What is more, sex and/or gender were explicitly brought to bear on their otherwise marginalized artistic production—for example, Susan Glaspell as Jig Cook's wife and assistant in his mission of organizing the Provincetown Players and as O'Neill's literary mother; Louise Bryant as Jack Reed's wife and O'Neill's mistress; Neith Boyce as Hutchins Hapgood's unfathomable counterpart in *Enemies*, incomplete and insufficient in herself, fulfilled only through the linguistic intervention of her husband; Edna St. Vincent Millay as the pretty-faced actress and Greenwich Village Muse; Sophie Treadwell as Elmer Rice's stylistic disciple. Djuna Barnes and Gertrude Stein proved so difficult to pigeonhole, especially in gender-specific categories, that they were totally absent from the traditional dramatic and theatrical canon.

Interestingly enough, many of the modernist women artists have gained significant critical appreciation for their contributions in other genres, especially fiction and poetry. Recent feminist revisions of the modernist canon have highlighted a female subtext of a stature commensurate to that of the "great" modernist "masters." It has alternatively been theorized as a subversion of patriarchal modernist structures and as a source of origin for "high" male modernism. Simultaneously, attention has been focused on the repression of women writers both in the construction of the dominant modernist paradigm and in the textual practices of the canonized modernists.[1] Stein and Barnes feature extensively here—they are currently considered exemplary representatives of *écriture féminine* and among the original sources of the modernist aesthetics.[2] In terms of dramatic output, however, it is only Glaspell and Treadwell that have successfully been incorporated in a feminist dramatic and theatrical canon while Barnes and Stein are rarely mentioned and Boyce, Millay, and Bryant hardly at all.[3] Whether it is a particular critical blindness or a perception of incompatibility among feminism, realism, and modernism in the theater, the fact remains that so far no consistent female subtext in modernist American drama and theater has been recovered.[4]

Here, I will consider works by three of those women playwrights only, Boyce's *Constancy* and *Enemies,* Bryant's *The Game,* and Barnes's *To the Dogs* in order to explore the diversity of female dramatic modernism and illustrate the contiguity of feminism, realism, and modernism in early-twentieth-century American drama and theater. Undoubtedly the analysis can be extended to include all the authors mentioned in the beginning with extremely gratifying results—Stein's works will be a perfect example of the destruction of familiar theatrical form, while Glaspell's of the mapping out of a specific space for female identity and subjectivity; Millay's and Treadwell's pieces can be seen as female interventions into "high" modernism. My selection is motivated as much by considerations of space, as by my desire to rescue Boyce and Bryant for a feminist discourse, and my understanding that Barnes's work is the epitome of the two tendencies I will be discussing.

In the process I will argue first, that modernism was not inconsistent with a female subject position and second, that theatrical realism as a mode of representation could accommodate both a strong feminist position and antinaturalistic modernist stylistic techniques. I will contend that these modernist women playwrights offered significant challenges and subversive strategies to the dominant dramatic and theatrical discourse and elaborated an idiosyncratic language and mise-en-scène, exploding the conventions of both traditional theater and modernist male drama. What is more, they also focused on the in-depth portrayal of female subjectivity by making women their primary interest and thus their dramas present forms of female identity construction within the very heart of modernism.

All these women stood in a rather ambiguous relation to both the mainstream and the experimental theater of the time. Boyce and Bryant entered the field accidentally, while Barnes's was to be a longer infatuation with somewhat disastrous effects. They were all associated with the Provincetown Players, one of the little theater groups, which produced *Constancy* (1915), *Enemies* (1916), *The Game* (1916), and three other plays by Barnes.[5] The emergence of independent theater groups willing to oppose the conventions of commercial Broadway[6] at the time was couched in the terms of delivering a long-promised salvation, through the conviction that "the theatre is a place for beauty, for design, for color, for imagination, for plays with spiritual content, for interpretation, for harmony of many parts, for a certain kind of poetry" (Moses 425).

The Provincetown Players were unique in their interest in producing exclusively American plays of high artistic merit.[7] The group was informally organized in 1915 by a group of radical intellectuals vacationing at Provincetown, in the center of which were George (Jig) Cram Cook and Susan Glaspell. Following the success of their productions in the summer of 1916, when O'Neill was first introduced to the group, they began to consider a move to New York. The impossible was realized in the autumn of 1916, and for eight seasons the group produced original plays by American authors that were refused or even not submitted for consideration at the commercial stage as part of their ideal of a new, serious, sincere, and original American drama and theater.[8]

As part of this experimental theater group, Bryant, Boyce, and Barnes were "modern" from the very beginning. They were, further, "female modern," because of the attention they paid to the novel construction of female subjectivity executed through a whole range of stylistic techniques, from naturalism, to symbolism, to impressionism. The degree to which traditional theatrical form was dissolved in their pieces differed considerably. In all of the works, experimental modernist form was intricately blended with naturalistic situations and characters.

Nowhere more so than in Boyce's *Constancy* and *Enemies*. The plays' settings are naturalistic, as is the action, which progresses quickly to its climax in the tradition of the well-made play. Both dramatize the clash between a man and a woman (Moira and Rex in *Constancy*, He and She in *Enemies*) at vital points in their relationships. Rex has come back to reclaim Moira's love after having broken their affair for love of another woman. In her turn, Moira has forgiven him his infidelity, but to his chagrin, receives him as a friend rather than an ex-lover. Determined to be rid of him, or of her love for him forever, she watches in amusement his attempts to accuse her of infidelity of the soul and sums him up as just a boy crying for what he cannot have.[9] Finally, Rex departs furiously with the promise to be back, refusing her forgiveness if it means she has stopped loving him. Moira replies, "That's the only sort [of forgiveness] anyone ever gets" (280) and watches, motionless, while he leaves.

He and She in *Enemies* are husband and wife concerned again with spiritual "infidelity." The husband feels abandoned and betrayed by his wife's indifference to him and her unwillingness to allow him in her inner world of loneliness:

> He: Our tastes and our vices are remarkably congenial, but our souls do not touch.
> She: Our souls? Why should they? Every soul is lonely.[10]

In a psychological analysis of their relationship that has obviously repeatedly been done, it becomes clear that She wants to reserve a territory of her own that will not necessarily correspond to his preconceptions:

> She: You have wanted to treat our relation, and me, as clay, and model it into the form you saw in your imagination. You have been a passionate artist. But life is not a plastic material. It models us. (135)

Reserved and at times ironic ("do be careful this time—get a good housekeeper" [132]), she assesses their relationship far more realistically ("what you want is to censor and control me, while you feel perfectly free to amuse yourself in every possible way" [128]) and is even ready to take him up on his suggestion that they separate—much to his surprise. What He fails to comprehend is that She is also an artist and needs a space that is not marked by her being his wife. At the end, they both agree they have at least never bored each other, and they have a truce, albeit an armed one.

As naturalistic as both *Enemies* and *Constancy* seem to us today, in their production context, they defied conventional illusionism since they dramatized not a possible or probable reality, not even reality as it should be, whether in its melodramatic or politicized versions. Neither did they present a subjective view of reality, a technique that would later characterize expressionist theater. What they did was transpose on the stage reality itself—the Hapgoods' marriage in both *Enemies* and *Constancy* and Mabel Dodge and Jack Reed's tumultuous affair in *Constancy*. From the numerous memoirs of the time, especially those of Dodge and Hutchins Hapgood, it is clear that they were "true," as "truth" was available to the group of artists and audience members at the time.[11] Not only did the incidents recounted in the pieces follow incidents that were familiar to the audience, but the performers themselves (Neith Boyce and Hutchins Hapgood portrayed She and He in *Enemies*) were implicated in them. That intimacy of content and form undoubtedly accounted for an almost therapeutic environment. By being ultrarealistic, they in fact destroy theatrical illusionism and bridge the gap between audiences and performers. All together get to relive a supposedly personal experience, so that the boundary between personal and public also dissolves. Theater becomes an intimate exploration of privacy, opening of the personal into the public in a way that changes its function from entertainment to therapy and drama's movement from the general, that is, the human principle, to the concrete, that is, the idiosyncratic crisis.

Contextually speaking, mainstream American theater and drama at the time offered as their standard fare formulaic pieces intent on preserving an illusionistic picture of the world. Realism of the type discussed here—a portrayal and exploration of an actual reality familiar to the audience—did not participate in the popularly or critically sanctioned canon. One can argue that Boyce merely wrote these pieces on a personally significant topic for purely utilitarian reasons. After all, the Provincetowners did not exactly have a great pool of scripts to choose from. Whatever the intentions behind *Enemies* and *Constancy*, however, they both accomplished a structural transcendence of illusionism. In a spectacular way, they collapsed the distinction between author/subject, character/object, and performer and epitomized the ideal of the unified work of art with a single source of creation, the Artist. In that sense they embodied the main principles of the modernist New Stagecraft—simplification, stylization, synthesis and unification.[12]

Theater as a unified artistic product is what was realized in Bryant's play, *The Game*. It is very often dismissed by historians and rarely mentioned in criticism,[13] but it was staged three times by the Players in their first two years, and what is more, was chosen to be on their opening New York season bill. This, I will argue, suggests that it was regarded one of the best available illustrations of what kind of theater they were trying to create.

It semiotizes the game of chance between Life and Death for the souls of Youth, a poet, symbolizing Art, and the Girl, a dancer, symbolizing Love. From the very beginning, the play relates to both the topical issues of the day, i.e., the war (both at the beginning and the end of the action, Life is seen counting her losses, thousands of war casualties) and to the aesthetic ideal of combining Art and Love to enrich Life, thus instantly inserting itself in the modernist search for a higher meaning in life, and the political radicalism of the times. Life wins the game for Youth despite his desire to die—he believes Love has betrayed him. As it will turn out, he had known Desire, not Love. The Girl, in love with the Poet and his art, can recognize true Love—it "understands." She establishes a common bond between the two of them—artists who sing to beauty and celebrate true Love. In an attempt to convince him that she understands, the Girl dances to his song "The Bird Calls," and he finally comes to realize the truth in her words:

> Youth: How beautiful! You do understand—you do—Wings flash and soar when you dance! You skim the sea gloriously, lifting your quivering feathery breast against the sunny wind. Dance again for me.[14]

Life's luck holds again and she wins a second time—the Girl and Youth walk off the stage, arm in arm.

The abstract character and symbolic action received an equally abstract production. The scenery was designed by William and Marguerite Zorach, who had come to Provincetown that summer to teach in the summer session of the Modern Art School. It reflected the artists' absorption in cubism[15] and their realization that "one is not confined to the small section of nature framed in the space of a canvas and seen from only one point of view but was free to use all the colors and directions of space and form" (Zorach 34). Among the Players, the Zorachs were particularly unhappy with O'Neill's insistence on stark realism, but failed to impress him with their reasoning that no real tree or real ocean can be installed on stage (Zorach 45). Bryant, however, was willing to let them free their imaginations, so the backdrop they designed was a "decorative and abstract pattern of the sea, trees, the moon, and the moon path" (Zorach 46), presenting a stylized version of the view from the Wharf Theater. The costumes and gestures were deliberately equally abstract. The announcement printed on the New York playbill and reprinted in the published version of the play took no chances of the audience missing the unifying intent: "The Game [*sic*] is an attempt to synthesize decoration, costume, speech and action in one mood. Starting from the idea that the play is symbolic of rather than representative of life, the Zorachs have designed the decorations to suggest rather than to portray; the speech and action of the players being used as the plastic element in the whole unified convention" (*The Game* 28). The published version also added: "As the gestures and decorations of this play are as important as the written speech it is essential that theaters wishing to produce The Game [sic] should send for photographs and directions" (28).

The vision of the New Art, both visual (the Girl's dances) and verbal (the Poet's songs), locked in an embrace of drama and production, provides the play's importance as a symbol for the synthetic theater that was to come. It was precisely because The Game offered such a synthesis of dramatic text and its theatrical realization that it proved so important in the Provincetown enterprise. Despite the attempts to discard The Game as a slight piece of purely historical interest only, which does not deserve serious scholarly attention, it is impossible to ignore the fact that it was the Provincetown Players' first truly nontraditional and one of their few modernist productions with its departure from crude realism in design and total abstraction of character. What is more, through its insistence on the synthesis of all theatrical elements into a unified whole, it embodied the philosophy of the New American Theater, simultaneously political and ethical, aesthetically meaningful and socially significant, dramatically and theatrically poetic.

Barnes's work offered a third model for the New Theater, one that most critics found difficult to understand, not to mention appreciate.[16] In all of her works there is a consistent dissolution of familiar theatrical practices—no action proper, no plot, no development, no change in characters, an abundance of descriptions and stage directions impossible to realize, and so on. It seems to me, however, that the problem the critics had was in the fact that Barnes was offering an entirely new theatrical conceptualization. A metaphor for this New Theater can be found in her *To the Dogs*.

It is typically actionless, the characters do not develop, there is no climax or denouement. All it offers is a verbal encounter between Helena Hucksteppe and Gheid Storm, her neighbor, in Helena's inner room. A long description of Helena's room and her appearance precedes the dramatic text, much of which is indeed the author's commentary rather than a straightforward description. "About this room there is perhaps just a little too much of a certain kind of frail beauty of object"[17] is a good example of the authorial uncertainty hovering over the piece—"perhaps," "just a little too much," "certain kind of." The symbolic atmosphere of the piece is enhanced by the description of Helena's gown as "a gown almost too faithful to the singular sadness of her body" (45).

While Helena is standing, one arm lying along the mantel, Gheid makes his entrance through the window, and the action of the play, that is, the verbal game is launched. Nothing Gheid ever says or does surprises Helena, despite or maybe because of his attempts to cast himself in a number of familiar roles—the ever faithful lover who has patiently been waiting for his beloved to notice him (46), the witty gentleman who respects ladies (47), or the man of the world who can understand women and forgive their sins (48).

Innuendo and implication reign supreme. When he realizes he is getting nowhere, Gheid appeals to a past night when Helena kissed him, but her reply further confuses him: "It was a dark night, and I ended it." Gheid's professed frankness with his son provokes Helena's cynical "Well, some day your son will blow his head off, to be rid of frankness, before his skin is tough" (50); his offer of his clean heart is intercepted by her "Things which have known only one state, do not interest me" (49).

Gheid has come to Helena because he has sensed a great lover, because he has been intrigued by the town gossip which has her driving a different man with a whip to her house, but also because he wants to explore and find himself. "Do you really want to know why I came?" (51), he asks her, and explains, "Because I need you——" (51). Unfortunately for him, Helena is not interested in his motives, in the same way in which she is not interested in his "clean heart." She makes it clear that it is not him the play is all about, but her: "I'm not interested in corruption for the many. . . . Nor in misplaced satisfaction—. . . . Nor do I participate in liberations" (51).

At this point, the alluring twist of Barnes's play should already have become obvious—from the familiar story of one man's inability to unravel the mystery of the woman, whose love he cherishes, it is transformed into an exploration of a female psyche that the audience is ever further encouraged to speculate about but is denied the eventual satisfaction of knowing. Gheid likes to imagine Helena as his audience, which would patiently listen to the exploration of his soul, but she blatantly refuses to be one. In this sense, the play can also be read as a theatrical metaphor, challenging the traditional roles of audience and actor. By declining to indulge Gheid in his soul probing, Helena displaces the interest on to herself. Behold, the audience metamorphoses into a self-exploring subject! Is it possible that what Barnes is saying is that the seduction of the audience is impossible? That theater is not about the drama or the author or the actors, but about the public?

On the other hand, of course, Gheid is also Helena's audience, though he does not readily admit it and is willing to insist to the very end that the path of exploration originates with and returns to him. To a very large extent, then, *To the Dogs* is a metatheatrical commentary in which play and audience symbolically change places, the boundaries between them are blurred, and the audience (Helena) turns the tables on the play (Gheid) and absorbs all the attention, weaving up a new play—one that does not develop gradually, does not rely on straightforward narrative, and hovers on the margins rather than at the center.

Following up on the suggestion of a theatrical metaphor, Barnes would seem to suggest a novel role for the theater, neither a place of corruption for the many, nor a place of pleasurable entertainment, nor, finally, a liberation of repressed emotions or an exploration of the familiar. In a sweeping move, she negates the whole history of the Western theater, and as usual does not provide new perspectives. What is theater there for? For knowledge, wisdom, understanding, the study of individuality? Perhaps. The study is never pleasurable or amusing, but resembles the objectivism of science:

HELENA: In the study of science, is the scientist angry when the fly possesses no amusing phenomena? (53)

Contrary to the communicative function of theater, *To the Dogs* is about noncommunication, because of Gheid's unfamiliarity with the communicative code and Helena's unwillingness to share it or relinquish it. She is not only beyond bitterness but also beyond communication, precisely because she is self-sufficient. Hence Gheid can simply call her "Helena," while he is "Gheid Storm" (49), complete only when associated with a family, a tradition, a context.

In a final (doomed) attempt at human communication, Gheid kisses Helena without a warning, but all he gets in return is her disdain:

> HELENA: And this, I suppose, is what you call "the great moment of human contact."
> (52)

He goes away, without having known Helena, this time through the door, for he is too exhausted to go through the window. Helena, also tired, takes her old position, back to the audience, the self-sufficient woman, who is not in need.

This image of women in which self-sufficiency furnished the grounding element of female subjectivity was not solely Barnes's prerogative. Exploring the New Theater, female dramatists offered the image of the New Woman. As conventional as Boyce's work might seem, it presents images of women that do not follow either the traditional theatrical representation or the newly elaborated radical conventions, in that they demand agency, a space of their own, an autonomy of some kind. Her women are self-sufficient, too, though certainly not as much as Helena is. Yet Moira can be seen as Helena at the beginning of her journey. She is also beyond need for she has found a place where Rex can no longer harm her. From that private female territory she is psychologically free to act in a way not expected of her. Instead of jealous fits and accusations, all Rex gets is the impenetrable surface of amused interest, another scientist at work. The surgically amputated emotion, the lack, the void completes this Woman who has only been complete through her love of Man before.

Women in these plays occupy positions they are not willing to relinquish, despite the pressure exercised on them. In *Enemies* She succumbs to neither her husband's demands of a more regular household nor his radical belief in the importance of sharing, of psychological "community of souls" between men and women. She urges the man to leave her by herself, much as Helena does. As different as *Enemies* and *To the Dogs* are, they operate on the same assumption of inherent female power and self-sufficiency, as well as on the belief in the existence of distinct female and male world views and communicative practices which do not intersect.

The contradictions at the heart of the enlightened "male feminists'" attitude toward marriage and gender roles required special efforts at preserving even a trace of free agency on the part of women artists. *The Game,* ostensibly not about women at all, in fact proves as deeply entangled in the radicals' contradictory ideas about women, and especially women artists, as *Enemies*. Through the portrayal of the Girl, it gave expression to a conflict experienced by a number of women artists at the time.

The bourgeois gender stereotypes have obviously already been eschewed—the Girl is an independent artist in her own right, but interestingly enough, the advanced radicals are also revealed as operating with a set of stereotypes. Youth presents the obsolete ideal of womanhood that the radicals of the group, who were also the piece's first audience, could not endorse: "Women do not have to understand. They must be fragrant and beautiful—like flowers" (33). Yet despite the realization that both the Girl and Youth are artists, somehow the female artist has to subordinate her art and creative work to that of her male friend. (Ironically Reed seems to have been among the few in the group who were genuinely concerned with the artistic success of their female associates, and with Bryant's in particular.) Her dances endure because they express the Poet's imagination. What is more, she is also ready to follow the Poet's lead into the beauty of creation forever, no matter whether she could expect eternal love in return. Undoubtedly, she is the New Woman, as often portrayed by the mass media—a great artist, passionate and loving, ready to flaunt social conventions for the sake of remaining true to her own heart. Yet she is also the New Man's private fantasy, a creative woman, who "understands," who does not expect him to be a provider or a faithful husband, but to be devoted to his art only. In this Life-and-Death struggle for art and love, Life wins at the expense of the woman artist. The only hope that remains in this profoundly ambiguous dramatization of the position of the New Woman artist is that somehow male and female could combine to produce Art that is not divisively but complementary gendered.

Of all the plays considered here, *To the Dogs* offers the fullest exploration of female subjectivity and the most unconventional image of a woman. At the beginning of the action, Helena is seen with her back to the audience, and at the end, she assumes the same position, in a symbolic gesture of refusal to be known, to be understood, or to be enjoyed as a good spectacle. On a certain level, the characters' names are metaphoric; Helena is the Helen of Troy who caused the most famous war of ancient times, the Woman all men will fight over, and Gheid Storm suggests some violence and profound transformation. On another level, they are also ironic, for who is there for Gheid to fight with other than himself? And what is there to win? Certainly not Helena. In Homer's text, of course, the original Helen of Troy receives scarcely a few lines. Famous for her beauty only, she is deprived of a voice and is without any subjectivity of her own, to say nothing of agency which is shared by the heroic warriors and the gods. In focusing on Helena, rather than Gheid, Barnes redresses the imbalance. If Troy was conquered, and Helen taken back to Greece as a prize for victory, this Helena is not. Even her silence, or "reticence," is of her own choice. It is not that she has been denied a voice, she simply renounces its conventional usage. Helena in fact acts in such a way as to preserve a sacred territory that cannot be invaded by Gheid, or by the audience for that matter. (Was this what Kristeva has in mind by the impossibility to represent woman?)

Female independence for Barnes presupposes a private sphere that is not for sharing, an individuality that does not need expression or the participation of an audience. Silence is power. In the private territory of the female subjectivity, social conventions are irrelevant, the familiar sign systems no longer hold. Helena is not an archetypal woman, however; she is a peculiar individual woman. Other images of women surface occasionally, as in the reference to Gheid's having been brought up by upright women, and to his wife whom he keeps in as good a trim as his lawns. Helena is like neither of those women, as Gheid is only too well aware. She is unnaturally calm, strange, unfathomable.

Helena's inscrutable meaning is problematic for Gheid, for his resort to conventional moves proves entirely useless. He claims to possess the past, but in fact all he has is yet another representation, constructed by the "starved women" of the town. Helena's definition of her constructed past is again replete with double entendre— "starved" here refers both to the women as having nothing better to do with their lives but indulge in idle gossip and, possibly, to their sex-starved psychological transpositions. In the visions of Helena, whip in hand, driving a different man in front of her every spring, they seem to be vicariously living out their own fantasies through the difference they attribute to her.

Helena and Gheid both construct their own images of the other which are not necessarily "objective." The difference is that Helena can also construct and reconstruct herself by refusing to be open for representation by the other. While Gheid does not believe in self-construction and reinventing—he is what he has been made out to be by his years of rigorous upbringing and socializing. His only problem is his attraction to Helena, but because he cannot transcend conventional models of male-female interaction (I know your shameful past, but I am prepared to forgive and forget), he is denied access to Helena's inner room. It is interesting to consider the physical representation of their interaction. At the beginning, Helena, her back to the audience, is stage right, near the fireplace, while Gheid enters through the window, stage left. There is no indication of when in the action they come closer, or of who approaches the other. Judging from the rest of the action, Helena seems to be rather immobile, so it would have to be Gheid who goes up to her when he later kisses her. Through the spatial relations on stage, an additional layer of commentary on the impossibility of those two ever meeting and understanding each other could further be underscored.

Toward the end of the piece, as if weary of his incapability to understand her or her ways, Helena finally makes him touch her only to prove that he does not even know how to touch women like her:

> HELENA— . . . Yet you would be my lover, knowing not one touch that is mine, not one word that is mine. My house is for men who have done their stumbling. . . .
> I cannot touch new things, nor see beginnings. (56)

Barnes's writing superbly illustrates the idea of the tip of the iceberg, where only a small part is seen on the surface and underneath remains a wealth of developments impossible to represent but open to the imagination of the reader/audience. She dramatizes the uncertainties of language by juxtaposing visual symbols and images to an implied meaning that is only to be guessed at and is never fully present. Choosing as her medium theater, among others, she obviously did not consider it theatrically incongruent that her plays do not have clear-cut characters, or conventional plot developments, or even action proper. They are not about acting, but about observing, much as Helena Hucksteppe observes the world around her.

In her interview with Helen Westley, Barnes compares her (or rather makes Westley compare herself) to the ancient Sphinx, mysteriously unfathomable and knowing, with a wisdom that comes from having always been present (Barnes, "The Confessions of Helen Westley" 261). That is what her female characters are, ancient sphinxes that understand with a wisdom come from age. But being ancient, they also seem unable to "see beginnings," to move on to a future. In fact none of them has any future; they all live in a continuous hopeless present. There is the fine smell of decay about them, an ennui, to borrow again from the Westley interview, a reconciliation with whatever comes. Maybe the climate of modernism was indeed hostile to the representation of women?

Boyce, Bryant, and Barnes struggle courageously to bring about the birth of the new modernist theater and a hope for representing the modernist woman. By focusing on a single moment rather than a gradually developing action toward a climax and then a denouement, they subvert the traditional theatrical form of the well-made play and partake of the experimental nature of theatrical modernism in a fascinating combination of realistic characters and unrealistic action. And even more courageously, they map out a territory of female subjectivity, a possibility of free female will, a female loneliness that empowers.

Notes

1. See, for instance, Jardine; Benstock; DeKoven; Gilbert and Gubar; and Scott, *The Gender of Modernism,* among many other studies devoted to the exploration of the ambiguities of modernism and feminism.

2. On Stein, see, for instance, Neuman and Nadel; Ruddick; and Secor. On Barnes, see the essays collected in Broe, *Silence and Power,* especially Burke 67–79; as well as the Barnes issue of *The Review of Contemporary Fiction* 13.3 (Fall 1993), especially Kent; Scott, "Barnes Being 'Beast Familiar'"; and Gerstenberger. See also Groves. Millay is in a category of her own, for her poetry has received critical attention from most diverse quarters.

3. Glaspell has steadily been gaining appreciation and by now the criticism on her is quite abundant. More recent pieces include Makowsky; Larabee, "Death in Delphi"; Dymkowski; Ben-Zvi. On Treadwell, see Bywaters and Strand. Barnes's and Stein's dramatic works receive recognition by critics interested in their overall output, and only occasionally as part of a canon. Excellent discussions of some of Barnes's plays can be found in Larabee, "The Early Attic Stage of Djuna Barnes," and in Dalton. On Stein, see, for instance, Robinson, and also Pladott. The only men-

tion of Bryant and Boyce outside histories of the Provincetown Players that I have come across is in Radel.

4. The perception that realism, or the so-called classical realism, is incompatible with a feminist agenda is particularly strong among some feminist critics. See, for example, Forte and Dolan.

5. Boyce was a journalist and a fiction writer who had her three pieces (*Enemies, Constancy,* and *Winter's Night*) produced because she and her husband were among the cofounders of the Provincetown Players. Bryant, also a journalist, was introduced to the Provincetown Players through her association with John Reed, who was especially active in the formal organization of the group in the summer of 1916. Barnes, on the other hand, besides being a journalist, novelist, and poet, served as a theater reporter and critic at least until 1931 and wrote over eighteen one-acts and three longer pieces, the last of which was *The Antiphon,* in 1958. The Provincetown Players staged her *Three from the Earth, An Irish Triangle,* and *Kurzy of the Sea* in their 1919–20 season. *The Dove* was produced at Smith College in 1925, and *The Antiphon,* which she considered her masterpiece, had a successful production in Sweden only.

6. Many of the artistic and organizational principles behind the new theater groups were synthesized in the manifesto of the Washington Square Players issued early in 1915: higher standards achieved through experimentation and initiative, absence of purely commercial considerations, honest work for the birth of an artistic theater in America, no endowment, subsistence through sale of tickets and subscriptions, democratic pricing, no set policy in the choice of plays other than producing pieces of "artistic merit," preferably, but not exclusively, American, as long as they were deemed unsuitable for or had already been rejected by the commercial managers. See Eaton 20–21.

7. In their first circular, the word "American" was repeated three times: "The PROVINCETOWN PLAYERS will open their first New York season with the production of three original one-act plays by American authors"; "during the summer of 1916, eleven original one-act plays by American authors had their first production in the Wharf Theater"; and "it is planned to give a season of twenty weeks, presenting ten bills of original plays by American authors." The first circular thus spanned the past, the present, and the future and inserted the Players firmly within the beginnings of constructing a specifically American context.

8. They felt themselves and were later considered to be part of the modern wave of creation that had swept the world before the war, comprising scientific discoveries, revolutions in the pictorial arts, architecture, city planning, mass communications, the psychological liberation of humanity, and a total transformation of sexual relations through the teachings of Freud, that is, the profound remaking of "the fabric of modern life," as Vorse later described it (116–17). For background information on the Provincetown Players, see Kenton's unpublished history in the Fales Collection of New York University; see also Deutsch and Hanau, *The Provincetown: A Story of the Theatre;* Sarlos; and Glaspell.

9. Boyce, *Constancy* 279. Further references are included parenthetically in the text.

10. Boyce, *Enemies* 124. Further references are included parenthetically in the text.

11. See Luhan.

12. See Macgowan, *The Theatre of Tomorrow.*

13. Sarlos refers to it as "a simple and not particularly brilliant morality play" (42); Deutsch and Hanau

see it as "not much in itself" ("When the Provincetown Group Began" 10); Gelb finds it "rather stiff" (89).

14. Bryant 37. Further references are incorporated in the text in parentheses.

15. Both had previously studied in Paris and had experienced the influence of the fauvists, and "more traditional modernists" such as Cézanne and Matisse, and both had met Picasso at Gertrude Stein's. They had subsequently moved to New York, exhibited in the Armory Show of 1913, and gotten involved with various groups of American modernists. See Zorach.

16. Woollcott, for instance, constantly remarked on the "unintelligibility" of her pieces. In his review of "Kurzy of the Sea," he quipped, "a mildly diverting Djuna Barnes pleasantly which is actually intelligible (possibly through oversight)." *Three from the Earth* elicited similar bewilderment: "It is really interesting to see how absorbing and essentially dramatic a play can be without the audience ever knowing what, if anything, the author is driving at and without, . . . the author knowing either." Neither was he alone in his bafflement. See Mantle's review of *Three from the Earth* or MacGowan's of the same piece.

17. Barnes, *To the Dogs* 44–45. Further references are included parenthetically in the text.

Works Cited

Barnes, Djuna. "The Confessions of Helen Westley." *Djuna Barnes, Interviews.* Ed. Alyce Barry. Washington, D.C.: Sun & Moon, 1985. 249–62.

———. *To the Dogs. A Night among the Horses.* New York: Horace Liveright, 1929. 44–58.

Benstock, Shari. *Women of the Left Bank: Paris, 1900–1940.* Austin: U of Texas P, 1986.

Ben-Zvi, Linda. "Susan Glaspell's Contributions to Contemporary Women Playwrights." *Feminine Focus: The New Women Playwrights.* Ed. Enoch Brater. New York: Oxford UP, 1989. 147–66.

Boyce, Neith. *Constancy. 1915, The Cultural Moment: The New Politics, the New Woman, the New Psychology, the New Art & the New Theatre in America.* Ed. Adele Heller and Lois Rudnick. New Brunswick: Rutgers UP, 1991. 274–80.

———. *Enemies. The Provincetown Plays.* Sel. and Ed. George Cram Cook and Frank Shay. Cincinnati: Stewart Kidd, 1921. 117–36.

Broe, Mary Lynn, ed. *Silence and Power: A Reevaluation of Djuna Barnes.* Carbondale: Southern Illinois UP, 1991.

Bryant, Louise. *The Game. The Provincetown Plays: First Series.* New York: Frank Shay, 1916. 28–42.

Burke, Carolyn. "'Accidental Aloofness': Barnes, Loy, and Modernism." Broe 67–79.

Bywaters, Barbara L. "Marriage, Madness and Murder in Sophie Treadwell's 'Machinal.'" *Modern American Drama: The Female Canon.* Ed. June Schuelter. New York: Associated U Presses, 1990. 97–110.

Dalton, Ann B. "'This Is Obscene': Female Voyeurism, Sexual Abuse, and Maternal Power in 'The Dove.'" *Review of Contemporary Fiction* 13.3 (Fall 1993): 117–39.

DeKoven, Marianne. *Rich and Strange: Gender, History, Modernism.* Princeton: Princeton UP, 1991.

Deutsch, Helen, and Stella Hanau. *The Provincetown: A Story of the Theatre.* New York: Farrar & Rinehart, 1931.

———. "When the Provincetown Group Began." *Drama Magazine* 21.9 (June 1931): 5–16.

Dolan, Jill. "Practising Cultural Disruptions: Gay and Lesbian Representation and Sexuality." *Critical Theory and Performance.* Ed. Janelle Reinelt and Joseph R. Roach. Ann Arbor: U of Michigan P, 1992. 263–75.

Dymkowski, Christine. "On the Edge: The Plays of Susan Glaspell." *Modern Drama* 31.1 (Mar. 1988): 91–105.

Eaton, Walter Prichard. *The Theatre Guild: The First Ten Years.* New York: Brentano's, 1929.

Forte, Jeanie. "Realism, Narrative and the Feminist Playwright—A Problem of Reception." *Modern Drama* 32.1 (1989): 115–27.

Gelb, Barbara. *So Short a Time: A Biography of John Reed and Louise Bryant.* New York: Norton, 1973.

Gerstenberger, Donna. "Modern (Post) Modern: Djuna Barnes Among the Others." *Review of Contemporary Fiction* 13.3 (Fall 1993): 33–40.

Gilbert, Sandra M., and Susan Gubar. *No Man's Land: The Place of the Woman Writer in the Twentieth Century.* 3 vols. New Haven: Yale UP, 1988, 1989, 1994.

Glaspell, Susan. *The Road to the Temple.* New York: Frederick A. Stokes, 1927.

Groves, Robyn. "Fictions of the Self: Studies in Female Modernism. Jean Rhys, Gertrude Stein and Djuna Barnes." Diss. U of British Columbia, 1987.

Hapgood, Hutchins. *A Victorian in the Modern World.* New York: Harcourt, Brace, 1939.

Jardine, Alice A. *Gynesis: Configurations of Woman and Modernity.* Ithaca: Cornell UP, 1985.

Kent, Kathryn R. "'Lullaby for a Lady's Lady': Lesbian Identity in *Ladies Almanack*." *Review of Contemporary Fiction* 13.3 (Fall 1993): 89–96.

Kenton, Edna. "History of the Provincetown Players." Ms. Fales Collection, New York University.

Larabee, Ann. "Death in Delphi: Susan Glaspell and the Companionate Marriage." *Mid-American Review* 7.2 (1987): 93–106.

———. "The Early Attic Stage of Djuna Barnes." Broe 37–44.

Luhan, Mabel Dodge. *Movers and Shakers.* Vol. 3 of *Intimate Memories.* New York: Harcourt, Brace, 1936.

Macgowan, Kenneth. Rev. of *Three from the Earth,* by Djuna Barnes. *New York Globe* 3 Nov. 1919: 14.

———. *The Theatre of Tomorrow.* New York: Boni & Liveright, 1921.

Makowsky, Veronica. *Susan Glaspell's Century of American Women: A Critical Interpretation of Her Work.* New York: Oxford UP, 1993.

Mantle, Burns. Rev. of *Three from the Earth,* by Djuna Barnes. *New York Evening Mail* 5 Nov. 1919: 15.

Moses, Montrose. *The American Dramatist.* C. 1925; New York: Benjamin Blom, 1964.

Neuman, Shirley, and Ira B. Nadel, eds. *Gertrude Stein and the Making of Literature.* London: Macmillan, 1988.

Pladott, Dinnah. "Gertrude Stein: Exile, Feminism, Avant-Garde in the American Theater." *Modern American Drama: The Female Canon.* Ed. June Schuelter. New York: Associated U Presses, 1990. 111–29.

Radel, Nicholas F. "Provincetown Plays: Women Writers and O'Neill's American Intertext." *Essays in Theatre* 9.1 (1990): 31–43.

Robinson, Marc. "Gertrude Stein, Forgotten Playwright." *South Atlantic Quarterly* 91.3 (Summer 1992): 620–43.

Ruddick, Lisa. *Reading Gertrude Stein: Body, Text, Gnosis.* Ithaca: Cornell UP, 1990.

Sarlos, Robert Karoly. *The Provincetown Players: Experiments in Style.* 2 vols. Ann Arbor, Mich.: U Microfilms, 1983.

Scott, Bonnie Kime. "Barnes Being 'Beast Familiar': Representation on the Margins of Modernism." *Review of Contemporary Fiction* 13.3 (Fall 1993): 41–52.

———, ed. *The Gender of Modernism: A Critical Anthology.* Bloomington: Indiana UP, 1990.

Secor, Cynthia. "Gertrude Stein: The Complex Force of Her Femininity." *Women, the Arts and the 1920s in Paris and New York.* Ed. Kenneth W. Wheeler and Virginia Lee Lussier. New Brunswick, NJ: Transaction Books, 1982.

Strand, Ginger. "Treadwell's Neologism: 'Machinal.'" *Theatre Journal* 44 (May 1992): 163–75.

Vorse, Mary Heaton. *Time and the Town: A Provincetown Chronicle.* New York: Dial, 1942. 116–17.

Woollcott, Alexander. Rev. of "Kurzy of the Sea," by Djuna Barnes. *New York Times* 4 Apr. 1920, sec. 6: 6.

———. Rev. of *Three from the Earth,* by Djuna Barnes. *New York Times* 9 Nov. 1919, sec. 8: 2:1.

Zorach, William. *Art Is My Life.* Cleveland: World Publishing, 1967.

The Unnatural Object of Modernist Aesthetics: Artifice in Woolf's *Orlando*

Suzanne Young

When Wyndham Lewis, in his 1934 book of literary criticism, *Men Without Art*, dismissed Virginia Woolf's contribution to British culture by concluding that she was a "matriarchal invert," his term would have resonated with his audience along a number of lines (168). "Invert" was the term coined by late-nineteenth-century sexologists to describe congenital lesbians whose "unnaturalness" was exhibited by their "mannish" behavior and clothes. The fact that Lewis chose this term testifies to the continued circulation of sexological terminology in the 1920s and 1930s; it also demonstrates how the medical and the literary were bound together in the cultural imagination of modernism. The label evokes modern anxiety about the kind of aggressive and overreaching woman the "invert" was supposed to be. Like her heterosexual counterpart, the "New Woman," the "invert" demanded "mannish" privileges that threatened to overturn traditional social hierarchies. "Matriarchal" refers to a specific instance of this anxiety—popular representations of the newly independent women as racially dangerous throwbacks to primitive matriarchies. The implication of Lewis's comment is that Woolf's rise to literary fame in the 1920s represented an unnatural and inverting ascendancy.

The "invert" as a figure of "nature gone wrong" gained dramatic public attention through the obscenity trial of Radclyffe Hall's *The Well of Loneliness* in 1928, the same moment that Woolf was publishing her own, very different novel about sexual ambiguity, *Orlando*. Women modernists such as Woolf and H.D. watched the trial anxiously, recognizing the importance of this public adjudication of "perverse" sexuality and women's writing.[1] Contemporary sources suggest that, with regard to the representative of the "intermediate sex," the opposite of the "natural" may be either the "unnatural" (which is, in fact, a subset of the natural) or the "artificial" (which implies a complete break from the natural). Hall, for example, deliberately placed her work in the first category by adopting a tone of factual sincerity in presenting what amounted to a "case study" of deviance, as Parkes, Rosenman, and others have suggested. *The Well* popularized an idea from late-nineteenth-century sexology that "mannish lesbians" were tragic figures, born as anomalies *within* the natural order, and therefore deserved pity rather than opprobrium.[2] Hall's earnest use of naturalizing scientific models was not the defining attitude among women modernists, however. The work of other writers, such as Djuna Barnes and Woolf herself, falls into the category of "artifice," and their lesbian writing is correspondingly more self-conscious and ironic. They exploit the confusion between sexual and social characteristics evident in medical and social discourse for parodic and political ends. In works such as *Ladies Almanack* and *Orlando,* Barnes and Woolf present female sexual identity as a social process that is shaped by, rather than defined in, contemporary popular discourse on sexuality.

This essay focuses on the way Woolf in particular negotiates the terms "unnatural" and "artificial," not by claiming a pitiable place for her sexually anomalous character in the natural order, but by refusing the ideology of the natural entirely.[3] Instead, she makes its negative terms—artifice and ornament—central elements of her style and characterization. *Orlando* confronts many of the epistemological questions of the modern era: the writer's claim to a unitary and original voice; the nature of time and its relation to narrative; the legibility of historical "facts"; and the ability of our senses to provide matter-of-fact proofs, particularly about sexual difference. Because it locates this questioning in the joint realms of sexuality and language, *Orlando* is particularly well suited for an analysis that connects the sexual politics of discourse on the "natural" to the textual status of "artifice" (nature's opposite) in literary modernism.

Orlando is an "anti-novel" not only in the ways J. J. Wilson has noted—its sendup of writerly authority, academic pretension, and conventional plot development—but also in its refusal to assign its protagonist a "natural" and fixed identity. The work tells the story of an aristocrat who begins life as a boy in the Elizabethan age and ultimately arrives as a middle-aged woman in the text's present, 1928. As a budding young writer, Orlando runs through standard masculine plots, winning various lovers and high political office. He eventually undergoes a mysterious transformation, while an ambassador to Constantinople, that makes him anatomically a woman but leaves his sense of gender completely unsettled. The changeling returns to England and lives out the Augustan, Victorian, and modern ages as a woman who must fight eighteenth-century courts to establish her identity and accommodate nineteenth-century social conventions in order to write. Her nonrestrictive marriage to a Victorian seafarer and the magical delivery of her son are followed swiftly by the "birth" of a long poem in the early twentieth century that represents centuries of artistic labor. Orlando's central transformation in Constantinople stands for all the other sex changes in the work—"her" own increasingly frequent costume changes, as well as those of other characters—and for the instability of foundational categories in the work in general.

Orlando denaturalizes sex and gender through fantastical sex changes in the same way that it denaturalizes the authorial voice through the shifting idiom of British literary tradition; the work tries on a breathtaking array of period styles, from the rhetorical ornament of Euphuism and the digressiveness of Sterne to the bizarre collages of surrealist prose. But the artifice of this sexual and stylistic masquerade led even positive contemporary reviewers to complain that Woolf risked becoming "too clever" through a style that was "artificial." J. C. Squire pointed to its ornamental surface in calling *Orlando* a "thread on which many bright beads are strung," and Conrad Aiken underscored what he saw as the work's frivolousness by characterizing it as "glibly rhetorical, glibly sententious, [and] glibly poetic." The reviews generally suggest that *Orlando* was too self-conscious, that Woolf was laying it on too thick. Aiken called its tone not merely "artificial," but "elaborately" so, and another reviewer lamented its "self-conscious facetiousness." The implicit call for naturalness, simplicity, and unselfconsciousness among these arbiters of modern culture suggests an attitude at odds with the emerging spirit of the age: modernity is noted for its self-reflexive, deliberately alienating art (dadaism, for example), its social instability (evidenced by the claims of workers' and women's rights groups), and its "sex-consciousness" (a result of women's growing presence in many male institutions). The modern is a period, in fact, most likely to produce a work like *Orlando*.

What I mean to emphasize in these reviews is the way that a nostalgic sense of the "natural" informs literary critical judgments (and, as I will argue, high modernist precepts) just as it does sexological theories of the period. Objection to *Orlando*'s supposed "artificiality" implies a desire for literary models that are timeless and self-evident, just as sexological objections to "deviant" sexuality demonstrate science's assumption of a preexisting natural order, and both discourses suggest that the "natural" is simple, unitary, and empirically ascertainable. Claiming the ground of "nature" makes for a powerful argument, whether discussing the foundation of literature or the foundation of a social order. Appeals to nature "fix us in a world of apparent solidity and truth . . . providing the benchmark for our resistance to what is corrupting, 'unnatural'" (Weeks 62). But "nature" and "biological sex" (the seemingly irrefutable site of nature) are social constructs: whatever we attempt to say about physical "matter" is always filtered through social discourse. As Judith Butler puts it, "[T]he category sex is a gendered category, fully politically invested, naturalized but not natural" (112). The formulations of the "natural" I have been pointing to in social discourse of the 1920s have their origin in the nineteenth-century tendency to make biology definitive of the self, and this "biologization" of bodies, roles, and personalities generally reduced women to their reproductive capacity (Nathanson 8). Through the turn of the century, doctors and public officials continued to use the claims of "nature" to counteract feminist demands for "masculine" rights and privileges: inversion and hereditary neurosis were said to occur more frequently among women of high intelligence; women's energies were seen to be governed by a rigid biological priority to reproduction; and any woman who favored her brains over her ovaries risked sterility, cancer, and insanity (Smith-Rosenberg

267, 271). By the 1920s, public officials and physicians had successfully collapsed social demands into sexual ones: the working woman's call for education and autonomy was conflated with the lesbian's supposed social and sexual aggression, and both were labeled "unnatural."

Coming of age during this heated argument about the nature of woman, Anglo-American modernists began what they termed a literary and cultural revolt against Victorian values. Many were attracted to the artificial writing experiments of European movements, such as futurism and dadaism, that sought to establish ties between literature and industrial culture. Despite their public rejection of nineteenth-century tradition and their formal avant-gardism, however, most Anglo-American modernists continued to make use of Victorian assumptions about nature, language, and sexuality. The linchpin of modernist doctrine was, in fact, like that of Victorian science, an unexamined faith in the "natural": Pound insisted that "the natural object is always the adequate symbol" ("Retrospect" 5), and Yeats formulated good writing as "the natural words in the natural order" (56). This natural or "common" language, as Eliot termed it, disallowed any "ornament," "bookwords," or "inversions," anything that smacked of "artifice." Rhetoric was redefined as the use of superfluous or obfuscating language—the "art of dressing up some unimportant matter," as Pound said. As Marjorie Perloff has noted, "[T]he declared enemy of modernism was said to be artifice, specifically the artifice of separating the word from the 'natural object' to which it ostensibly refers" (30). Although their practice was often at odds with their poetics (Yeats, for example, advocated a natural language but worked from elaborate symbolic systems),[4] these statements of modernist poetics suggest a nostalgic will to nature in the face of rapid industrialization. This ideology of the natural in language was spurred, I argue, by the same pressures as the ideal of a natural and foundational social order. The problem of artifice in both cases is that it is seen to dress up, confuse, or conceal some fixed "truth"—either the truth of the unmediated natural world or the truth of biological sex differentiation.

Not only was the "natural object" capable of being expressed through language that was transparent rather than mediating, it was assumed to be available and evident to perception. It has been noted that modernist aesthetics privilege the visual,[5] from the attention to the look of the poem on the page in the work of Pound, Marianne Moore, and William Carlos Williams to Pound's interest in the Chinese ideogram. Ford Madox Ford's literary impressionism drew from the sister art of painting in rendering dramatic situations through the immediacy of visual impression. Joyce's idea of epiphany formulated in *Stephen Hero* centered on a moment of supreme "focus": Stephen's "glimpses" of the material world are "the gropings of a spiritual eye which seeks to adjust its vision to an exact focus" (Joyce 211). As the *point de repère* of modernist aesthetics, the imagist movement eschewed traditional poetic interest in narrative, character, or philosophical development in favor of "the images themselves" (Levenson 46). The Poundian formulation of the image—"an intellectual and emotional complex in an instant of time" ("Retrospect" 4)—assumed in an unselfconscious way that the thing itself is available to perception and that the writer's apprehension of it, indeed, his visionary experience of it, is unproblematically assured. Pound's inattention to the ambiguities of perception[6] lead him to a circular assertion of epistemological confidence: "An image . . . is real because we know it directly" (qtd. in Kenner 185). There is no split between subject and object in this idealist formulation; the surface of the object, offering no resistance to the probing of the aesthetic eye, is perfectly self-revelatory.

By contrast, sartorial and sexual masquerade, like the rhetorical excess and stylistic masquerading in *Orlando,* offers complex resistances to this masterful eye: cross-dressing signals the "unnaturalness" of its wearer (an androgyne or "mannish" lesbian), as well as exposing the artifice of supposedly reliable markers of sexual difference. In *Orlando,* this visual confounding of sexual identity through masquerade rewrites the history of lesbian invisibility or "derealization" (Castle, *Apparitional Lesbian* 34) for parodic ends. What I want to suggest is that *Orlando* deliberately plays on this epistemological, and specifically visual, uncertainty the lesbian raises by opposing it to the visual confidence of high modernism. The hiddenness of her sexuality, like the hiddenness of female genitalia, associates her with the mysterious and the "grotto-esque," as Mary Russo notes of woman in Western imagination (1). As a particular subject of psychoanalytic discourse, the lesbian is aligned with the "secretiveness" and "insincerity" that woman's "impenetrable obscurity" suggests in masculinist culture (Freud, qtd. in Lawrence 255). The fact that she has been stubbornly misperceived or waved away, as Castle notes, has limited the ability of heterosexual culture to grant her existence.[7] Just seven years before the publication of *Orlando,* in fact, the British law courts dismissed a proposal to extend the 1885 Labouchère Amendment, which outlawed "acts of gross indecency" between men, to include lesbian offenses, because the House of Commons was unwilling to contemplate sex between women (Parkes 434). Given that "the standard of vision . . . of *what can be seen*" (de Lauretis, "Sexual Indifference" 170–71) has excluded the lesbian in Western culture, *Orlando*'s critique of sexual normalcy must include a critique of high modernism's metaphorics of visibility.

Orlando's use of stylistic and sexual masquerading to unsettle foundational categories is typical of masquerade in general: As Castle has suggested in her work on the eighteenth-century masked ball, masquerade projects "an anti-nature, a world upside-down, an intoxicating reversal of ordinary sexual, social, and metaphysical hierarchies" (*Masquerade* 6). When masquerade regained prominence in the late nineteenth and early twentieth centuries, it again promised (or threatened) inversions of all kinds tied to the imagined ascendancy of marginal or alienated groups, in this period specifically to the homosexually coded Decadents. By the 1910s and 1920s, when male artists began to dispense with their aesthete styles, lesbian artists continued to write and dress in ways that signaled their professional and personal allegiance to an "intermediate sex" and to the "soft" and "ambiguous" sexuality of the nineties.[8] By the time *Orlando* was published in 1928, masquerade was clearly, though not exclusively, associated with female homosexuality.

My larger argument is that masquerade represents a specific instance of the general epistemological uncertainty of the modern age, a particularly powerful one that overturns systems of gender and perception. The signifying power of masquerade often noted by scholars of modernism takes on a new aspect when considered in the social and sexual context I have been framing. Reading the problematics of masquerade as simply a sign of the "war between the sexes," as Sandra Gilbert and others have done, wrongly separates the problem of how the moderns understood sexual difference from the interconnected problem of signifying and language use, and it pays only glancing attention to the gender war's parallel site of contestation, female sexuality and lesbianism. In *Orlando* Woolf treats sexual artifice and masquerade as continuous with rhetorical artifice—the status of one reflects the status of the other. Given the extent to which representing the "thing itself" free of ornament or artifice depends on true seeing and a faith in traditional representational systems, the lesbian artificer is doubly threatening to high modernist aesthetics in her undermining of both sex differentiation and Western confidence in the eye. What *Orlando* shows us is that, for the moderns, dressing up—either sartorially or rhetorically—is threatening because it obscures recognition of the external world and, what is more, calls the stability and naturalness of that world into question.

What follows is a reading of *Orlando* that addresses the ways homosexually coded artifice, ornament, and masquerade relate to aesthetic method in the modern period. I begin with a discussion of aesthetic mode—contrasting Woolf's relationship to language in this experimental lesbian text to the high modernist aesthetic ideal of a natural and unadorned language. I then recast this discussion in terms of masquerade to show how Woolf challenges the heterosexualized opposition between false costumes and true selves in male modernist writing. Specifically, I suggest that *Orlando* questions the naturalized surface/depth dichotomy of modernism's visual focus on the natural object, a dichotomy that makes lesbian desire seem insubstantial or unreal.

At the opening of the work, we find our hero acting the part of "the artist as a young boy"—he is dreamy, intense, and in search of a poetic style. Despite his youth, he has the "audacity," the ubiquitous narrator tells us, to pause in his writing of nature poetry and look out the window at the "thing itself," the object of his artistry: "[I]n order to match the shade of green precisely he looked . . . at the thing itself, which happened to be a laurel bush growing beneath the window. After that, of course, he could write no more" (17). Rather than offering inspiration, authentic reality deflates Orlando's creative work. "Nature and letters seem to have a natural antipathy," the narrator states (17). And indeed, Orlando's very prosody is disrupted by this incursion of the "real": "The shade of green Orlando now saw spoilt his rhyme and split his metre" (17). He puts aside this wrestling with the art of poetry in favor of a stroll in Nature. There is more than a little humor here directed at "nature" writers who stay locked up indoors. More important, though, I would argue that the aim of the passage is to burlesque the traditional definition of language as a window on nature—if we want "nature," Woolf seems to say, we might just as well go out among the fields and experience the "thing itself." Where Pound and others taught that good writing was based on the "thing itself," the natural object unfettered by obscuring language or artificial ornament, *Orlando* sends up the idealism of treating language as a transparent medium for the expression of an essence. This first flight outdoors sets a pattern for the narratorial voice, and each of the "biographer's" subsequent forays outdoors ironically becomes a flight into a progressively more "literary," more "artificial," realm, marked by whimsical playfulness and self-conscious rhyming. Each flight of fancy underscores the impossibility of retreat to a readily available "nature," or to the authenticity of the original, at this late date in literary history.

Although a conception of good art as that which takes the "natural object" as the "adequate symbol" assumes a ready link between the natural and artistic worlds, in fact, the question whether we can simply go into the fields and experience the "thing itself" unmediated by language was a pressing problem for the moderns. Rather than a faith in word-to-world correspondence, Woolf's work in general explores the idea that words are less signposts for a "reality" outside the text of language than things in themselves.[9] In the passage discussed above, for example, she presents art and nature as antipathetic in the extreme; nature (though it still exists "out there") works comically to disarm artistic pursuit. Repeatedly during the novel, Woolf uses Orlando's linguistic experimenting to show that even attempting to write in an unadorned and "natural" way is merely another pose, rather than a stripping down to a foundational language.

After an early romance with metaphor, Orlando decides to adhere to the precept (which we recognize as a tenet of the "men of 1914") that metaphor—treating everything in relation to something else and therefore not seeing it in itself—is the enemy of good writing.[10] Despite this attempt at austerity, Orlando comes to compare the inevitability of metaphor in thought to "a lump of glass which, after a year at the bottom of the sea, is grown about with bones and dragon-flies, and coins and the tresses of drowned women" (101). In other words, all he discovers in this first stage of his vexing search for unadorned Truth is yet "another metaphor." It is a silly one at that, about dragonflies attached to glass at the bottom of the sea, which, according to a scientific view, is also "manifestly untruthful" because it could not occur in nature. Orlando decides, nonetheless, to make a second attempt at the "austere spirit of poetry." In a work that consistently denaturalizes givens like sex and identity, Orlando's confidence in the empirical watchwords "truth" and "simplicity" locates him in this scene as a foil for Woolf's satire. The joke is on Orlando because he cannot even think about literature and truth without embellishing the relationship: As soon as he asks himself "if literature is not the Bride and Bedfellow

of Truth?" he cries out against saying "Bedfellow" when he has already said "Bride."
And the very terms of the metaphor suggest Woolf's awareness of the persistent
gendering of mimesis in Western culture.

Orlando's experiment in austerity reaches a crisis when he attempts to "simply
say what one means and leave it." As if to ward off rhetorical excess he takes as his
mantra the seemingly transparent and undeniable statement that "the grass is green
and the sky is blue." When he looks up from this ritual, however, he sees to the
contrary that "the sky is like the veils which a thousand Madonnas have let fall from
their hair; and the grass fleets and darkens like a flight of girls fleeing the embraces
of hairy satyrs from enchanted woods" (102).

If Woolf is laying it on a bit thick, as her critics claimed, she always does so with
a deliberate end in view. Despite its romantic rhetoric (and all the metaphysical
associations of such mysticism), this passage introduces the destabilizing axiom at
the center of Woolf's work. Orlando realizes from his outbreak of romantic metaphor that austerity is "no more true" than ornamentalism, that "both are utterly false"
(102). Here, language is neither a barrier nor disguise to the "real" outside textual
mediation; it is reality for us. Writing is profoundly "artificial," and a "natural style"
unencumbered by interferences is merely, as the poet Charles Bernstein has suggested, "a preference for a particular look" that suggests honesty, artlessness, and
spontaneity (42).

Woolf's treatment of writing as artifice clearly has implications for traditional
theories of meaning: a practice of writing as masquerade, a series of borrowings,
flouts the possibility that meaning can be immediately and authentically present,
unitary, or fixed. The ideology of the natural is based on a faith in representation
that both masquerade and rhetorical excess call into question, precisely because they
resist ultimate meanings or fixed positionings. Rather than assuming a transcendental
meaning for language in "nature," Woolf resolutely sees writing as style—historically determined and temporally fragile. In my introduction, I suggested that "nature" was a powerful foundational category for both the Victorians and the moderns;
the moderns' faith in a "natural" language represents an extension into the realm of
language of the foundational belief that sex or biology is definitive of a recognizable
natural order. When Woolf undermines the possibility of a natural language in *Orlando* she is also cracking the foundations of biological determinism for all women
in the modern period. The gap between language and "reality" represents the (mul-
tiply signifying) gap between costume and the body it covers. Each costume/sex
change in *Orlando* in turn stands for the ultimate indeterminacy of language.

This gap, this highlighting of the artifice of style in *Orlando,* also has particular
meaning for the lesbian, not merely because of the work's confounding of the sex
dichotomies on which heterosexual desire is predicated, but more specifically because of the meaning of the artificial style at this moment in literary history. The
analogy J. C. Squire's review suggests between sentence and ornament—Woolf's
style is like a "thread on which many bright beads are strung"—shows that contem-

porary readers recognized *Orlando*'s rhetorical and sartorial "dress up." Like Barnes's *Ladies Almanack,* a comic tale of a 1920s lesbian community that also borrows from historical styles, Woolf's tribute to English literary tradition—her stylistic masquerade—would have suggested established connections between "artifice," the homosexual, and the writings of aesthetes such as Wilde, Pater, and Swinburne.[11] Just as masquerade divides the representation from the original so as to ironize the very notion of origins, rhetorical mimicry posits the signifying context of language not as the thing itself but as other *language.* As Eliot wrote of Swinburne, his "morbidity [was] not of human feeling but of language. . . . It [was] in fact the word that give him the thrill not the object" (Eliot 285, 284). This "unhealthy" use of language as style was, in fact, the central tenet of one widely recognized definition of Decadent writing by the 1910s: "A decadent style is one where the unity of the book decomposes to give way to the independence of the page, where the page decomposes to give way to the independence of the word" (Paul Bourget, qtd. in Schor 43).

Although the high-spirited tone of *Orlando* is unlike the fatalistic tone that characterizes fin-de-siècle writing, Woolf's work does highlight linguistic artifice through its ironic and playful treatment of language as an entity in itself. What escaped the censors—the pervasive queer sensibility of a work that seemingly broached the subject of same-sex attraction only indirectly[12]—would have been clear to critics of *Orlando*'s glib artificiality, rhetorical excess, and stylistic masquerading, if only through literary association.

Like her questioning of a transparent link between word and world, Woolf's treatment of gender and masquerade in *Orlando* works to undermine a "metaphysics of substance."[13] Just as ornament and "excess" are seen as dangerous because they seem to separate the word from the thing in the referential view of language, so too does masquerade seem to be a false or concealing veneer for a fixed self in an essentializing view of gender and sexual identity. In "Costumes of the Mind," Sandra Gilbert suggests that male modernists such as Eliot, Joyce, Yeats, and Lawrence oppose costume, which is seen as "false or artificial," to either "true clothing" or nakedness. Women modernists, on the other hand, have more invested in changing the gender restrictions signaled by costume and therefore tend to "experiment more radically with costume as metaphor" (195). Instead of opposing false costume to "true" nakedness, women writers treat "'selves' as costumes and costumes as 'selves'" (196). The first, essentializing view implies a fixed and readily identifiable truth, the truth of natural sex differentiation that parallels the empiricist's faith in the accessibility of the unmediated external world. The implication of treating gender as masquerade, on the other hand, is that no one "can or should be confined to a . . . single form or self" (196). The ideology of the false costume/true self that *Orlando* calls into question is based on the same surface/depth or appearance/reality dichotomy which reviewers summoned when critiquing Woolf's work as superficial and glib, as lacking sincerity, depth and naturalness. Ironically, however, the masquerade trope at the center of *Orlando* dispenses with such oppositions as a way to rethink the naturalness of heterosexuality, among other foundational assumptions. Even when the Lady Orlando and her lover Shelmerdine have doubts about the other's sex and "put the matter to the proof" by immediately disrobing, no conclusive gender dichotomy emerges that might put their questions about sexual identity and orientation to rest (258). The work treats costume in a variety of ways, but always maintains the difficult postulate that the self is merely a series of costumes, that sexual poses, like literary styles, are all "false" in the sense that there is no one "true" self. What I emphasize is that *Orlando*'s denaturalizing of identity through masquerade questions heterosexual norms as well as conventional gender categories.

Woolf uses Orlando's sex and costume change in Constantinople to suggest that gender is the product of social rather than natural forces, as critics have noted. It is only as a woman that Orlando's movements and opportunities seem to become more restricted. As the demands of gender begin to dawn on her on her way back to England, Orlando concludes that "women are not . . . obedient, chaste, scented, and exquisitely appareled by nature," but rather must gain this status "by the most tedious discipline" (157). The femininity she finds she must attain is the product of schooling and studied artifice; this continuous movement across gender boundaries is figured, at the level of narrative, in Orlando's crossing and recrossing of national borders (Lawrence 256). Rather than a foregone conclusion of the "natural" order, Orlando's "true" sex after her transformation is held comically in suspension so that she is anonymous for a time, her identity literally and legally nonexistent. When a British court of law decrees Orlando a woman, though, she loses all claim to the family property, demonstrating how concretely social and legal discourse can manifest its power.

Given *Orlando*'s constructionist vision of gender, the question whether it is also a lesbian text—usually posed as the question whether Orlando, the character, is ever a woman who loves women—seems to miss the point by literalizing identity. I have already discussed the text's pervasive "queerness" at the level of style. Here I suggest that highlighting artifice in gender identity similarly queers the work's treatment of sexuality by raising the problem of self-identification in the desiring exchange. When the woman Orlando returns by ship to the country she left as a man, for example, she maintains her love for her previous lover, Sasha: "[T]hrough the culpable laggardry of the human frame to adapt itself to convention, though she herself was a woman, it was still a woman she loved" (161). In creating a character whose identity is indeterminate, Woolf does not avoid perverse desire so much as reconstitute it. Unlike Hall, whose lesbian is a fixed, psychologically interior identity, Woolf treats sexual identifications and desires as enmeshed in and enabled by social conditions. Rejecting the surface/depth dichotomy of the natural ideology, in fact, is what defines *Orlando* as a lesbian project, since the "true" self to be uncovered is normatively understood as heterosexual.

The opposite of the self created by language and costume—social convention—is the original and masterful creative eye ("I"), evident, as I have argued, in the visual aesthetics of high modernism. In *Orlando,* we see this confident Western eye figured in the person of Queen Elizabeth when she visits Orlando's family estate. Rather than becoming the object of the gaze, as the usual economy of spectacle and pageantry demands, the Queen herself has a bold look: her eyes are described as "wide open," and she looks at her favorite, Orlando, with such intensity that she seems to "pierce his soul" (24). Although the Queen, it is said, "[knows] a man when she [sees] one" (11), even the wide open eyes of this royal power cannot assure us of eternal and absolute truths. From the opening sentence of the work that introduces the young Orlando, in fact, visual confidence, especially with regard to gender identity and sexual orientation, is under siege: "He—for there could be no doubt of his sex, though the fashion of the time did something to disguise it—was in the act of slicing at the head of a Moor which swung from the rafters" (13). Costumes frequently confuse gender identity and sexual desire: Orlando's Russian mistress Sasha wears a "loose tunic and trousers of the Russian fashion [that] serv[e] to disguise the sex," driving Orlando mad with the possibility that he loves a man (37). Orlando's suitor, the Archduchess Harriet, undergoes miraculous changes of sex and costume that keep pace with Orlando's own so that the courtship always seems strictly heterosexual; the "vulture" of lust that Harriet's courtship inspires in Orlando suggests a "perverse" aspect to the relationship which is later confirmed when, as the Archduke Harry, the suitor confesses that he "was a man and always had been one" (179). Archduke Harry can laugh off his appearance as a woman earlier in the narrative, now that the specter of homosexuality has been lifted by Orlando's own sex change, but the reader remains skeptical of this avowal of safely heterosexual desire, given the pervasive instability of identity in the work. The gender/sex dichotomy of heterosexual desire has been so thoroughly undermined by this point in the novel that all relationships (including Orlando's later marriage to the seafaring Shelmerdine) begin to seem thoroughly queer. Like the mistaken identities central to Shakespearean comedy, misperception is what motivates action and creates meaning in *Orlando.*

Critics have discussed the centrality of masquerade as a trope for the instability of gender identity but paid little attention to visual exchange itself or to the implications of this exchange for sexual identification and desire. The self-affirming view of the observer implied in the modern privileging of the eye is part of the novel's larger satire on the distinction between the "false" or "unnatural" costume and the natural, heterosexual body. Like the cross-dressed, sexually ambiguous woman of the 1920s, Orlando disrupts the relation between subject and object at both ends of the exchange: when the object of (aesthetic) contemplation has become "unnatural" through the artifice of cross-sex dress (and the same-sex identification this induces), the viewer can no longer be assured of his knowledge of even the foundational assumption of sexual difference. He cannot, as Woolf's great queen would have it, "know a man when he sees one" (or a woman, for that matter). The positivist underpinning of modernist aesthetics expressed in Pound's formulation that "[a]n image . . . is real because we know it directly," like the confidence with which sexology divides the normal from the abnormal on the basis of scientific observation, is consequently undermined.

The exotic scene of Orlando's transformation from man to woman is important to examine because it takes this play of false and true sexual identity to a comic extreme.[14] The fanfare of the veiled dancers and the trumpets blaring "Truth" amount to a sort of metaphysical striptease that encourages and then frustrates the mastery of the gaze. We, the readers, are clearly positioned as spectators of this mock primal scene in which the new woman Orlando eventually stands in complete "nakedness before us" (137). The staginess that pervades *Orlando* comes to the fore in the explicitly dramatic conventions of this scene. The figures making up the drama are allegorical personifications, from the dancers who represent Purity, Chastity, and Modesty, to the trumpets that eventually blast these "Horrid sisters" (like Shakespeare's weird sisters) off the stage with the winds of "Truth." Dramatic entrances and exits are effected to the archly mannered stage direction, "Avaunt," and the slamming of doors. The veils and towels that the dancers wave in an effort to conceal themselves, cover the mouths of the trumpets blaring "Truth," or hide the naked form of Orlando all double as mini-stage curtains, each one promising a final and absolute unveiling. But the deflationary aspects of this broadly comic and allegorical scene ensure that the naked body never represents a "true" or unambiguous identity.

The language of revelation and the hushed expectation that develops once the final door has shut and the last trumpet has blasted create an air of sincerity and awe unlike *Orlando*'s usual tone. As the naked Orlando stands on display, we are told that "[n]o human being, since the world began has ever looked more ravishing and the silver tongues of truth seemed to caress his body" (137). But Orlando is hardly born before the winking narrator undercuts this reverent atmosphere. For, though "silver tongues" encase her, as it were, in "truth," they also suggest associations between female voicedness and lesbian sexuality that other "perverse" works, such as Barnes's *Ladies Almanack,* exploit. And, in fact, worldly knowledge has already separated the scene's protectors of womanhood—Purity, Chastity, and Modesty—from their charge, given Orlando's firsthand knowledge of manhood and sexual freedom prior to this moment. The scene closes on a deflationary note as the narrator announces that she will "take advantage" of this pause created by the wonder Orlando's beauty inspires to "make certain statements"; these amount to an ambiguous and, at times, contradictory lecture on the meaning of sex change and gender identification that purposely leaves the reader bewildered. Not only are we robbed of the frisson of witnessing a moment of originary wonder, we are also refused the truths that the spectacular unveiling has led us to expect.

Just as Woolf literally disarranges the spectatorial gaze in *Between the Acts* by holding up a shattered mirror to her audience, she uses Orlando's unveiling to disrupt the masterful eye and its quest for whole and absolute knowledge. What becomes clear is that this rebirth of Orlando as a woman complicates rather than clarifies questions about gender and sexual identity: What do we make of a man who becomes a woman but still cherishes the memory of Sasha, the woman with mannish qualities whom he once loved? Or of the paradox that although "Orlando had become a woman," "in every other respect he remained precisely as he had been" (138)? The scene of unveiling is merely the most dramatic instance of *Orlando*'s critique of modernity's confidence in visibility, from the objective eye of modernist aesthetics to the clinical observations of sexologists. It is not simply a matter, as Hall's work seems to suggest, of exposing "the lesbian" to public view as she exists in an essential state and asking for tolerance. Rather, treating the lesbian as a paradigmatic figure of the gender and sexual "inversions" of the 1920s, Woolf suggests that it is not clear where and how we might find her from one moment to the next.

What Woolf called "sex-consciousness" was both a problem and a provocation for modernist art. On the contested ground of literary modernism, artists often chose to explain creativity through biological metaphors that tended to reinforce an array of social codes. Pound asserted that the brain, as a source for new images and ideas, was "a great clot of genital fluid held in . . . reserve" ("Translator's Postscript" 206). In her 1919 essay "Notes on Thoughts and Vision," H.D. postulated that the source of artistic vision was the "womb-brain" (95). And as early as 1909, T. E. Hulme distinguished feminine "sentimentality" from the "virile thought" that marked the best in modern writing (69). Not only were literary modes persistently figured in terms of gender and biological difference in the modern period, but, as I have been suggesting, the writer's ideal relation to the word was heterosexualized. Given the queer significance of the "artificial" and "unnatural" by the 1920s, an aesthetic theory based on the natural object was implicitly posed in opposition to nonnormative and nonreproductive sexualities. When Pound and Eliot proposed the "natural object" as a poetic ideal and endorsed a "natural language" with which to present it, part of what they opposed in decrying ornament was the challenge that the "intermediate sex" represented to the natural (heterosexual) order. And when male modernists such as Pound decried elaborate styles as a sign of excess or irrelevance, maintaining, for example, that "Rhetoric [was] the art of dressing up some unimportant matter" (*Gaudier-Brzeska* 83), ornamental language was explicitly linked to threatening or trivializing gender masquerade. Ornament and artifice were the enemies of the artistic order in the same way that "unnatural" or "deviant" sexuality was the enemy of the naturalized order constructed around heterosexual pairing. In *Orlando,* Woolf refuses this ideology of the natural and instead presents both selves and styles as successive tryings on, as masquerades.

What some theorizers of the 1920s and many now suggest is that all women (not simply lesbians) are to some extent members of an intermediate sex that is poised ambiguously between the poles of a dichotomized gender system. In a 1929 essay entitled "Womanliness as Masquerade," psychoanalyst Joan Riviere suggests that women who have trespassed on male privilege by gaining education and professions feel they must ward off male anger by acting out a caricatured form of femininity—displaying coquetishness and embarrassment—immediately following any assertion of their professional authority. What is striking about Riviere's essay, which predates current theorizing about performative femininity by half a century, is that although she focuses on what her contemporaries would recognize as a "mannish" professional woman, she really views all femininity as a mask: "The reader may now ask how I define womanliness or where I draw the line between genuine womanliness and the 'masquerade.' My suggestion is not, however, that there is any such difference; whether radical or superficial, they are the same thing" (94). And, more recently, Makiko Minow-Pinkney has suggested that because woman is "situated at once outside and inside the dominant order," she is forced to "attain an androgynous position" that works to deconstruct the dominant male discourse (10). She is, as Woolf suggests in *A Room of One's Own,* necessarily "alien and critical" (146). The trajectory of Orlando's sex change—from man to woman and not the reverse—is significant in this regard; like most women who grow up identifying with the universalized male point of view, Orlando approaches femininity from a defamiliarized position, thus literalizing this androgynous aspect of female development. In suggesting that all women were (and still are) members of an "intermediate sex" in relation to social discourse, I do not intend to blunt the specifically lesbian meanings of either Woolf's work or my argument, but rather to show how all women are implicated in aesthetic and scientific discourses that treat the supposedly narrow category of "deviance."

By the 1920s, woman as such was becoming increasingly, and to some alarmingly, associated with the "artificial" and the "unnatural," as I have suggested. In fact, the figure of the "mannish" lesbian was considered merely an extreme point on a continuum of gender rebellion, and abusive public rhetoric about such "deviants" was often used as a way to contain the ambitions of all women.[15] The movement of women away from their "natural" sphere and into the mechanized public realm originated far earlier, however, in the same period as the ideology of "separate spheres."[16] As significant numbers of women entered the public work force in the nineteenth century, the differences of sex idealized in Victorian social codes were already beginning to collapse: "Women [became] mass-produced, widely available commodities with the 'massification' of industrial labor and society, . . . losing their 'natural' qualities" (Buci-Glucksmann 222). Well into the 1920s, social observers warned that the "artificial life of the great cities" must prove a "strain on the nerves of the weaker sex" and exhorted women to return to the natural rhythms of country life (Dane 27). By this point, though, woman was firmly linked to artifice through the efforts of commerce: manufacturers of everything from automobiles to cigarettes courted the newly independent woman who tended to marry late or not at all, had a career, and, presumably, disposable income. The rise of the film industry and the Hollywood star system in this period also contributed to the "artificing" of woman by circulating images of female perfection that were highly posed and artificially enhanced through lighting and makeup. And the cosmetics industry, which had flourished even before the first World War, became a $1 billion business in the United States by the late 1920s (Leach 269). Woolf herself posed during this period wearing a slash of dark lipstick, suggesting that the brash artifice of makeup went hand-in-hand with the "newness" of the modern intellectual woman.

Despite the problematic influence of capitalist forces in women's separation from the claims of "nature," the project of exposing femininity as masquerade was a liberating process for many women writers of the early twentieth century. *Orlando*'s manipulation of social codes through costume change, for example, is clearly meant to represent the expansive potential of the modern age: "Her sex changed far more frequently than those who have worn only one set of clothing can conceive; . . . the pleasures of life were increased and its experiences multiplied" (221). Woolf's other works of the 1920s show a similar interest in the passing of the Victorian spirit of the "natural" woman in favor of the self-constructions of modern women. Although her attitude toward Mrs. Ramsay's femininity in *To the Lighthouse* is complex, Woolf does expose this "angel in the house" to criticism through Mrs. Ramsay's own doubts about the unaffected naturalness of her behavior. Mrs. Ramsay wonders if her selflessness and philanthropy might be a role she plays before an adoring audience: "[A]ll this desire of hers to give, to help, was vanity" (65). Her eventual death represents, as many have noted, the passing of the ideal of separate spheres already under attack in the work, and her heir, Lily Briscoe, demonstrates a social awkwardness and refusal to accommodate men that throws into question the naturalness of this role. Lily's alienation from heterosexual codes and her love for Mrs. Ramsay, in fact, place her as a figure of gender and sexual inversion in the novel; her completion of the painting in the culminative scene of the novel can be seen as an embrace of the liberatory possibilities of artifice. No longer the representative of nature, this modern woman's final stroke signifies her ability to construct her world in a new way. The meaning of the balance that Lily's painting restores is unclear, but the hopefulness of the gesture casts artifice as the heir to nature.

Recent feminist scholarship has established gender as a crucial category of inquiry in the modern period. Critics have pointed to gender bias in the formation of the modernist canon, examined the gendering of particular genres or modes, discussed the mentoring habits of major modernists, and uncovered the heretofore unrecognized role of women publishers and small magazine editors.[17] While avoiding the tendency of feminist scholarship to appropriate lesbian culture,[18] it is also important that our gendering of modernism consider the heterosexual/homosexual opposition Eve Kosofsky Sedgwick has noted in twentieth-century culture. In this essay, I have treated gender and sexual identity as overlapping but not identical categories in showing how philosophical questions about language, empirical fact, perception, and sexual difference took on not simply gendered but particularly "perverse" meanings in the modern period. To write in a rhetorically excessive style, to dress up or masquerade in style as in sexuality, was not so much to write as a woman as to write as a homosexual, to invert the natural order of language, as of sexual difference. By the 1920s, one motivator of this intellectual anxiety about the foundations of language and its relationship to the world was the perceptual ambiguity raised by the figure of indeterminate masquerade, the lesbian artificer.

I have suggested that the artifice that characterizes all language use forced some moderns toward a romantic ideal of language as capable of presence and immediacy. Others, like Woolf, recognized that both our bodies and our minds are written by culture and that, as the poet Lynn Hejinian puts it, "the limits of language are the limits of what we might know" (278). This understanding of language as constitutive rather than merely instrumental allowed her to reclaim "excess" and "artifice" in an era when the dominant aesthetic treated the "natural" in language and in sexuality as the foundation of great art. By queering our view of sexual identity and word-to-world relations through the indeterminate Orlando, Woolf asserts the fact of textual and sexual mediation—of artifice—against the invisibilizing pressures of a natural ideology.

Notes

1. See Adam Parkes for an account of Woolf's comments on and attendance at Hall's trial. Though unconvinced of the aesthetic merit of Hall's novel, Woolf was quite concerned about how its lesbian content would be treated. Susan Stanford Friedman reports in *Penelope's Web* that, according to H.D.'s friend Sylvia Dobson, *The Well*'s trial had a chilling effect on the lesbian artistic community, which included H.D. and Bryher: "We didn't call ourselves homosexuals in those days. We had to be very, very careful" (381 n. 3).

2. Although Hall's portrait of the lesbian as a doomed male spirit in a female body who became what she was partly through faulty socialization (parental treatment, the pursuit of horse riding, etc.) seems to hearken to outdated sexological theories, those theories still held sway in the 1920s. However, one of Hall's contemporaries, the journalist and celebrity Janet Flanner, has critiqued Hall's literal interpretation of the "folklore" of sexology, demonstrating that some contemporaries of Woolf, like Woolf herself, recognized the ridiculousness of the discourse meant to define the "lesbian" as a man manqué: "[Hall's] whole analysis [of the lesbian] was false and based upon the fact that the heroine's mother, when expecting her, had hoped for a boy baby, which as a daughter, Miss Hall interpreted literally" (48).

3. The natural and artificial are, of course, overlapping and mutually dependent categories. On this point, see Judith Butler's reading of the category of "sex" as necessary to and created by the dominant gender system in order to naturalize the social order. See also Mary Russo on woman and/as "freaks": The grotesque as bodily category "emerges as a deviation from the norm" (11–12). That is, people who are born with physical deviations from the norm are defined as and become "freaks" through the process of social normalization that rests on their exclusion.

4. Two such examples are Yeats's use of Rosicrucian symbols in the early poems and the system of symbols he worked out from his wife's "visions" late in his writing career. Perloff notes in her discussion of poetics versus practice that the idea of "'natural speech' was itself a carefully crafted simulation" (221 n. 7).

5. Elizabeth Hirsch discusses the New Critical emphasis on "visualist and spacialist" readings of modernist aesthetics and the way that this type of criticism tended to privilege the "classicizing, reactionary strains of High Modernism, recuperating Modernist texts as 'timeless' artifacts and self-sufficient objects of aesthetic contemplation" (2–3). Marjorie Perloff has also discussed what she sees as a shift from the modernist image to the artifice of the word in the development of poetics over the course of the twentieth century.

6. Recent poststructuralist and feminist readings have critiqued the "occulocentrism" of Western discourse in its entirety, linking "the sense of sight, the eye, to the constitution of the 'I,' and [indicting] both as instruments for the repression of (feminine) difference" (Hirsch 1). In this sense, modernist emphasis on seeing rightly is not merely an inattention or an oversight, but part of the overall rejection of the "feminine" in high modernist aesthetic discourse.

7. Castle traces the various ways in which the lesbian has been "ghosted"; she is seen to haunt others until she fades into obscurity (as in Diderot's *Nun* and James's *Bostonians*) or is driven to distraction herself by the "ghosts" that signal her unnaturalness to the reader (as in Diderot's work and the conclusion of *The Well of Loneliness*). Castle also notes the way that the existence of lesbian sexual practices has alternately been denied by officials as impossible or censored as dangerous to the public good.

8. See Cassandra Laity on the identification many lesbian modernist felt with the writing and ethos of the nineties. Along with H.D., Laity discusses writers such as Katherine Mansfield and Renée Vivien. Djuna Barnes's entire oeuvre is strongly marked by Decadent visual and linguistic imagery, but see, especially, *The Book of Repulsive Women; 8 Rhythms and Five Drawings.*

9. Pamela Caughie presents the most sustained study of Woolf's use of postmodern language practices.

10. The problem with metaphor (or any poetic figure of speech) is complicated in modern aesthetics. I have been discussing what many moderns saw as the tendency of the figure of speech to place the "thing itself" at one remove through analogy, rather than enacting an (impossible) identity between perceiver and perceived or between word and thing. Metaphor also smacked of stale literary convention for many moderns (including Pound, Williams, Moore, and Woolf herself). Modernism is notable for its renunciation of the traditional uses and associations of poetic language; writers such as Eliot, Pound, Hulme, and Ford Madox Ford positioned the new writing in relation to science as a way to "cleanse" it of "literary" associations.

11. As I have noted, lesbian modernists continued to read and incorporate the work of the Decadents in their own writing well into the 1920s. The late 1920s saw a general resurgence of Decadent style that was noted in fashion and home-decorating columns. In the art world, this renewed interest, though not a major movement, is evident in a little magazine entitled *Two Worlds,* published in the late 1920s, that featured writings of Oscar Wilde, memoirs and commentary by Arthur Symons, and imitations of the Decadent style in verse, drama, and prose by new writers. Though such writing may have seemed outdated to contemporary readers, it

is my sense that this borrowed stylistic context actually permitted writers to focus on the very modern theme of sexuality, and especially homosexuality.

12. Sherron Knopp covers the conflicting critical opinions over the extent of *Orlando*'s lesbian content and makes a persuasive argument for its lesbian allegiances.

13. I borrow this term from Judith Butler (10).

14. Karen Lawrence reads this scene in relation to Orientalist imagery and as a "comic deflation of the Freudian paradigm" of female castration (255).

15. See Faderman on the discrediting of social activists and first-generation new women through the accusation of "lesbianism" often leveled against women living together in settlement houses and colleges. My point here is not to defend or refute such claims but rather to draw attention to the way the vocabulary of sexology has been used for political ends; the category of the so-called sexual deviant works to police all women.

16. For the classic statement of "separate spheres," see John Ruskin, who argues that man is "the doer, the creator, the discoverer, the defender," while woman's "intellect is not for invention or creation, but for sweet ordering, arrangement, and decision." "The man, in his rough work in [the] open world, must encounter all peril and trial. . . . But he guards the woman from all this; within his house, as ruled by her[,] . . . need enter no danger, no temptation, no cause of error or offense."

17. See, for example, Bonnie Kime Scott's collection of essays and stories by female and male modernists, *The Gender of Modernism;* Suzanne Clark's study of neglected sentimental writing by women modernists, *Sentimental Modernism;* Susan Stanford Friedman's contextualizing study of H.D.'s prose, *Penelope's Web;* Shari Benstock's social and literary history of women writers in Paris, *Women of the Left Bank;* and Rita Felski's theoretical analysis of the meaning of gender in modernism, *The Gender of Modernity.*

18. Teresa de Lauretis has called this impulse of feminist scholars to appropriate lesbian culture in problematic ways "the seductions of lesbianism"; see *The Practice of Love* 149–202.

Works Cited

Aiken, Conrad. Rev. of *Orlando,* by Virginia Woolf. *Dial* Feb. 1929: 147–49.

Barnes, Djuna. *The Book of Repulsive Women: 8 Rhythms and Five Drawings.* 1915. Los Angeles: Sun & Moon, 1989.

Benstock, Shari. *Women of the Left Bank: Paris, 1900–1940.* Austin: U of Texas P, 1986.

Bernstein, Charles. "Stray Straws and Straw Men." *The L-A-N-G-U-A-G-E Book.* Ed. Bruce Andrews and Charles Bernstein. Carbondale: Southern Illinois UP, 1984. 39–45.

Buci-Glucksmann, Christine. "Catastrophic Utopia: The Feminine as Allegory of the Modern." *The Making of the Modern Body.* Ed. Catherine Gallagher and Thomas Laqueur. Berkeley: U of California P, 1987. 220–29.

Butler, Judith. *Gender Trouble.* New York: Routledge, 1990.

Castle, Terry. *The Apparitional Lesbian.* New York: Columbia UP, 1993.

———. *Masquerade and Civilization: The Carnivalesque in Eighteenth-Century English Culture and Fiction.* Stanford: Stanford UP, 1986.

Caughie, Pamela. *Virginia Woolf & Postmodernism.* Urbana: U of Illinois P, 1991.

Clark, Suzanne. *Sentimental Modernism: Women Writers and the Revolution of the Word.* Bloomington: Indiana UP, 1991.

Dane, Clemence. *The Women's Side.* New York: George H. Doran, 1927.

de Lauretis, Teresa. *The Practice of Love: Lesbian Sexuality and Perverse Desire.* Bloomington: Indiana UP, 1994.

————. "Sexual Indifference and Lesbian Representation." *Theatre Journal* 40.2 (1988): 155–77.

Eliot, T. S. "Swinburne as Poet." *Selected Essays.* New York: Harcourt Brace Jovanovich, 1950. 281–85.

Faderman, Lillian. *Odd Girls and Twilight Lovers.* New York: Penguin, 1991.

Felski, Rita. *The Gender of Modernity.* Cambridge: Harvard UP, 1995.

Flanner, Janet. *Paris Was Yesterday: 1925–1939.* Ed. Irving Drutman. New York: Viking, 1972.

Friedman, Susan Stanford. *Penelope's Web: Gender, Modernity, H.D.'s Fiction.* Cambridge: Cambridge UP, 1990.

Gilbert, Sandra. "Costumes of the Mind: Transvestism as Metaphor in Modern Literature." *Writing and Sexual Difference.* Ed. Elizabeth Abel. Brighton: Harvester, 1982. 193–219.

Hall, Radclyffe. *The Well of Loneliness.* 1928. New York: Doubleday, 1990.

H.D. *Notes on Thought and Vision and The Wise Sappho.* San Francisco: City Lights Books, 1982.

Hejinian, Lyn. "The Rejection of Closure." *Writing / Talks.* Ed. Bob Perelman. Carbondale: Southern Illinois UP, 1985. 270–91.

Hirsch, Elizabeth A. "'New Eyes': H.D., Modernism, and the Psychoanalysis of Seeing." *Literature and Psychology* 32 (1986): 1–10.

Hulme, T. E. "A Lecture on Modern Poetry." *Further Speculations.* Lincoln: U of Nebraska P, 1962.

Joyce, James. *Stephen Hero.* New York: New Directions, 1963.

Kenner, Hugh. *The Pound Era.* Berkeley: U of California P, 1971.

Knopp, Sherron E. "'If I Saw You Would You Kiss Me?': Sapphism and the Subversiveness of Virginia Woolf's *Orlando.*" *PMLA* 103 (1988): 24–34.

Laity, Cassandra. "H.D. and A. C. Swinburne: Decadence and Sapphic Modernism." *Lesbian Texts and Contexts: Radical Revisions.* Ed. Karla Jay and Joanne Glasgow. New York: New York UP, 1990. 217–40.

Lawrence, Karen R. "Orlando's Voyage Out." *Modern Fiction Studies* 38 (1992): 253–77.

Leach, William. *Land of Desire: Merchants, Power, and the Rise of American Culture.* New York: Pantheon Books, 1993.

Levenson, Michael. *A Genealogy of Modernism.* Cambridge: Cambridge UP, 1984.

Lewis, Wyndham. *Men Without Art.* London: Cassell, 1934.

Minow-Pinkney, Makiko. *Virginia Woolf and the Problem of the Subject.* New Brunswick: Rutgers UP, 1987.

Nathanson, Constance A. *Dangerous Passage: The Social Control of Sexuality in Women's Adolescence.* Philadelphia: Temple UP, 1991.

Parkes, Adam. "Lesbianism, History, and Censorship: *The Well of Loneliness* and the Suppressed Randiness of Virginia Woolf's *Orlando.*" *Twentieth Century Literature* 40 (1994): 434–60.

Perloff, Marjorie. *Radical Artifice: Writing in the Age of Media.* Chicago: U of Chicago P, 1991.

Pound, Ezra. *Gaudier-Brzeska: A Memoir*. 1916. New York: New Directions, 1970.

———. "A Retrospect." *Literary Essays of Ezra Pound*. Ed. T. S. Eliot. New York: New Directions, 1968. 3–14.

———. "Translator's Postscript." *The Natural Philosophy of Love*. By Remy de Gourmont. New York: Boni and Liveright, 1922.

Riviere, Joan. "Womanliness as Masquerade." *The Inner World and Joan Riviere: Collected Papers, 1920–1958*. Ed. Athol Hughes. London: Karnac Books, 1991.

Rosenman, Ellen Bayuk. "Sexual Identity and *A Room of One's Own:* 'Secret Economies' in Virginia Woolf's Feminist Discourse." *Signs* 14.3 (1989): 634–50.

Ruskin, John. "Of Queens' Gardens." 1865. *Sesame and Lilies*. Philadelphia: H. Altemus, 1897.

Russo, Mary. *The Female Grotesque*. New York: Routledge, 1995.

Schor, Naomi. *Reading in Detail*. New York: Columbia UP, 1987.

Scott, Bonnie Kime. *The Gender of Modernism*. Bloomington: Indiana UP, 1990.

Sedgwick, Eve Kosofsy. *Epistemology of the Closet*. Berkeley: U of California P, 1990.

Smith-Rosenberg, Carroll. "The New Woman as Androgyne: Social Disorder and Gender Crisis, 1870–1936." *Disorderly Conduct: Visions of Gender in Victorian America*. Oxford: Oxford UP, 1985. 245–96.

Squire, J. C. "Prose-de-Société." *Observer* 21 Oct. 1928: A6.

Weeks, Jeffrey. *Sexuality and Its Discontents*. London: Routledge & Kegan Paul, 1985.

Wilson, J. J. "Why is *Orlando* Difficult?" *New Feminist Essays on Virginia Woolf*. Ed. Jane Marcus. Lincoln: U of Nebraska P, 1981. 170–84.

Woolf, Virginia. *Between the Acts*. London: Harcourt Brace Jovanovich, 1941.

———. *Orlando*. London: Harcourt Brace Jovanovich, 1928.

———. *A Room of One's Own*. London: Harcourt Brace Jovanovich, 1929.

———. *To the Lighthouse*. London: Harcourt Brace Jovanovich, 1927.

Yeats, W. B. *Letters on Poetry from W. B. Yeats to Dorothy Wellesley*. London: Oxford UP, 1964.

～ Contributors

JOSEPH O. AIMONE is Lecturer in English at the University of California at Davis, where he received his Ph.D. in English with a designated emphasis in critical theory in 1996.

DAGNY BOEBEL teaches in the Department of English and is Director of Gender Studies at Manchester College. She has published essays and presented papers on a wide variety of authors, including Shakespeare, Milton, Aphra Behn, Anne Sexton, and Monique Mojica.

MARIA FRAWLEY is Assistant Professor of English at Elizabethtown College, Elizabethtown, Pennsylvania. where she teaches Victorian, modern British, and women's literature. She is the author of *A Wider Range: Travel Writing by Women in Victorian England* (Associated UP, 1994) and *Anne Brontë* (Twayne Publishers, 1996). She is currently working on a study of nineteenth-century invalid literature.

ELIZABETH JANE HARRISON is author of *Female Pastoral: Women Writers Re-Visioning the American South* (University of Tennessee Press, 1991). Her areas of research include southern women authors, autobiography, and American regionalism. She is a reviewer for *The Women's Review of Books* and has published articles in *South Atlantic Review, MELUS, and The Southern Quarterly.* Currently she teaches at DePauw University in Greencastle, Indiana.

MICHAEL KAUFMANN teaches literature and film at Indiana University–Purdue University Fort Wayne. He has explored the innovative use of print in modernist fiction in his book *Textual Bodies* (Bucknell University Press, 1994) and has written on T. S. Eliot, Gertrude Stein, James Joyce, Virginia Woolf, and other twentieth-century writers. Currently he is at work on the way in which Modernist writers/critics defined Modernism in their critical writings.

LORALEE MACPIKE is Chair of the English Department at California State University, San Bernardino. She is the author of *Dostoevsky's Dickens* and editor of *There's Something I've Been Meaning to Tell You* (essays by lesbian and gay parents about coming out to their children). She is also the founding editor of *The Lesbian Review of Books,* an international quarterly review of books by, for, and about women. Her current work focuses on the construction of lesbian identity in British and American fiction of the 1920s and 1930s.

GENEVIÈVE SANCHIS MORGAN recently completed her Ph.D. at the University of California, Davis. She has published articles on Vanessa Bell and Dora Carrington and is working on a book-length study of the domestic artist.

SHIRLEY PETERSON is Associate Professor of English at Daemen College in Amherst, New York, where she teaches modern British and Irish literature, and gender and literature. She has published essays on the literary representation of the British women's suffrage movement, women and freaks, and women and film. She is currently researching feminism and freaks in literature.

CHRISTINE W. SIZEMORE is Professor of English at Spelman College, Atlanta, Georgia. She is the author of *A Female Vision of the City: London in the Novels of Five British Women* (Knoxville: U of Tennessee P, 1989). She has also published articles on twentieth-century novelists, most recently an article on Virginia Woolf and Doris Lessing in *Breaking the Mold,* edited by Ruth Saxton and Jean Tobin.

JULIE ANNE TADDEO completed her Ph.D. in history and gender studies at the University of Rochester in 1996. She currently is Visiting Assistant Professor of history at Temple University.

KORNELIA TANCHEVA is Senior Assistant Professor of English at Sofia University, Bulgaria. She recently defended her Ph.D. dissertation on American modernist drama in the 1920s at Cornell University and is currently working on a study of female modernist drama.

SUZANNE YOUNG is an Instructor at the College of Charleston. She has published an article on H.D.'s 1930s prose in *Tulsa Studies in Women's Literature* (Fall 1995). She is completing her dissertation at the University of Virginia on the intersection of sexological and aesthetic discourses in late 1920s texts by Djuna Barnes, H.D., and Virginia Woolf.

Index

Unmanning Modernism was designed and typeset on a Macintosh computer system using PageMaker software. The text is set in Perpetua and chapter ornaments are set in Minion Ornaments. This book was designed by Kay Jursik, composed by Kimberly Scarbrough, and printed and bound by Thomson-Shore, Inc. The recycled paper used in this book is designed for an effective life of at least three hundred years.